W9-BAQ-963

KAUFMAN FIELD GUIDE TO BIRDS OF NORTH AMERICA

KENN KAUFMAN

with the collaboration of
RICK and NORA BOWERS
and
LYNN HASSLER

Illustrated with
more than 2,000 images
digitally edited
by the author
and based on photos
by more than
80 top photographers

HOUGHTON MIFFLIN COMPANY

DUCKS, GEESE, SWANS

OTHER SWIMMING BIRDS

AERIAL WATERBIRDS

BIRDS OF PREY

CHICKEN-LIKE BIRDS

WADING BIRDS

SHOREBIRDS

MEDIUM-SIZED LAND BIRDS

HUMMINGBIRDS, SWIFTS, SWALLOWS

FLYCATCHERS

TYPICAL SONGBIRDS

WARBLERS

TANAGERS, BLACKBIRDS

SPARROWS

FINCHES, BUNTINGS

PICTORIAL TABLE OF CONTENTS

WHEN YOU SEE AN UNFAMILIAR BIRD:
1. Try to figure out which group it belongs to. (Hint: in defining these groups, a bird's *shape* is usually more important than its colors.)
2. Go to that section of the book. Find the pictures that match best.
3. Check the range map for the bird you've picked, to see if it's likely.
4. Read the text for that bird to get further information.

BIRDS OF PREY, PAGES 108–137

CHICKEN-LIKE BIRDS, PAGES 138–149

WADING BIRDS, PAGES 150–163

SHOREBIRDS, PAGES 164–193

MEDIUM-SIZED LAND BIRDS, PAGES 194–219

HUMMINGBIRDS, SWIFTS, AND SWALLOWS, PAGES 220–233

FLYCATCHERS, PAGES 234–249

TYPICAL SONGBIRDS, PAGES 250–301

WARBLERS, PAGES 302–327

TANAGERS AND BLACKBIRDS, PAGES 328–343

SPARROWS, PAGES 344–363

FINCHES AND BUNTINGS, PAGES 364–370

QUICK KEY TO THE RANGE MAPS

Colors on the maps show where a bird may be found at each season:

There are only three colors to remember: red for summer, blue for winter, gray for migration. For more details, see page 16.

summer
all seasons
spring and fall migrations
winter

Colors are paler if the bird is rare or hard to find:

summer (rare)
all seasons (rare)
migration (rare)
winter (rare)

DEDICATION

TO THREE WHO ARE GONE BUT NEVER FORGOTTEN

JOHN YATES KAUFMAN
JOAN BADER KAUFMAN
ROGER TORY PETERSON

ALL, IN THEIR OWN WAYS, THE GREATEST OF TEACHERS

Copyright © 2000 by Hillstar Editions L.C.
All rights reserved

For information about permission to reproduce selections from
this book, write to Permissions, Houghton Mifflin Company,
215 Park Avenue South, New York, New York 10003.

Visit our Web site: www.hmhco.com.

LIBRARY OF CONGRESS CATALOGING-IN-PUBLICATION DATA

Kaufman, Kenn.
Birds of North America / Kenn Kaufman ; with the collaboration
of Rick and Nora Bowers and Lynn Hassler Kaufman.
p. cm. — (Kaufman focus guides)
ISBN 0-395-96464-4
ISBN 0-618-07324-8 (cloth)
ISBN 0-618-57423-9 (flexi)
1. Birds — North America — Identification. 2. Birds —
North America — Pictorial works. I. Title.

QL681.K36   2000
598'.097 — dc21   00-056717

Book design by Anne Chalmers
Typefaces: Minion, Univers Condensed
Illustrations and maps for this guide were produced in Tucson, Arizona,
by Hillstar Editions L.C. and Bowers Photo.

PRINTED IN CHINA

SCP 22 21 20 19 18 17 16

GETTING STARTED IN BIRDING

Birdwatching, or birding, is among the most rewarding pursuits in the world. It can be mentally
challenging and physically strenuous, or it can be
relaxing and casual. At any level, it gets us away
from stressful and trivial parts of modern life, putting us back in touch with the real world of nature.

Birding, birdwatching: What's the difference? These two terms mean
practically the same thing, although "birding" implies a somewhat more
active, extreme, or radical approach. Birding is the attempt to find and
identify different species of birds in the wild, and it often includes an effort
to find as many different kinds as possible. Birdwatching can be the same
thing – or it can be more passive and peaceful, involving just watching one
bird for a long time and not worrying about finding more. Still, most of us
use these terms interchangeably. I'm glad to consider myself both a birder
and a birdwatcher.

Whatever we call it, it's the most fascinating pursuit imaginable. More
than 700 kinds of birds live in North America and more than 10,000
worldwide, enough variety to keep anyone fascinated for a lifetime. I've
been birding since I was six years old, and I still see amazing things every
time I go outdoors. After all, birds have wings. They show up in totally unexpected places. You never know for sure what you're going to find. You
may see some exotic bird that has strayed far from its normal range, or
you may see a familiar bird doing something completely unexpected. But
the birds are not just wandering around at random. They are respond-
ing to rhythms that have been established over thousands of generations.
When it's time for birds to migrate north in spring, they may be delayed by
weather or chance, but we can be certain that ultimately they will arrive. So
in some ways birding is reassuringly predictable, but it has enough unpredictable elements to keep us on our toes.

Birdwatching also gives us an extra measure of independence. Modern
life has become so commercialized that we are often regarded not as citi-
zens but as consumers. Collectively we're often viewed not as a society or a
civilization but as a market to be exploited. We are constantly bombarded
with advertising. But when we go birding, we free ourselves from all that.
If we can find a place to watch wild birds, no corporation, no government
can control what we will see. This is why birdwatching is not mere escap-
ism. Rather, it allows us to connect with the real world, the natural world.
In fact, we could summarize the benefits of birding this way:

Birding is not an escape from reality. Birding IS reality!

How to be a great birder: Birdwatching is something that we do for enjoyment, so if you enjoy it, you are already a good birder. If you enjoy it *a lot*,
you are a *great* birder! But by sharpening your skills, you still may increase
your enjoyment. In the following pages, I share some advice on improving
your skills, so that you can find and identify more birds and understand
more of what you're seeing outdoors.

WHERE, WHEN, AND HOW TO FIND BIRDS

Where to look: Even a city street will have a few birds, but you'll see more in natural habitats. Most birds are choosy about habitat. A species that is common in a marsh may never show up in a woodlot a mile away; others live mainly in fields, or deserts, or on the shore. By visiting more different habitats, you'll see more different species. But it doesn't require wilderness travel: even cities like Los Angeles, Chicago, Toronto, and New York have great birding spots close to downtown. And if you don't even want to travel across town, any backyard or park will have birds worth watching.

When to look: Most birds are most active early in the morning. Many that are elusive later in the day may be conspicuous at dawn, coming out in the open, singing and calling. A lesser peak of activity often occurs in the evening. But with patience, you can find plenty of birds even at noon. Waterbirds that live in the open are less affected by time of day than songbirds; hawks and other soaring birds may be most active during the warmer hours of midday. Also, the rule about good birding at dawn becomes less important in winter, when activity may stay about the same all day.

Birdlife changes with the seasons, so if you go out at different times of year, you'll see different species. Spring and fall migration seasons can be especially rewarding: billions of little birds are on the move, many going long distances, and they may stop over anywhere. Even a tiny park might be visited by birds on their way from South America to northern Canada.

Of course most of us would rather be out in nice weather, but bad weather sometimes makes for good birding, especially in migration season. Storms may drive seabirds close to the coast, or cause "fallouts" of migrating songbirds. Passage of a cold front may trigger a major movement of waterfowl or other birds.

On the search: A brisk hike is a great way to exercise and see a few birds, but you may see more if you slow down. The ideal way is to be relaxed but alert, pausing occasionally next to patches of good habitat.

Some birds sit blatantly in the open, but a lot of them don't; instead, they move about in tall grass or dense trees. Birders learn to watch for movements among the foliage and wait for the birds to show themselves.

Birds are very aware of sounds, so birders should be too. Listening is one of the best ways to find birds. Even if you don't recognize them by sound, you can still locate them by listening keenly for songs at a distance or soft callnotes in the foliage nearby. So birders have two powerful reasons for staying quiet outdoors: so they can hear the birds, and so they don't scare them away.

When birds are nesting and raising young (mostly in spring and summer), most kinds will be divided up into pairs, defending their own little territories. But at other seasons, birds are often in mixed flocks containing several species. You may walk through the woods for a while without seeing or hearing any birds at all and suddenly find a pocket of activity. Learn to listen and watch for such flocks and you'll find more birds.

You can sometimes call birds closer to you, or get them to come out of dense cover, by making "squeaking" or "shushing" noises (try saying "pssh, pssh, psshh" — it's best to practice this when you're alone!). If you can learn to imitate your local screech-owl or pygmy-owl species, that will often bring an excited response from small birds. And many birds will respond to good imitations of their own voices. Any bird-calling method should be used with moderation; in particular, avoid harassing nesting birds.

In some situations, birding by car can be very effective. It's a good way to cover a lot of territory in open country, looking for hawks and other large birds. It's a good way to cruise backcountry roads in search of flocks. Often you can approach birds more closely in your car than on foot. Still, in most places you'll find more birds when you're out of the car and walking.

Clothing for birding should be chosen for comfort. Birding gives you an excuse to put on beat-up old clothes and just be comfortable. The other birders don't care what you look like, and neither do the birds. (One tip, though: if you will be seeking shy forest birds, you may get closer to them if you wear dull, muted colors instead of bright colors or whites.) In cool weather, wearing several layers rather than one heavy coat will make it easier to adjust to changes in temperature.

Sneakers are good footwear in many situations, but waterproof boots are sometimes necessary, and hiking boots may be better in thorny or rocky terrain. Waterproof and windproof jackets are often necessary, but try to avoid those that squeak every time you move. If you're buying a jacket for birding, check to see if the pockets are big enough for this field guide!

A wide-brimmed hat will not only keep the sun out of your eyes but will help you avoid sunburn. Even with a hat, sunscreen is a good idea. In warm weather, it's always a good idea to carry insect repellent, even if you don't wind up using it very often. If you'll be walking through tall grass or dense brush in warm weather, it may be wise to spray repellent around your ankles first, to keep ticks and chiggers from biting.

Using this field guide: Experienced birders can slip this book into the pockets of their field jackets without a second thought as to how to use it. But if you are new to birding, consider these pointers. First, if you have found an unfamiliar bird, look at the bird, not at the book! Try to take in as much detail as possible. Then, to get to the right section of this field guide, go to the **Pictorial Table of Contents** in the front. This guide is arranged by groups of birds, and if you can narrow your bird down to one group, you will only have to flip through a few pages. If you think you know what the bird is, the **quick one-page index** at the back of the book can take you there fast, or you can follow the **color tabs** on the edges of the pages to the right section. Once you've found pictures that look like your bird, always check the **range map** to see if that species is likely to occur where you are. And remember that pictures can't tell the whole story, so always **read the text** for key points about the bird's habitat, behavior, or special field marks.

THE TWO ESSENTIALS: A FIELD GUIDE AND A BINOCULAR

Birding doesn't really require much in the way of equipment or supplies. But two items are practically essential: a field guide and a binocular. Newcomers to birding may realize that they need some kind of book with pictures, but a **field guide** is a particular type of book like this one: compact enough to be carried in a large pocket or day pack. Its focus is on how to tell different kinds of birds apart – it won't have room to include much other information about them, but it does illustrate or describe their distinguishing features. The book is set up to make it easy to find mystery birds or to compare those that are similar. It includes all the birds likely to be seen in a particular area.

Choosing a binocular: A binocular is not absolutely necessary for birding. (Technically it's correct to say "a binocular," not "a pair of binoculars.") Anyone can enjoy watching large birds at a distance, or small birds outside the window, without a binocular. But this one piece of equipment can make a world of difference in your birding.

Literally hundreds of models of binoculars are available today. The most expensive ones are all good. But to get a good binocular for less than $500, you need to shop carefully. Here are some things to consider.

Binoculars with two types of internal prisms are easily recognized. (Without these prisms, you would see magnified images that were upside down and backward.) **Porro prisms,** the old standby, bend light through a "dogleg," while **roof prisms** bend the light

Porro

Roof

differently and deliver the image straight out the other side in a more compact but more complicated design. Most of the most expensive binoculars (in the $1,000-plus range) use roof prisms, but lower-priced roof prism binoculars should be approached with caution. It is more expensive to make good roofs than good porros, so of two lower-cost binoculars with the same price, one with porro prisms is likely to be better.

All binoculars have **specifications** like 7x35, 10x40, etc. The first number is the **magnification:** a 7x binocular will make the bird look seven times closer. One might expect more powerful binoculars to be better, but above 10x they become very difficult to hold steady; you may get your best view with a 7x or 8x binocular. The second number (after the "x") is the **diameter of the objective (front) lens,** in millimeters. If the front lenses are small (as in a compact 8x24 binocular), they may not let in enough light for good views. Larger lenses make for a heavier binocular, though. Modern coatings for lenses make them much better at transmitting light, so a large objective lens is not as important for birding as it used to be.

Having a wide angle of view is less relevant for birders than for football fans, but **minimum focus** is important. Often we want to look at a bird that is close to us, and it's irritating to have to back up to focus. Most good binoculars today can focus closer than 15 feet, and some can focus down to three feet (making them excellent for butterfly watching too).

The **eye relief,** or the distance from the lens of the binocular to your eye, is important, especially if you wear glasses. Most of the better binoculars have eyecups that can be adjusted to change the eye relief. If you wear glasses, be sure to check on this feature before you buy a binocular.

Waterproof binoculars cost more, of course, but they can be worth the expense if you want to go birding in all kinds of weather.

Before you buy a binocular, check the **alignment**—that is, are both barrels aimed at the same point? Your eyes can compensate if the binocular is slightly out of alignment, but this will put strain on your eye muscles and can create headaches after a day in the field.

Finally, there's the issue of your personal preference: what type fits well in your hands, how easily your fingers can reach the focusing wheel, the **weight** of each model. A heavy binocular on a thin strap can be literally a pain in the neck after a few hours. But if your favorite binocular is a heavy one, you can buy a wide padded strap to reduce the direct pressure on your neck. There are even binocular harness arrangements that will loop over your shoulders and take the weight off your neck entirely.

Using a binocular: Many people have different strength of vision in each eye, and with good binoculars you can compensate for that. The binocular will have a central focusing wheel that focuses for both eyes at once, and a separate adjustment on one eyepiece (usually the right). You need to set this individual eyepiece to account for the difference between your eyes. First look through just your left eye and focus on a particular object using the central focusing wheel. Then look at the same object with just your right eye and sharpen the view using just the individual focus of the right eyepiece. Thereafter you shouldn't have to touch the individual focus; just use the central focus and the image should be sharp for both eyes.

One of the biggest challenges at first is aiming the binocular at the bird you want to see. If you put the binocular up to your eyes and then start trying to aim, you'll only find the bird through sheer luck. A better approach is to stare fixedly at the bird while you bring the binocular up smoothly in front of your eyes. If you have kept your gaze directly on the bird, when you get the binocular positioned in front of your eyes, you should have the bird in your sights. You can practice aiming the binocular at anything (you don't have to wait for a bird to appear), and after a while you'll be able to zero in on birds instantly.

Spotting scopes: For some kinds of birding, such as watching shorebirds or waterfowl, a telescope can be very useful. Most of the best ones for birding are of the refractive type (straight through the lenses), not the mirror telescopes useful for astronomy. A 20x eyepiece, or a zoom eyepiece that goes as low as 20x, will be the most versatile.

BIRD TOPOGRAPHY AND FIELD MARKS

You don't have to learn a lot of jargon to identify birds. At times, though, it helps if we're using the same terms to describe the various parts of a bird. The diagrams below will cover all of the major terms that are used in the text in this book, and then some. Words in parentheses are not used much in this guide but will show up often in more technical works.

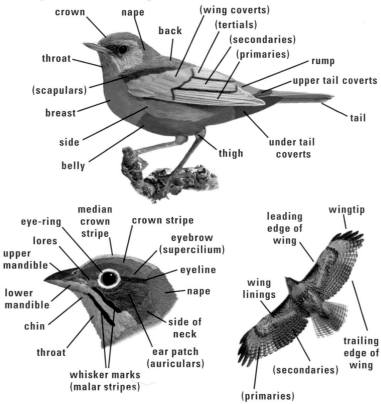

Young birds often look slightly different from adults. The term "immature" in this book applies to any bird that is not an adult yet. Sometimes to be technically accurate I use "juvenile," a specialized term for a bird in its very first set of feathers. The two words don't mean the same thing: a Herring Gull, for example, is a juvenile for only a few months, but it continues to be an immature until it reaches adult plumage at the age of three and a half years. The definition is of interest mainly to scientists, and in most cases it's simpler to refer to all young birds as immatures.

WHAT TO LOOK FOR ON AN UNFAMILIAR BIRD

When we see an unfamiliar bird, it's easy to be distracted by one conspicu-ous feature (say, a bright yellow bill) and forget to notice anything else. This can lead to frustration when the bird flies away and we realize that dozens of birds scattered through the book have bright yellow bills. To avoid such frustration, we need to look at a variety of things on any unknown bird.

Size is given in this book as a length in inches, from the tip of the bill to the end of the tail. For some birds, a measurement for wingspan (from one wingtip to the other) is also given. These are average lengths, and a species will vary. Size can be a helpful mark, but it also can be misleading. A lone bird — especially on the water or in the air — may be much larger or much smaller than it seems. If your mystery bird is with other birds that you can recognize, try to get a direct comparison of their sizes.

Bill shape is not always easy to see, but it goes a long way in getting you to the right *group* of birds. If you see a small yellow bird, for example, it helps to see whether it has the thin bill of a warbler or the thick bill of a finch. If you see a swimming bird, it's important to notice whether it has the typical bill shape of a duck or some completely different bill shape. Even within groups of birds, the shape of the bill is often a key mark.

Shape and posture are often among the best clues for identifying birds at a distance. Experts can recognize hundreds of species by silhouette alone. In some difficult groups of birds, such as small flycatchers, female ducks, or female hummingbirds, subtle differences in shape are among the most reliable distinguishing features. Such subtleties are hard to see without practice, but even first-time birders should try to notice whether a bird is chunky or slim, short-tailed or long-tailed, etc., and try to learn the typical shapes of each group of birds.

Behavior can be important in identification. Is the bird part of a flock, or is it solitary? If it's on the ground, does it walk or hop? Does it perch hori-zontally, or upright with the tail down? If it's swimming, does it stay on the surface or dive underneath? Does it bob its tail up and down while perched, or bob its head back and forth while swimming? Such clues, added to the typical shape and posture, can help to make some birds recognizeable from far away. I try to mention such behavioral clues in the text for each group of birds in this guide, or for the individual species.

Habitat is the key to finding various birds, as mentioned on p. 8, and it's also a good clue for identifying the ones you've found. A thin-billed brown bird on the ground in deep forest might be a thrush, while another on the ground in an open field might be a pipit instead. Always read the text for clues on habitat. But remember that birds sometimes show up in the "wrong" habitats, especially during migration season.

Field marks are often referred to as "the trademarks of nature." Most birds have particular markings that help to distinguish them from all others, and the trick is to know which ones are important. On the illustrations in this guide, pointers indicate the key markings, so that you can quickly check the book in the field to see what to focus on. In the text, important marks are mentioned in *italic* type. But in all cases you should take a good look at

the bird first — it may fly away while you're checking the book! Look for markings on the *face*, such as an eye-ring, whisker marks, or an eyebrow stripe. If the face is totally plain, lacking in obvious markings, that could be considered a field mark as well. The *wings* may show prominent wing-bars or a patch of contrasting color, or they may be plain. Many birds have some white in the tail, most obvious when the bird flies; this may consist of white

Field marks on a Northern Water-thrush, including a pale eyebrow, thin dark whisker mark, streaks on the underparts, and no wing-bars

outer edges or corners or spots partly concealed halfway up the tail. Many birds are paler below than above; the pale underparts may be plain or may have lengthwise streaks, crosswise bars, round spots, or some other pattern. In all cases, the more details you can notice, the better chance you have of identifying the bird.

Bird voices are distinctive, but it can be hard to match sounds to the written word. I include voice descriptions for most species anyway, since they can help give you confirmation on a bird that you have heard and seen. In a few groups of birds (such as flycatchers, dowitchers, owls), voice is the only sure way to tell some species apart, and it should be noted with care.

For many birds I describe both songs and callnotes. Songs are given mostly by males, mostly in spring and summer, to defend nesting territories and attract mates. Calls may be given by any member of the species in any season. Not all birds have songs, and some are not very vocal at all.

Pitfalls of bird identification can trip us up at times. Even if we know what a particular bird is supposed to look like, we can be misled. It's easy to misjudge sizes, as mentioned on p. 13, but colors can be tricky as well. Odd lighting can make brown birds look reddish or make gray birds look blue. Birds also get discolored in various ways. They may be stained on their faces or bellies if they have been eating sticky fruit or wading in mud. Then there are birds that have abnormal colors, such as albinos or partial albinos, patched with white. Finally, the process of molt changes the appearance of birds. Most healthy wild birds replace all their feathers at least once a year, in an orderly way, a few feathers at a time. During this molt their plumage may be a patchwork of old and new feathers, or their tails or wingtips may be oddly shaped. Birds in this condition don't have to be confusing if you understand what's going on.

Variation in birds: If you look closely at birds, you'll see some that don't look quite like the pictures in this guide. At first it may seem unsettling that the birds don't look like they are "supposed to," but this is normal. Part of this is owing to regional variation, the fact that bird populations look different in different places (see p. 22). But even on a local level, no two individuals look *exactly* alike — and the appearance of a bird will change subtly through the year. To demonstrate, here are some normal variations in the familiar House Finch (p. 366).

. . . but they're all House Finches!

The final ingredient: I commented earlier that birding is something we do for enjoyment, so if you enjoy it a lot, you're already a great birder. But there is one other essential element. I have met a lot of outstanding birders, and they all had one thing in common: a strong sense of birding ethics.

Good birding ethics mostly just involve common sense. If you're birding with others, be considerate and try to help others see the birds. Be considerate toward the general public, too. They may not understand your excitement, but you can be courteous, and maybe you can show them something that will spark their interest. Never trespass on private property without permission, and in places like parks and refuges, respect those areas that are closed to the public. Finally, be considerate toward the birds themselves and avoid harassing them or damaging their habitats. By taking a responsible approach, we can help to make sure that birding will continue to be the most rewarding pursuit in the world.

BIRDS IN PLACE AND TIME

You can find birds everywhere, but you will not find the *same* birds everywhere. Each species has its own distribution, its own range. And each place has its own particular combination of bird species. One of the keys to identifying birds is knowing what to expect at a given place and time.

Range maps: The range maps in this guide are color-coded to show you where and when to expect each bird. Lighter colors show where the bird is scarce or especially hard to find.

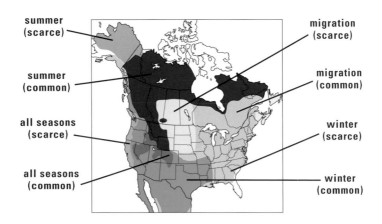

summer (scarce)

summer (common)

all seasons (scarce)

all seasons (common)

migration (scarce)

migration (common)

winter (scarce)

winter (common)

At first glance this might seem like a lot of colors, but there are really only three to remember: red for summer, blue for winter, gray for migration. (Put the summer red and winter blue together, and you have purple for the birds that stay all year.)

Birds do wander outside their normal ranges at times, so you may see a bird far from where it's "supposed" to be. (In general, migratory birds are far more likely to stray than birds that are permanent residents, wherever they live.) But if you're trying to figure out a new bird that you've seen, you should always check the maps right away to see which possibilities are most likely where you are.

The value of local information: One of the most helpful things you can get is a local bird checklist. Such lists are available for most wildlife refuges and parks, and many local bird clubs also publish lists of the birds of their regions. Often these checklists are annotated with the season of occurrence for each species and its commonness or rarity. A detailed list like this will tell you exactly what birds you should expect to see, with far greater precision than the range maps in this book. You may even want to mark up this book with your own codes for birds likely in your area.

Birds through the year: Birding sharpens our awareness of the seasons. In winter, birds are often in flocks, and the flocks may break up in late winter as birds prepare to choose nesting territories or to migrate north. Spring brings a great rush of migration, with huge numbers of little birds moving north across the continent. Many birds are in bright breeding plumage, and the males are singing. By late spring, when some birds are still heading north to the Arctic, others are actively building nests and raising young. Summer is the peak of nesting activity in the north. By late summer, identifying birds can be a challenge: adults may be in worn, faded plumage, and their youngsters can look odd as well. There is far less singing in late summer and fall. Adult birds molt into fresh new feathers, so they may be easier to identify again, except for those whose fall plumages are confusingly different from spring garb. Migration stretches over a longer period in fall than

male Song Sparrow singing to defend his nesting territory

in spring, with some shorebirds southbound in July, some waterfowl and sparrows not moving until November. By late fall, most birds have settled in where they will spend the winter. Watching this ageless cycle can give us a reassuring sense of being connected with the natural world.

Keeping lists: We humans have an instinct to collect things. Birders often satisfy this collecting urge by keeping lists of the birds they have identified. The most common type of list is the life list, a tally of all the bird species seen in one's lifetime; a bird seen for the first time is a "lifer." But other types of lists are popular as well. A yard list, or a list for any other small area, may grow to surprising numbers in time. Active birders often keep lists for their state or province or county, or for the birds seen in one year. The extreme listing event is a "big day," an attempt to find as many species as possible in one 24-hour period: a bit absurd, maybe, but lots of fun!

Writing it down: It may sound like homework, but there can be a special pleasure in going beyond mere lists and writing notes on what you've seen. After a few years, you'll be able to compare exactly when your local migrants returned every spring or relive birding experiences on vacation trips. And over a long period, detailed notes can even have scientific value.

Birding events: Cooperative bird surveys that are open to anyone include the Christmas Bird Count (CBC), held in late December or early January, and the Great Backyard Bird Count (GBBC), held in February. CBCs take place at over 1,500 locations, while anyone can take part in the GBBC from anywhere. Find information on both at www.birdsource.org. In May, International Migratory Bird Day celebrates the travels of birds all over the globe, reminding us that "our" birds are a resource that we share with the rest of the world. Many communities now hold local bird festivals, which are often in spring or fall but can be at any time of year.

FEEDERS AND OTHER MEANS OF ATTRACTING BIRDS

Feeding birds is tremendously popular, and rightly so: a bird feeder can bring nature right to our windowsills, allowing us to appreciate the beauty and intensity and fascinating behavior of birds from inches away. In most cases, wild birds could get along fine without this artificial food source, so we are really feeding them for our own sake, not theirs, but there is nothing wrong with this. For many people, especially for children, such a chance to watch birds up close may spark a lifelong interest in nature.

A feeder can be as simple as an open tray with a roof to keep the rain off. Sunflower seeds are very attractive to grosbeaks, cardinals, jays, chickadees, and others. Millet, especially white proso millet, is a good all-around food for most seed-eating birds, including finches, buntings, and sparrows. Nyjer ("thistle") seeds are favored by small birds such as goldfinches, siskins, and redpolls. It is worthwhile to buy these seed types separately, or to check the ingredients carefully if you buy mixtures. Generic birdseed mixtures may include cheap "filler" seed that will go to waste.

Suet (beef fat) is a standard food for attracting woodpeckers, nuthatches, jays, and other insect-eating or omnivorous birds. It can be put up in a wire mesh cage on a post or tree trunk to make it easy for these birds to reach it. In place of suet you can use a mixture of peanut butter and corn meal, which can be presented in various ways — even spread over a pine cone.

Hummingbird feeders are becoming very popular. Filled with a mixture of one part sugar to four parts water, they may attract orioles and others as well as hummingbirds. Most such feeders have red on them to catch the attention of the hummers; it's best not to put red coloring in the water.

Keep in mind that if you maintain a feeder, *you have a responsibility to keep it clean.* Most feeders need to be cleaned out every week or two. Hummingbird feeders may have to be cleaned every couple of days, especially in hot weather. Birdbaths should be washed out each time they're refilled. If you don't keep these sites clean, you might help spread disease through the bird population, doing more harm than good.

Planting for birds: If you have any space for gardening, the best way to attract birds is to plant for them. Exactly what to plant will vary depending on where you live. Many botanical gardens and arboretums have demonstration areas or information on how to plant for birds, butterflies, or other wildlife, and there are local publications on the subject for many regions.

Ideal choices for a bird garden are plants that will provide food in some way — in the form of edible seeds or berries, or good flower nectar for hummingbirds — as well as providing shelter. It's always best to use native plants when possible — plants native to your own particular region. They are already adapted to your local climate, so they won't require special care. Best of all, these plants will attract native insects without being overwhelmed by them, and insects are the best bird food of all. Of course, you should never use pesticides in a garden where you hope to attract birds.

CONSERVATION

Bird watching can thrive only as long as we have birds to watch. It seems too obvious to mention, but many birders appear to ignore this idea. Bird populations face serious threats, and we can't assume that some organization or government agency will deal with the problems. Birders need to be advocates for the birds, to speak up and support their conservation.

Endangered species: You will never know the thrill of seeing the Passenger Pigeon, Carolina Parakeet, Great Auk, or Labrador Duck, because those birds have all ceased to exist — that is, they have become extinct — within the last couple of centuries. Eskimo Curlew, Ivory-billed Woodpecker, and Bachman's Warbler are almost certainly extinct as well. Those birds are lost to us forever, and it is too late to help them.

However, we still have a chance to save *endangered species* (those in imminent danger of becoming extinct). Several North American birds are seriously endangered. Whooping Crane, California Condor, Kirtland's Warbler, Golden-cheeked Warbler, and Red-cockaded Woodpecker are all birds that could disappear within a few years without active protection. We also need to pay attention to *threatened species* (those at risk of becoming endangered), from the Florida Scrub-Jay to the California

Roseate Tern: classified as endangered in eastern Canada and northeastern U.S., threatened in southeastern U.S.

Gnatcatcher, birds that are especially vulnerable. In addition, several states and provinces keep lists of *species of special concern:* not yet threatened or endangered but with risk factors that make them worth monitoring.

Literally millions of dollars have been spent in the effort to pull the California Condor back from the brink of extinction. To those of us who care about nature, this is money well spent, because we don't want to lose a single species. But it is much easier and less expensive to save species while they are still common. For this reason, birders need to take responsibility for monitoring all bird populations, so that we will know if any of them start to slip. And we need to support the laws that protect endangered species, at the national, state, or provincial level, and demand that our politicians do nothing to weaken those laws. We owe it to the birds, and to future generations of bird watchers.

Habitat: One of the most important things that birding can teach us is the relation between birds and their habitats. Some birds are adaptable, found in many habitats, and such birds are usually very common — for example, the American Crow. Others are much more specialized. Kirtland's Warbler will nest only in stands of young jack pines of a certain age, and this bird is rare and endangered, finding suitable habitat mostly in just a few counties in Michigan. Kirtland's is an extreme case, but it stands to reason that birds that rely on scarce habitats will be scarce themselves.

An area of bird habitat will have a specific *carrying capacity* — that is, the number of birds that can find enough food, water, and shelter there. A woodlot that supports two pairs of Wood Thrushes will not suddenly support ten pairs. This is why people who care about birds have to focus their attention on protecting habitat. If that woodlot is cut down, those two pairs of Wood Thrushes are probably doomed. They can't just move into another forest, because that habitat is likely to be occupied already.

Obviously, sometimes we have to destroy habitat, since humans need room to live also. But we need to be aware of the value of rare habitats and the specialized birds (and other living things) that make their homes there. Some types of habitats have become particularly rare. Vast areas of marshes, both coastal salt marshes and inland freshwater marshes, have been drained or filled, and marsh birds have declined in numbers. Only a tiny fraction of our native prairies survive today; some prairie birds have adapted to pastures and farm fields, but others have become rare. Most of our old-growth forest has been cut down, and while replanting is a good idea, a tree farm is not the same thing as a real forest. The few old-growth forests that remain should be kept intact. With some careful planning, we can have progress and prosperity without losing our wildlife heritage.

Most of us are not in a position to buy large tracts of natural habitat, but even a small yard can be made into better habitat (see "Planting for birds" on p. 18). Here are other ways that individuals can help birds.

Shade-grown coffee: The kind of coffee that you drink can have an impact on bird populations. Traditional coffee is grown in deep shade in the tropics, and a plantation can look almost like a native forest with the undergrowth replaced by coffee bushes. These traditional coffee farms support many birds, including both tropical residents and migrant birds that nest here in North America and winter in the tropics. However, there are now cultivated varieties of coffee that can be grown in full sun. This sun coffee may produce slightly higher yields per acre, but it generally requires far more chemicals (fertilizers and pesticides), making it unhealthier for the workers in the fields, and sun coffee plantations support practically no birds at all. Buying shade-grown coffee for use at home and asking for it in restaurants may be a little inconvenient, but by increasing the demand for it, we can help to maintain good bird habitat in the tropics.

Cats indoors: House cats that are allowed to roam outside kill staggering numbers of wild birds — scientists estimate that the death toll runs into the hundreds of millions every year in North America. Cats that are well fed do not lose their hunting instincts; they are just stronger and faster, better able to kill more birds. Putting a bell on the cat's collar, or even declawing the cat, may not help much, because these crafty little predators can usually learn how to overcome such obstacles. It's best just to keep them indoors. Cats that are kept inside tend to live longer and be healthier than those that roam outdoors, so this is an issue on which cat lovers and bird lovers should be able to agree.

The problem is even more serious with feral cats that live outdoors all the time. Well-meaning people who feed these cats are only making the problem worse. House cats have no place in any natural ecosystem on this continent, not even suburban ecosystems, and birders and nonbirders alike have a responsibility to keep them indoors.

Ecotourism as a force for conservation: In some cases, we can contribute to conservation just by going birding, if we do it in the right way. Studies have shown that visits by bird watchers may pump millions of dollars into local economies in some places; but until recently, very few communities realized this. The establishment of official birding trails, with marked birding stops along a driving route, has helped to make more communities, businesses, and chambers of commerce aware of the economic impact of birdwatching. Ideally, they will realize that to keep the birders coming, they have to protect habitat for the birds. When you travel, at hotels and other tourist facilities, be sure to mention that you are visiting to see birds and that you appreciate local efforts to protect natural habitat. If you are lucky enough to travel farther afield and to visit ecotourism sites in other countries, such as jungle lodges, research these ahead of time and try to choose those that are locally owned, that employ local people, and that benefit local communities.

Organizations that deserve support: Many organizations work to conserve bird populations, and there is not room here to list all of them. Here are a few that work over wide areas of North America. The **National Audubon Society** (www.audubon.org) has worked for over a century on bird conservation. Its strength is in its many local chapters and a growing network of nature centers. Also extremely effective are some independent state organizations, notably New Jersey Audubon and Massachusetts Audubon. **The Nature Conservancy** (http://nature.org) has a focus on saving habitat by buying it, a direct approach that has had a huge impact on saving rare and endangered species. The **American Bird Conservancy** (www.abcbirds.org) works on a wide variety of issues and helps to coordinate the activities of diverse groups through its Bird Conservation Alliance. **Nature Canada**, formerly the Canadian Nature Federation (www.cnf.ca), works to protect all of nature, including birdlife, through its programs and its affiliates throughout Canada. The **Natural Resources Defense Council** (www.nrdc.org) takes on some of the most difficult issues in protecting birds and other wildlife in the United States. The work of **Birdlife International** (www.birdlife.net) is worldwide in scope, and in some places this is virtually the only organization trying to save endangered birds. The **Cornell Lab of Ornithology** (http://birds.cornell.edu) is a center for research and education that gets the public involved in research and conservation. Finally, the **American Birding Association** (www.americanbirding.org) is not only a great club for serious birders but also an active voice for protecting bird populations. In addition to these, there are many local and regional organizations devoted to conservation, and some of these are highly effective.

For more ideas on how you can support bird conservation, visit my website and look at www.kknature.com/conservation.

HOW BIRDS ARE CLASSIFIED AND NAMED

The sheer variety of nature is wonderful and amazing, but it is also potentially confusing. To make sense of this dizzying diversity, scientists classify living things into categories such as order, family, genus, and species. The color-coded sections in this guide are built around families of birds. For birding, the category you will usually want to know is the species — the basic "kind" of bird that you might write on your life list of sightings.

Species of birds: Whole books have been written to define precisely what a species is. No definition fits perfectly, because there are many borderline cases, forms that appear to be in the process of becoming species but are not quite distinct enough. In general, though, members of a species are isolated from members of other species in terms of reproduction. Different species often can interbreed (and may even produce fertile offspring) but typically don't. Willow and Alder Flycatchers (p. 244) are extremely similar, but they don't interbreed even where they live side by side. "Yellow-shafted" and "Red-shafted" Northern Flickers (p. 218) look obviously different, but they interbreed randomly wherever they meet: just east of the Rockies, almost all flickers are intergrades between the two forms. Baltimore and Bullock's Orioles (p. 340) also interbreed on the western plains, but much less often; they are considered separate species.

Subspecies (races): Members of a species may not all look the same — they can vary from place to place. In eastern North America, Hairy Woodpeckers change gradually from larger in the north to smaller in the south. The northern and southern birds are classified as different subspecies (or races), but the division between them is somewhat arbitrary. In the northeast, Newfoundland hosts a form that is more distinctly different, with more black in the plumage, but it is still clearly a Hairy Woodpecker; it too is classified as a subspecies. In this book I illustrate those races that look strikingly different, but the vast majority of subspecies can't be identified in the wild, and most birders will find it easier to ignore this topic.

Scientific names are applied to every known species. In Latin or Latinized Greek, these names are recognized by scientists working in any language. Names are usually written in italics: *Picoides villosus* is the Hairy Woodpecker. The first word is the genus: *Picoides.* The Arizona Woodpecker, *Picoides arizonae,* also belongs to this genus, so it's related to the Hairy. If a scientific name has three words, the third word is the subspecies. *Picoides villosus terraenovae* is the race of Hairy Woodpecker in Newfoundland.

English names of birds don't always seem logical. Some are named for things you can detect only with the bird in hand (like Sharp-shinned Hawk). Some are named on a global perspective: Common Sandpiper is rare in North America but common in the Old World. The Northern Cardinal is found mainly in the south (but there are other cardinals in South America). So don't expect to identify birds by their names.

Standardized names: Opinions differ on naming and classifying birds. If each expert followed his or her own preference, we'd have chaos in our bird guides. Fortunately, names are standardized by the Committee on Classification and Nomenclature of the American Ornithologists' Union (AOU). This committee of experts, a sort of supreme court of bird classification, reviews all published research and periodically issues the *AOU Check-list of North American Birds.* All bird names in this Field Guide follow the AOU's latest *Check-list* (1998) and its supplements issued since then (published in the July issues of *The Auk,* the AOU's scientific journal, in 2000, 2002, 2003, and 2004).

Checklist order: Besides official names, the AOU establishes the official sequence of lists. By tradition, official lists put the most primitive birds at the beginning and the most advanced ones at the end. This order changes over time, based on new research. Unless you plan to become a professional ornithologist, there's only one reason to keep up with the official sequence: most published checklists follow AOU order. If you want to check off birds you've seen on a list, it helps to know the order they're arranged in. This Field Guide is arranged so that similar kinds of birds are close together for comparison, so it departs from the AOU order in several places, but it is close enough that a familiarity with this book should allow you to find the species on published checklists as well.

Changes in how birds are classified: The classification of birds at any one time reflects the best current knowledge, but as our total knowledge continues to change, so do our bird lists. The sequence of bird families on the list has changed many times. For example, for many years, the loons and grebes were the first two families of birds on the North American list. The experts on the AOU committee reviewed all recent evidence and decided to change the sequence in 2003, and now the family of ducks, geese, and swans is the first group on the official

Canada Goose: divided into two species in 2004

list, as it is in this field guide. Changes at the species level occur even more often. As ongoing studies tell us more about the relationships of various birds, one species may be split into two, or two may be lumped into one. For example, most of the forms of juncos shown on p. 361 were considered separate species until they were lumped in the 1970s. More recently, the Black-crested Titmouse was officially split from the Tufted Titmouse in 2002, while the seemingly well-known Canada Goose was split into two species (Canada Goose and Cackling Goose) in 2004. This constant shuffling of the list can seem distracting at times. But you can ignore it if you wish — regardless of what's official, we're free to call the birds whatever we choose — or you can do as I do, and welcome each opportunity to think about some familiar bird from a new perspective.

DUCKS, GEESE, AND SWANS

(family Anatidae) begin next, on p. 26. These familiar waterfowl can be divided into several groups, as detailed below.

Among the **TRUE DUCKS**, males usually show bright patterns. Females wear subtle camouflage and are harder to identify; look at head shape, bill shape, and bill color. Males depart soon after courtship, leaving the females to care for the young. In late summer, many ducks molt into a drab **eclipse plumage**, and even males may become hard to identify.

American Wigeon:

spring male   female   male in eclipse plumage

Dabbling ducks (beginning p. 26) feed at the surface or tip up to reach underwater; they rarely dive. Also often feed on land. Common on small ponds, marshes, large lakes; fewer on coastal bays. They take flight by springing up directly from the water.

some dabbling ducks:

Mallard   Blue-winged Teal   Northern Pintail tipping up

Diving ducks (beginning p. 32) feed at the surface or dive deep underwater. Common on large lakes, coastal bays; in summer, also on marshes. To take flight, they usually must run across the surface of the water.

some diving ducks:

Lesser Scaup   Canvasback   scoter   eider   merganser

Black-bellied Whistling-Duck

GEESE, p. 46, tend to be larger than ducks, and have short thick bills. Most feed on land as well as in water.

Mute Swan

Canada Goose

WHISTLING-DUCKS, p. 44, are odd birds of tropical climates, not closely related to the true ducks.

SWANS, p. 50, are huge, long-necked, and usually white.

compare OTHER SWIMMING BIRDS (beginning on p. 54)

This category includes several unrelated families of birds. Many of these may look like ducks at first glance, but they often have different bill shapes.

Coots and gallinules, p. 54. Bob their heads as they swim or walk. Mostly on fresh water.

Grebes, p. 54. Great swimmers and divers, helpless on land. On fresh or salt water.

Auks, p. 50. Ocean birds, mostly in north. Great swimmers and divers.

Loons, p. 66. Large, low-slung divers. Strong in flight. Bold pattern in summer, drab in winter.

Cormorants, p. 68. Slinky divers of lakes and sea. May perch with wings spread to dry.

Many **AERIAL WATERBIRDS** (beginning p. 72) also may be seen swimming:

pelican

gulls

And here are a couple of part-time swimmers from unrelated families:

rail, p. 160

phalaropes, p. 190

25

feed in the shallows by dipping their heads in the water or by upending with head down and tail straight up. Males of most have bright patterns (except in late-summer eclipse plumage). Females are best identified by head shape, bill color, and (in flight) wing pattern.

MALLARD   *Anas platyrhynchos*

typical Mallard

"Mexican Duck"

The most familiar duck of the Northern Hemisphere, ancestor of many domestic ducks, very common and widespread in the wild. Besides wild populations, many Mallards live in semiwild state around cities, parks, farms; these birds are often larger than wild Mallards, and plumage may vary (see p. 52). ▶ Male's green head contrasts with yellow bill, white neck ring, reddish chest, gray body. Female mottled brown, with *black* smudges on *orange* bill. Both sexes show patch (speculum) on trailing edge of wing, *blue with white borders*. Note: in the northeast, Mallard and American Black Duck often crossbreed, producing intermediates. Near the Mexican border, a local form of Mallard (formerly called **"Mexican Duck"**) has male and female patterned alike, with mottled brown plumage, though male still has bright yellow bill. ♪ **Voice**: thin *rreeb* (male), noisy quacking like barnyard ducks (female).

AMERICAN BLACK DUCK   *Anas rubripes*

Common in the northeast, but declining in areas away from the coast as its range is invaded by the Mallard. Favors woodland ponds, coastal salt marshes. ▶ Both sexes suggest female Mallard, but with much darker body, gray head. Speculum on wing dark purple, *lacks* bold white edges shown by Mallard; in flight, the *white underwings* are striking in contrast to the dark body. Male has yellow bill, female's is duller. Often interbreeds with Mallard, so hybrids are frequently seen in the northeast. ♪ **Voice**: like Mallard's.

MOTTLED DUCK   *Anas fulvigula*

A warm-weather duck, the only typical dabbler to nest regularly in Florida and on the Gulf Coast. Introduced in coastal South Carolina, and rare inland on southern Great Plains. ▶ Both sexes look like a darker version of female Mallard, but bill is bright yellow (male) or dull yellow (female); blue wing patch (speculum) lacks broad white borders. At a distance, looks much like American Black Duck (rare in deep south), but body paler, head more buff. Similar birds in southwest (west Texas to Arizona) are "Mexican Ducks" (see under Mallard, above). ♪ **Voice**: like Mallard's.

DABBLING DUCKS

male

Mallard
23"

female
with
young

female

male "Mexican Duck"
(southwestern Mallard)

male hybrid,
American Black
Duck X Mallard

male Mallard in
eclipse plumage

**American
Black Duck**
23"

male

female

Mottled Duck
22"

male

female

are often rather vocal. Males and females usually make different sounds. While females mostly do variations on basic quacking, the males' calls may be very distinctive and are worth noticing.

NORTHERN PINTAIL *Anas acuta*

A trim, elegant dabbler, very common on marshy ponds and lakes, especially in the west. Likes very open habitats and usually is wary, hard to approach. ▶ Male has *white stripe* running up long neck onto brown head; gray body, long tail. Female mottled buff-brown; known by pointed tail, long neck, gray bill. In flight, shows narrow white trailing edge on inner part of wing. ♪ **Voice**: mellow *chooop* and high thin note (male), and quacking much like Mallard's (female).

GADWALL *Anas strepera*

Sometimes overlooked (it is confusingly plain) but fairly common, especially in the west. Likes large shallow ponds with lots of marsh plants. ▶ Male mostly gray, with contrasting *black stern*. Female mottled brown, with gray and orange bill. Note head shape, with steeper forehead than female Mallard (previous page). Square white patch on trailing edge of wing obvious in flight, sometimes visible while swimming. ♪ **Voice**: short *ghenk* (male), high nasal *quack* (female).

AMERICAN WIGEON *Anas americana*

Also called "Baldpate" for male's white cap. Common, especially in the west. Flocks often graze on land near ponds, including on parks, golf courses. On deep water, sometimes steals food from coots or diving ducks when they come to the surface. ▶ Male has *white crown stripe*, green ear patch on gray head; pink chest and sides. (In early fall, male may be plainer, more rust-colored.) Big white wing patches show in flight. Female has gray head contrasting with more pinkish body. Note rather *small blue-gray bill*. ♪ **Voice**: far-carrying whistle, *whee-WHEEW-wheew*, second note highest (male).

EURASIAN WIGEON *Anas penelope*

Mostly a winter visitor, uncommon in the northwest and Alaska, rare in the northeast, very rare elsewhere; native to Europe and Asia. In North America, almost always with flocks of American Wigeon. ▶ Male has bright *rusty head* with *buff* crown stripe; mostly gray body. Compare to male Redhead (p. 34). Rare hybrids with American Wigeon have intermediate patterns (but American can have buff on crown also). Female very much like female American Wigeon, may have browner head.

Northern Pintail
20"–26"

female

males

male,
late summer

Gadwall
20"

female

male

American
Wigeon
19"

male

male, early fall

female

male

Eurasian Wigeon
20"

TEALS AND SHOVELER

are small dabblers that often feed by swimming forward slowly in the shallows with their bills partly submerged.

GREEN-WINGED TEAL   *Anas crecca*

Common in marshes, the Green-wing is our smallest dabbler. Flocks in flight look very fast, twisting and turning in the air. ► Male has *chestnut* head with *green* ear patch, white bar on side of chest, yellow "tail-light." Female known by small size, strong eyeline, gray bill. **"Eurasian" Green-wing** is resident on islands of western Alaska, also rare winter visitor in northwest and northeast; male has white back stripe, lacks white chest bar. Female not safely identified. ♪**Voice**: far-carrying, squeaky *chyerk* (male), sharp quack (female).

BLUE-WINGED TEAL   *Anas discors*

A summer duck, common in marshy ponds east of the Rockies. Strongly migratory, it avoids cold weather more than most ducks. ► Pale blue wing patch mostly hidden when swimming, obvious in flight. Male has *white crescent* on *gray face* in spring. In fall, many are in drab eclipse plumage, look like females. Blue-wing and Cinnamon females very similar. ♪**Voice**: high peeping whistle (male), hoarse quack (female).

CINNAMON TEAL   *Anas cyanoptera*

Common in western marshes, but departs from colder regions in winter. ► Bright chestnut male unmistakable in spring. Female very much like female Blue-wing, with same wing pattern, but has slightly heavier and longer bill, plainer and browner face. Many males in fall still wear drab eclipse plumage, looking much like females except for their red eyes. ♪**Voice**: weak whistle (male), hoarse quack (female).

GARGANEY   *Anas querquedula*

Very rare visitor from Eurasia, but might show up on any marshy pond, especially in spring. ► Male has long white stripe on brown head. Female very much like female Blue-winged Teal, but with stronger face pattern.

NORTHERN SHOVELER   *Anas clypeata*

Common in shallow ponds, this front-heavy duck may swim with its head low, pushing its spatula bill through the water to strain out food. Despite heavy look, shovelers often fly around for no obvious reason. ► Male has green head, *white chest,* rusty sides; female mottled brown, with *big* gray and orange bill. Blue wing patch obvious in flight. Molting male may show pale face crescent. ♪**Voice**: throaty *thook-thook* (male).

TEALS AND SHOVELER

male

Green-winged Teal
14"

female

"Eurasian" form male

female

males

Blue-winged Teal
15"

female

Cinnamon Teal
16"

male

male

Garganey
(rare)
15"

female

male

Northern
Shoveler
19"

31

find much of their food by diving and swimming underwater. Unlike the dabbling ducks, they are awkward on land, and usually need to have a running start to take flight from the water. Also unlike the dabblers, they are silent most of the time.

LESSER SCAUP *Aythya affinis*

Scaup (or "bluebills") are very common in winter on lakes, bays. The two species are very similar: males with black head and whitish back, females with sharp white patch around base of bill. Lesser is usually more common on inland lakes in winter, Greater along coast, but there is overlap. Lesser spends summer at marshes in forest or prairie regions. ▶ Head shape is best mark: Lesser has peak at back of crown, slightly smaller bill than Greater Scaup. In flight, note shorter white wing stripe of Lesser (reaches halfway out wing). Male Lesser often shows purple gloss on head in good light.

GREATER SCAUP *Aythya marila*

Big flocks (or "rafts") of scaup gather in winter on open waters. This species is mainly along coast, less common inland. Nests at lakes in far north. ▶ Very much like Lesser Scaup, but different *head shape* (more rounded, with highest point toward front of head), larger bill. In flight, shows longer white wing stripe. Male often shows green (not purple) gloss on head, and sides may look whiter than on Lesser Scaup. Females of both scaup may show pale ear patch in summer.

RING-NECKED DUCK *Aythya collaris*

Favors sheltered waters more than most divers. Often in small flocks on small tree-lined ponds in winter. In summer, favors similar ponds in north or high country. ▶ Male has black head and back; *white bar* separates *gray sides* from black chest. Despite name, brown neck ring is very hard to see, but *rings on bill* are obvious. Female mostly gray-brown. Shows wide pale area near base of bill, usually less contrasty than on female scaup; similar to female Redhead (next page) but grayer, with more peaked head, more obvious bill ring.

TUFTED DUCK *Aythya fuligula*

Very rare winter visitor in northeast and northwest, more frequent as a migrant in Alaska. Usually seen with other diving ducks on ponds or lakes. Native to Europe and Asia. ▶ Tuft on head may be long or short, sometimes missing. Male shows strong contrast of *white* sides, *black* back. Female resembles other female divers, mostly dark brown, sometimes with white around base of bill; not safely identified unless she has obvious head tuft.

DIVING DUCKS

immature

Lesser Scaup
16½"

female

male

female
(summer)

Greater Scaup
18"

male

female
(winter)

Ring-necked Duck
17"

female

males

Tufted Duck (rare)
17"

33

The first three species below are related to the divers on the previous page. The Long-tailed Duck is very different, a hardy Arctic diver, often gathering in great flocks on icy seas of the north.

CANVASBACK *Aythya valisineria*

This elegant diver nests on prairie marshes, winters on lakes and bays, sometimes in large flocks. Wary and swift in flight, often flying high in V-formation. Like some other ducks that nest on northern prairies, the Canvasback was once much more numerous than it is today. ▶ Larger than related species of diving ducks. Shape is best field mark: most easily recognized by the long *"ski-jump" profile* of the head and bill. Male has *chestnut* head, black bill, black chest, *whitish back*. Female has pale tan head and neck contrasting with dark bill and grayish body.

REDHEAD *Aythya americana*

Although classified as a diving duck, the Redhead often dabbles in shallow water. Seen in small numbers in most areas, but huge flocks gather in winter on lagoons along Texas coast. In summer, on prairie marshes, the female often lays eggs in the nests of other waterbirds (other duck species sometimes do this also). ▶ Both sexes told from Canvasback by *rounder* head, shorter bill with pale band near tip. Male has back *gray* (not white). Female suggests female Ring-necked Duck (previous page) but browner, usually plainer on face, and lacks the Ring-neck's high, peaked head shape.

COMMON POCHARD *Aythya ferina*

Alaska only; a scarce visitor to islands of western Alaska. Common across northern Europe and Asia. ▶ Male combines field marks from Redhead and Canvasback (somewhat rounded head, whitish back) but has black bill with pale blue-gray stripe. Female plain gray-brown, may resemble female Redhead, but usually shows the Pochard bill pattern.

LONG-TAILED DUCK *Clangula hyemalis*

A unique duck of cold waters, sometimes abundant in far north. Noisy, especially males in spring flocks. Typically stays offshore when not nesting; only a few show up on lakes in the interior. Formerly called Oldsquaw. ▶ Has very different summer and winter plumages. Adult males with long tail, striking pattern. (Compare to Northern Pintail, p. 28.) Females and young males less distinctive, usually *pale* overall, with squarish head and stubby bill. All plumages show solidly *dark wings* in flight. ♪ Voice: musical yelping, *yow-owdle-ow*.

DIVING DUCKS

Canvasback
21″

female

male

Redhead
19″

female

male

Common
Pochard
(rare)
18″

male

Long-tailed
Duck
16″–22″

female (summer)

female (winter)

male
(summer)

male
(winter)

SCOTERS AND HARLEQUIN

Scoters are bulky dark sea-ducks. South of their Arctic nesting areas, they are seldom seen away from the coast or the Great Lakes. When migrating, flocks of scoters fly low over the water well offshore, paralleling the coastline. A few scoters may linger through summer far to the south of their nesting range. The Harlequin Duck is a unique little diver of northern rivers and rocky coasts.

SURF SCOTER *Melanitta perspicillata*

Common in some coastal areas in winter, especially along Pacific Coast. Often some distance offshore, although small flocks will also float sluggishly near piers and jetties. ▶ Male has striking pattern with white head patches (sportsmen's nickname is "skunkhead coot"), orange and white on bill, otherwise all black. Female dark sooty brown, with two whitish patches on face. At close range, notice how base of bill is shaped. ♪ **Voice**: usually silent, sometimes low whistles or croaks.

WHITE-WINGED SCOTER *Melanitta fusca*

Common along some coastal areas in winter, but less numerous toward the south. ▶ *White wing patch* conspicuous in flight, often hidden while swimming. Adult male has small white teardrop. Female and young male very dark, with paler face patches, pattern in front of eye different from female Surf Scoter's; at a distance, these birds are hard to tell from Surf Scoter unless the small white wing patch happens to show. ♪ **Voice**: usually silent, sometimes low whistles or croaks.

BLACK SCOTER *Melanitta nigra*

Fairly common in winter along central Atlantic Coast and northern Pacific Coast, but scarce toward the south. ▶ Adult male all black except for *orange bill knob*. Female and young male dark, with contrasting *pale face* and foreneck. Winter male Ruddy Duck (p. 40) smaller and paler, with relatively bigger bill. ♪ **Voice**: clear whistles, croaks. More vocal than other scoters.

HARLEQUIN DUCK *Histrionicus histrionicus*

This clown-patterned duck thrives in turbulent waters: rushing streams in summer, surf-pounded rocky coast in winter. Usually in small flocks. Flight is swift and low. ▶ Male unmistakable. Female dark brown, with two or three white face spots; compared to scoters (above), looks smaller with much shorter bill. See female Bufflehead (p. 40), female scaup (p. 32). ♪ **Voice**: various squeaks and whistles (sometimes called "sea mouse").

female

male

young
male

Surf Scoter
20"

female

young male

male

White-winged Scoter
21"

female

Black Scoter
19"

male

female

Harlequin Duck
16½"

males

37

are big hardy sea-ducks of northern coastlines. Their soft, dense down feathers protect them in frigid weather, and the female eider plucks her own down feathers for an insulating layer around the eggs in her nest (the insulating quality of eiderdown is well known to humans also).

COMMON EIDER *Somateria mollissima*

More commonly seen than other eiders, regularly south to New England and Long Island in east, to southern Alaska in west. Dense flocks (or "rafts") float offshore, rest along rocky coastlines. Despite their heavy look, eiders are swift in flight. ▶ Adult male distinctive; bill color varies from orange (Alaska) to olive-gray (northeast). Female known by large size, long sloping bill, heavy barring on sides; overall color varies from grayish to rusty brown. Young males go through various stages including dark-headed, white-chested look. ♪ Voice: low crooning, short growl.

KING EIDER *Somateria spectabilis*

A tough duck, abundant in parts of high Arctic. Only a few straggle south to where most birders live. Nests on tundra, winters at sea, some as far north as there are openings in pack ice. ▶ Adult male has orange frontal shield, powder blue head, much black on back. Female much like Common Eider but has different head shape, more *scalloped* look (not bars) on sides. Young male can look much like young male Common Eider but has shorter bill, more square-looking head.

SPECTACLED EIDER *Somateria fischeri*

Alaska only. This oddly beautiful goggle-eyed duck is uncommon to rare in summer on coastal tundra. Its wintering area was discovered only recently: it winters in flocks among pack ice, far out in Bering Sea. Declining in numbers, may be endangered. ▶ Male has bold "spectacles" on green head; white back, black chest and underparts. Female mottled brown, shows a strong hint of the male's face pattern.

STELLER'S EIDER *Polysticta stelleri*

Alaska only. Uncommon, nesting on tundra; declining in numbers. Winters along coast, usually in tight flocks. Lone birds may associate with Harlequin Ducks or other divers. ▶ The smallest eider. Adult male shows unique pattern, with peachy chest, black neck ring and eye spot, green and black knob on crest. Female confusing, plain dark brown, suggests a female scoter (previous page) or dabbling duck; notice square head, white borders on blue wing patch.

EIDERS

young male

Common Eider
25″

males

females

young male

King Eider
23″

male

female

female

Spectacled Eider
22″

male

female

Steller's Eider
18″

male

39

GOLDENEYES, STIFFTAILS

The two goldeneyes and the Bufflehead are big-headed diving ducks of cold waters. They usually nest in holes in trees. Stifftails (Ruddy and Masked) are small diving ducks with big flat bills. Their stiff, spiky tail feathers are often raised above the water.

COMMON GOLDENEYE   *Bucephala clangula*

A sharply patterned duck of lakes, rivers, coastal bays. Usually in small flocks in winter. Wings make whistling sound in flight. ▶ Male has roundish *white spot* before yellow eye, black head and back contrast with white chest and sides. Female has chocolate brown head contrasting with gray body, often has yellow tip on black bill (but bill may be all dark in summer). Young male resembles female through middle of first winter.

BARROW'S GOLDENEYE   *Bucephala islandica*

A cold-water duck of the northwest and northeast, usually less numerous than Common Goldeneye. Wings make a whistling sound in flight. ▶ Smaller bill and steeper forehead than Common Goldeneye. Male has *white crescent* (not a round spot) before eye, more black on back. Female not always safely identified; often has bill all pinkish yellow, may have darker brown head than female Common, and head shape is good clue.

BUFFLEHEAD   *Bucephala albeola*

A diminutive diver, like a toy duck. Usually in small flocks on lakes or shallow bays in winter. Found along northern rivers and bogs in summer, often nesting in old Northern Flicker holes. ▶ Adult male has white "scarf" on round black head. Female has gray head with white ear spot; young male is similar, but white spot is bigger. See Hooded Merganser (next page).

RUDDY DUCK   *Oxyura jamaicensis*

An odd little duck, common in many areas. Sluggish, sitting around on ponds, lakes, bays, sometimes in large flocks. Takes flight with difficulty, flies with fast buzzy wingbeats. In courtship, male bobs head, makes odd croaking rattle. ▶ Male has contrasting dark cap and *white cheeks;* ruddy brown body color and bright blue bill in breeding season. Female's pale cheeks crossed by smeary *dark line.* Wings solid dark in flight.

MASKED DUCK   *Nomonyx dominicus*

Rare visitor to Texas and Florida, extremely rare elsewhere. Secretive; hides in marshes along edges of shallow ponds. ▶ Breeding male reddish with black face; female and nonbreeding male with *two strong dark stripes* on buffy face. White wing patch shows in flight.

GOLDENEYES, STIFFTAILS

Common Goldeneye 18½"

female

male

young male

female in summer

Barrow's Goldeneye 18"

female

male

female

males

Bufflehead 13½"

winter male

Ruddy Duck 15"

summer male

female

female

Masked Duck 13½"

breeding male

41

are among the few ducks that regularly eat fish. Slender and long-bodied, they dive and swim underwater. Serrated edges on their bills (sportsmen call them "sawbills") help them grasp slippery minnows. In flight they look stretched out and thin.

COMMON MERGANSER *Mergus merganser*

Mostly on fresh water, favoring rivers and lakes in all seasons. In forested country in summer, often nesting in large tree cavities. In winter, sometimes in very large flocks on reservoirs. ► Male mostly white with black back, green head. Other green-headed ducks (Mallard, p. 26, Shoveler, p. 30) have different body pattern and shape. *Red bill* is thick at base, elongated and narrow toward tip. Female gray, with bright rusty head, sharp white throat. Compare to female Red-breasted Merganser (below), male Redhead (p. 34).

RED-BREASTED MERGANSER *Mergus serrator*

Mainly on salt water in winter, often seen around coastal jetties and beaches. Flies fast and low over the water. ► Male not as white as Common Merganser, with *gray* sides, dark red breast. Shaggy crest not obvious at distance, but *white collar* is conspicuous. Female is much like female Common, but shows *less contrast* between whitish throat and *duller* brown head; also lacks Common's contrast between brown neck and white chest. (Note: young Common Mergansers in summer can look very similar.) Thinner bill of Red-breasted Merganser, with different feathering at base, may be noticeable at close range.

HOODED MERGANSER *Lophodytes cucullatus*

Favors small lakes, ponds, especially those surrounded by trees, but also ponds in coastal marshes in winter. Uncommon, never in large flocks. Nests in holes in trees, sometimes in Wood Duck nest boxes. ► Male's elaborate crest, white with black border, may be raised high or flattened. Compare to Bufflehead (previous page). Female smaller than other mergansers, more uniformly dark, with mostly *dark bill;* paler bushy crest shows at back of long flat head.

SMEW *Mergellus albellus*

Rare visitor to western Alaska during migration and winter; extremely rare winter visitor elsewhere in North America. Widespread in Eurasia. ► Male is mostly white, with black pattern on face, crest, wings. Compare to Long-tailed Duck (p. 34). Female has two-toned head, bright red-brown with white lower face and throat. Shorter bill than other mergansers.

MERGANSERS

Common Merganser
25"

female

male

male

Red-breasted Merganser
23"

female

male

Hooded Merganser
18"

males

female

female

Smew
(rare)
16"

male

Unlike most ducks, these four all perch in trees at times, and three of these nest in tree holes or nest boxes. Whistling-ducks are gangly waterfowl of the tropics, not closely related to the true ducks. Sexes of whistling-ducks look alike, and both parents care for the young.

WOOD DUCK *Aix sponsa*

A beautiful duck of wooded swamps, shady ponds, quiet rivers. Common in parts of the east and northwest, uncommon elsewhere. May perch high in trees. Wood Ducks frequently use nest boxes put up for them. ► Colorful adult male unmistakable for most of year. Female has hint of crest, dark back, *white eye-patch* on gray head. Male in eclipse plumage resembles female, with more distinct white throat. In flight, Wood Ducks look long-tailed and dark, with a white trailing edge on inner part of wing. ♪ **Voice:** shrill, hoarse *oowheak!* on taking flight (female), thin *djeee* (male).

FULVOUS WHISTLING-DUCK *Dendrocygna bicolor*

Locally common in southern marshes, rice fields, lakes, and other wide-open habitats. Flocks often fly around at dawn and dusk. A few may wander far north of normal range. Unlike others on this page, usually nests on the ground. ► Butterscotch color with *gray* bill, long neck, *white stripe* on flanks. Compare to young Black-bellied Whistling-Duck, also to female Pintail (p. 28). In flight, black underwings and white crescent above tail contrast with buff body. ♪ **Voice:** hoarse whistle, *ka-wheeeah*, often given while flying.

BLACK-BELLIED WHISTLING-DUCK *Dendrocygna autumnalis*

Mostly near Mexican border but increasingly common, especially in Texas; also established in Florida. Often nests in nesting boxes put up near water. Active at dawn and dusk and also forages at night, and flocks may be heard calling in the dark as they fly to their feeding grounds. ► Adults unmistakable: chestnut, gray, and black, with bright pink bill. White wing patch striking in flight. Young bird has gray bill, muted colors, but shows hint of adult pattern. ♪ **Voice:** squeaky whistles, *costa-REEcah, chi-chi-chi.* Often calls in flight.

MUSCOVY DUCK *Cairina moschata*

Most Muscovies seen in North America are escapees from domestic stock (see p. 52). A few wild ones stray from Mexico to Falcon Dam area, south Texas. Wild Muscovies are big wary ducks of wooded riverbanks, swamps. ► Very large, black. White wing patches obvious in flight, not when swimming. Male larger, glossier than female, with knob above bill.

PERCHING DUCKS

Wood Duck
18"

females

males

Fulvous
Whistling-Duck
20"

adults

juvenile

adults

Muscovy
Duck
28"

Black-bellied
Whistling-Duck
21"

GEESE

are sociable waterfowl, usually seen in flocks. Most geese will forage on land as well as in the water. Unlike typical ducks, the sexes of geese are usually patterned alike, and both parents help to care for the young.

CANADA GOOSE   *Branta canadensis*

Common and familiar, and becoming more so. Once mainly a wilderness bird, the "honker" is adapting to life on golf courses and city parks, extending its year-round range. Many of these new feral flocks are permanent residents; northern wild flocks still migrate, flying in lines or V-formation. ▶ Basic pattern unmistakable, with *white chinstrap* on black head and neck. Different populations vary greatly in size and body color (from white-chested to very dark). See Cackling Goose (below). ♪**Voice:** deep musical honking.

CACKLING GOOSE   *Branta hutchinsii*

Only recently (2004) recognized as a separate species from Canada Goose. Nests mainly in tundra regions, winters in west and south. ▶ Most distinctive populations are *very small,* hardly bigger than Mallards, with *stubby bill.* Smallest races of Canada can be nearly same size as largest races of Cackling, so intermediate-sized birds not safely identified. ♪**Voice:** honking or cackling, usually higher-pitched than voice of Canada Goose.

GREATER WHITE-FRONTED GOOSE   *Anser albifrons*

Very common in parts of the west and midwest, nesting on Arctic tundra, wintering in warm climates. Flocks may feed in open farm fields in winter. ▶ Adult has white band around base of bill, variable *black barring* on belly. Young bird in fall is all gray-brown; separated from immature blue-morph Snow Goose (next page) by pale bill and legs, white on rump. Some domestic geese resemble White-fronts; see p. 52. Some stray White-fronts on Atlantic Coast are from Greenland, slightly more orange on bill (difference is hard to see). ♪**Voice:** high-pitched laughing, *ah-HAH-uh-huh.*

BRANT   *Branta bernicla*

A small goose that hugs the coast, where flocks feed in sheltered bays during winter. A few show up inland during migration to and from Arctic tundra. ▶ Black head and neck with *small* white neck spot, dark back. Two types: eastern birds (also scarce in northwest) have white belly contrasting with black chest; western "Black Brant" has much darker belly (hard to see when birds are swimming). Young birds during first winter have pale bands on back. ♪**Voice:** hoarse, low honking.

GEESE

Canada Goose
34"–46"

smallest Canada Geese and
largest Cackling Geese are
very similar in size

**Greater
White-fronted
Goose**
28"

adult

Cackling Goose
22"–33"

"Aleutian" form

immature

adult Atlantic (pale-bellied) Brant

Brant
24"

adult
"Black
Brant"

immature
"Black Brant"

SMALLER GEESE

SNOW GOOSE   *Chen caerulescens*

Abundant in certain areas, nesting on Arctic tundra, wintering in marshland and open country in warmer climates. Follows traditional routes in migration, may be seldom seen outside these corridors of travel. Flocks often forage on land in farm fields, marsh edge, tundra. Two color morphs; the gray-bodied, white-headed form, **"Blue Goose,"** was once considered a separate species. ▶ Typical adult white with black wingtips, pink-orange bill and legs. Compare to white domestic geese and ducks (p. 52). Immature grayer. Immature of blue morph is mostly dark brown, with *dark* bill and legs; compare to White-fronted Goose (previous page). ♪ **Voice:** nasal honking, *owk-owk,* heard constantly from flocks.

ROSS'S GOOSE   *Chen rossii*

A smaller cousin of the Snow Geese, usually seen with them but almost always outnumbered by them. Ross's Geese are uncommon in the west, rare in the east, but increasing; might show up anywhere in migration or winter. ▶ Smaller than Snow Goose. Much shorter bill *lacks* black "grinning patch," often has bumpy blue-gray area at base. Head rounder, eye more centrally located in face, for more gentle expression. Young Ross's is much whiter than young Snow. Blue morph of Ross's is quite rare. Snow and Ross's sometimes hybridize, producing intermediates. ♪ **Voice:** higher-pitched and softer than honking of Snow Goose.

EMPEROR GOOSE   *Chen canagica*

A rare Alaskan specialty, nesting on coastal tundra, wintering in flocks along shorelines of Alaska Peninsula and Aleutians. Very rare winter stray to Pacific Northwest. ▶ Somewhat like "Blue Goose," above (gray body, white head), but has *black foreneck and chin,* scaly pattern on body plumage. Juvenile in first fall has all-dark head, neck, and bill. ♪ **Voice:** a musical *quah-haah,* often given in flight.

BARNACLE GOOSE   *Branta leucopsis*

Nesting in Greenland and wintering in Europe, Barnacle Geese may very rarely stray to northeastern North America, but most seen on this continent are probably aviary escapees. These may associate with wild Canada Geese or other waterfowl. ▶ Black neck and cap surrounding white face, small dark bill, barred gray back.

GEESE

white morph juvenile

white morph adult

Snow Geese flying (Ross's are similar)

Snow Goose 28"

blue morph juvenile

adult blue morph ("Blue Goose")

adult

juvenile

Ross's Goose 23"

Emperor Goose 26"

adults

Barnacle Goose (rare) 27"

49

include the largest of waterfowl. Most swan species are pure white. Both parents help to incubate the eggs and care for the young.

MUTE SWAN   *Cygnus olor*

Native to the Old World, introduced in North America. Populations on Atlantic Coast increasing and spreading, displacing native birds in some cases. Still localized around Great Lakes and farther west. ► Orange bill with raised black knob. Often swims with neck held in graceful S-curve, sometimes with wings arched above its back. Young bird duller, may be brownish gray, with gray bill. ♪ **Voice:** usually silent (sometimes hissing and grunting), but wingbeats noisy in flight.

TUNDRA SWAN   *Cygnus columbianus*

Nests on Arctic tundra; winters commonly in a few traditional regions, but only a scarce wanderer elsewhere. Flocks sometimes seen flying high overhead, calling. North American race formerly known as Whistling Swan. ► Adult has *black* bill (not orange as in Mute Swan), usually with a small *yellow spot* at base of bill, before the eye. Juvenile dull gray-brown, with pink tinge on bill; plumage becomes whiter by midwinter. (Eurasian race, "Bewick's Swan," a very rare visitor in the west, has much more yellow at base of bill, but less than Whooper Swan, below.) ♪ **Voice:** nasal or musical honking, often three-noted.

TRUMPETER SWAN   *Cygnus buccinator*

This huge swan weighs more than any other native bird. Formerly endangered; now doing well in the northwest and being introduced into areas farther east (including northern plains, Great Lakes region). ► Quite similar to Tundra Swan, not always safely identified. Trumpeter is larger, with massive all-black bill. *Lacks* yellow spot before eye (but so do some Tundra Swans). In summer, Trumpeter is mostly farther south than Tundra, but the two overlap in migration and winter. The size difference is apparent when the two species are together. ♪ **Voice:** rich bugling notes, lower-pitched than calls of Tundra Swan.

WHOOPER SWAN   *Cygnus cygnus*

This Old World swan is a regular visitor to the Aleutian Islands, Alaska, and rarely shows up at other points in western Alaska. Escapees from captivity may be seen elsewhere in North America. ► Huge (size of Trumpeter Swan), with bill extensively yellow at base. See note regarding "Bewick's Swan" under Tundra Swan account, above.

SWANS

juvenile

adult

Mute
Swan
56"

Tundra Swan
53"

adult

juvenile

juvenile

adult

Trumpeter
Swan
60"

Trumpeter

Tundra

Mute

Whooper
Swan
58"

51

The tame ducks and geese living in barnyards and around city park ponds are mostly descended from the wild Mallard (p. 26), Muscovy (p. 44), Swan Goose (below), and Greylag Goose (native to Eurasia), but may look very different from their wild ancestors.

In addition, many exotic waterfowl are kept in captivity. Escapees are sometimes seen wandering in the wild. A few examples are shown here.

Black Swan
Cygnus atratus
native to Australia

Swan Goose
Anser cygnoides
(domestic form)
native to Asia

Egyptian Goose
Alopochen aegyptiacus
native to Africa

EXOTIC DUCKS

male

Mandarin Duck
Aix galericulata
native to China

female

male

Ringed Teal
Callonetta leucophrys
native to South America

White-cheeked Pintail
Anas bahamensis
native to American tropics

female

male

Red-crested Pochard
Netta rufina
native to Eurasia

female

male

Ruddy Shelduck
Tadorna ferruginea
native to Old World

Northern Shelduck
Tadorna tadorna
native to Old World

all favor marshy ponds. Coots, moorhens, and gallinules act like ducks when they are not walking on land or climbing in marsh plants; related to rails **(family Rallidae,** p. 160). Grebes are introduced on next page.

AMERICAN COOT — *Fulica americana*

In many regions, every lake, pond, and marsh has coots — sometimes by the hundreds. Noisy and feisty, may become tame on park ponds, golf courses. Mostly on fresh water, also coastal bays in winter. ▶ Charcoal gray with blacker head, *thick white bill*, with white and chestnut frontal shield up forehead. Nods its head as it swims; walks on land, showing big feet with lobes along toes. Immature paler gray; downy young has red head.
♪**Voice:** varied; clucking, whining, and chattering notes.

COMMON MOORHEN — *Gallinula chloropus*

Not as outgoing as the coot, usually less common, prefers ponds with more marshy cover. ▶ Adult slaty with browner back, *white stripe along side.* Thick bill and frontal shield usually *red and yellow,* sometimes all yellow or brownish. Legs greenish. Immature paler gray with dull bill and legs, but shows white stripe on side.
♪**Voice:** varied; nasal whining and clucking notes.

PURPLE GALLINULE — *Porphyrio martinica*

A colorful marsh bird of warm climates. Swims, walks on shore, climbs in marsh plants and in waterside trees.
▶ Adult is mostly purple and green, with pale blue shield above red and yellow bill. Undertail coverts noticeably *white;* legs *bright yellow.* Immature much plainer, buff-brown and olive; note bill shape, white undertail coverts. ♪**Voice:** sharp wails, whines, clucks.

PIED-BILLED GREBE — *Podilymbus podiceps*

On ponds and lakes everywhere except far north, this little diver is common, but not seen in flocks. Sometimes swims submarine-style, with only its head above water. ▶ Compact and short-necked, with *thick bill.* In breeding season, bill is white with black ring ("pied"); at other seasons, bill is dull and pale. Brownish overall, with rusty tinge in winter, black throat in summer.
♪**Voice:** odd gobbling *kuh-kuh-kuh-kowp, kuh-kowp.*

LEAST GREBE — *Tachybaptus dominicus*

South Texas specialty, singly or in pairs on small marshy ponds, usually a bit secretive. Very rare visitor to Arizona. ▶ Smaller than Pied-billed, dark, gray-faced, with small *thin* bill and bright *yellow eyes.* Throat blackish in breeding plumage. Some Eared Grebes (next page) in winter plumage are quite dark and may have yellow eyes. ♪**Voice:** sputtering metallic trill.

POND SWIMMERS

immature

American Coot
15"

chick

adult

adult

adult

immature

Common Moorhen
14"

adult

Purple Gallinule
14"

immature

adult

chicks

winter

Pied-billed Grebe
13"

winter

Least Grebe
9½"

breeding

breeding

55

GREBES

(family Podicipedidae) are highly aquatic and swim very well underwater but are almost helpless on land. Often build floating nests. Pied-billed Grebe (page 54) is the most widespread grebe in North America.

HORNED GREBE *Podiceps auritus*

Nests on northern lakes and marshes, winters on coastal bays or large lakes. ▶ Summer plumage known by reddish neck, buffy-gold "horns" on black head. Winter plumage can be much like Eared Grebe, but usually looks cleaner black and white, with *white cheeks,* pale spot before eye, thicker bill. Much more compact than last three on this page, with darker bill.

EARED GREBE *Podiceps nigricollis*

On ponds and lakes in the west, often very common, nesting in colonies and wintering in large flocks. Rare visitor in the east. ▶ Summer plumage known by black neck, buffy-gold "ears" on side of black head. Winter plumage like Horned but duller, dingier, with darker cheeks, gray on neck, *whitish ear patches* near back of head. *Bill thinner,* slightly upturned; head more peaked.

RED-NECKED GREBE *Podiceps grisegena*

Generally an uncommon bird, but can be conspicuous in summer at marshy ponds of far northwest. Winters mostly in coastal waters. ▶ Told from Western and Clark's by color on neck, from Horned and Eared by *yellow* on bill (sometimes hard to see in winter) and more elongated shape. Pale cheeks contrast with reddish neck in summer, gray cheeks in winter.

WESTERN GREBE *Aechmophorus occidentalis*

This graceful swimmer is common on many freshwater marshes in the west, also on coastal bays in winter. Many grebes have courtship dances, but Western and Clark's perform spectacular splashy race across water, with loud calls. ▶ Slender, long-necked, long-billed, sharply black and white. Compare to Clark's Grebe, also to loons in winter plumage (p. 66). ♪**Voice:** reedy, grating *krrrik krrrikk,* sharply two-noted.

CLARK'S GREBE *Aechmophorus clarkii*

A close relative of Western Grebe, often found with it, but usually less common. ▶ Very much like Western, but white on face extends narrowly above eye; bill brighter orange-yellow. Voice also differs. In winter, some birds appear to have intermediate face patterns, may not be safely identified. ♪**Voice:** reedy, grating *krrr-rrrrr,* slurred but usually not sharply two-noted.

GREBES

Horned Grebe
13½"

summer

winter

Eared Grebe
12½"

winter

summer

Red-necked Grebe
20"

winter

summer

Western Grebe
25"

**Clark's
Grebe**
25"

57

These gaudy-beaked seabirds introduce the Auk family **(Alcidae)**, which includes murres, guillemots, puffins, murrelets, and auklets. All are ocean birds, often spending most of their time far from land, using their short wings to "fly" underwater more gracefully than they do in the air. For nesting, they often gather at large colonies on offshore islands. Most auks are rather quiet away from their nesting colonies.

ATLANTIC PUFFIN   *Fratercula arctica*

Famous, but not often seen except around some islands in Maine and eastern Canada in summer; winters out at sea. Puffins nest in burrows or crevices of offshore islands. ▶ Summer adults unmistakable (no range overlap with other puffins). In winter, bill is somewhat smaller and less colorful (after outer plates are shed), face is grayer. Immatures have bill even smaller, but still recognizably different shape from other auks in Atlantic.

HORNED PUFFIN   *Fratercula corniculata*

Alaskan specialty, seldom seen farther south. Common around islands in Bering Sea and off southern Alaska. May move south in winter, far out at sea; sometimes found far from the California coast.▶ Suggests Atlantic Puffin (no overlap in range) but has simpler bill pattern, more obvious fleshy "horn" above eye. In winter, adult's bill becomes smaller and plainer, face becomes gray. Immature's bill even thinner and darker.

TUFTED PUFFIN   *Fratercula cirrhata*

The widespread puffin of the west coast, but seen more easily in southern Alaska than elsewhere; has become less common in southern part of range. Nests in burrows on offshore islands, may dig a tunnel more than seven feet long. ▶ Blackish body, big bright bill. Summer adult has white face, golden head tufts. In winter, face gray, tufts reduced or lacking, bill may be red or yellow. Immature has smaller yellow bill.

RHINOCEROS AUKLET   *Cerorhinca monocerata*

Fairly common off the northern Pacific Coast, the "Rhino" may go far out to sea or may forage rather close to shore, often in large flocks. ▶ Yellow bill, two white face stripes (less apparent in winter). Horn on bill is worn only in spring and summer. Winter birds look fairly plain dark gray, known by big-headed look, bill shape and color. Tufted Puffins in winter can be very similar but have thicker bills and larger, rounder heads. Cassin's Auklet (p. 62) is much smaller.

PUFFINS AND RHINO

Atlantic Puffin 13"

immature

summer

winter

summer

Horned Puffin 14½"

summer

winter

winter adult

immature

Tufted Puffin 15"

summer

summer

Rhinoceros Auklet 14"

winter

COMMON MURRE *Uria aalge*

Murres, our largest surviving auks, nest in colonies on island cliffs, often packed close together on narrow ledges; gather in large flocks far offshore. This murre is fairly common along west coast, but in east is only a rare visitor south of Canada. ▶ Charcoal above, white below, sharply two-toned in summer but with more white on face in winter. Compare to loons, p. 66. Thick-billed Murre is very similar.

THICK-BILLED MURRE *Uria lomvia*

This bulky diver is abundant in the high Arctic, but only a few move south in winter—to New England waters in east, rare south of Alaska in west. ▶ Much like Common Murre. Seen close, slightly thicker bill shows *white mark at gape.* Blacker back (hard to see without direct comparison). In summer, Thick-billed may show white coming up higher in point on chest; in winter, it may have more black on face than Common.

RAZORBILL *Alca torda*

A big chunky diver of the North Atlantic. Nests on cliffs of northern islands and coasts, often in same colonies as murres. Winters in large flocks far offshore, but may be seen from shore during storms. ▶ At close range, adults known by *white band* across *massive bill.* Young birds and distant adults in winter resemble Thick-billed Murre but have even thicker bill, bigger head, longer tail often held up above water when swimming.

PIGEON GUILLEMOT *Cepphus columba*

Guillemots stay closer to shore than most other auks, with small numbers swimming around wave-washed rocks, nesting in coastal rockpiles or under debris. Pronounced "GILL-uh-mott." ▶ In breeding plumage, black with big *white wing patches,* orange-red feet. Smaller than White winged Scoter (p. 36), with much bigger wing patch. Juveniles and winter adults gray to whitish, paler than most auks.

BLACK GUILLEMOT *Cepphus grylle*

This auk hugs the coastline of northern and eastern Canada, extending south into New England, with some reaching Massachusetts in winter. ▶ Very much like Pigeon Guillemot, best known by range (they overlap only in northwest Alaska). Pigeon often shows *dark wedge* across wing patch, Black does not. Underside of wing (seen in flight) is dusky on Pigeon Guillemot, mostly white on Black Guillemot.

LARGE AUKS

winter

Common Murre
17"

summer

summer

Thick-billed
Murre
18"

winter

winter

Razorbill
17"

summer

winter

Black Guillemot
13"

summer

Pigeon Guillemot
13"

winter

summer

61

CASSIN'S AUKLET   *Ptychoramphus aleuticus*

Numerous off west coast but seldom seen from shore. Nests in burrows on offshore islands, disperses out at sea. ▶ Small, compact, and dark. Pale spots above and below eye and on base of bill, visible at close range. Whitish belly is visible only in flight. Flying birds look stubby and dingy, with fast fluttery wingbeats. All of the murrelets (below) look stronger in flight.

ANCIENT MURRELET   *Synthliboramphus antiquus*

Common off British Columbia and Alaska; some move south in winter as far as California coast. Nests in burrows on offshore islands. Unlike other auks, a few stray far inland almost every fall, have even reached Atlantic Coast. ▶ Distinct *gray back* contrasts with white underparts and black on head. Short, thick bill is noticeably *pale*. In breeding plumage, smeary white eyebrow. In winter, less black on throat.

MARBLED MURRELET   *Brachyramphus marmoratus*

In sheltered coastal waters, these murrelets often swim in pairs. If disturbed, they dive underwater or fly away with fast, deep wingbeats. Unlike other auks, they nest on high branches in old-growth forest, and are threatened in many areas by loss of habitat. ▶ In breeding plumage, dark mottled brown all over. In winter, black and white with a white stripe over wing. Note: a similar Asian bird, Long-billed Murrelet (*B. perdix*), has been found inland in North America several times.

KITTLITZ'S MURRELET   *Brachyramphus brevirostris*

Alaska only, scarce and local along southern coast, especially near glaciers. ▶ In summer, like Marbled Murrelet but more golden brown above, with *entire belly white* (most easily seen in flight). At close range, looks distinctly shorter-billed. Easier to tell in winter, when Kittlitz's has *white face.*

XANTUS'S MURRELET   *Synthliboramphus hypoleucus*

This and the next are warm-water auks. Xantus's (pronounced "zan-TOOSS-es") nests on islands off southern and Baja California, almost never seen from mainland. Pairs are seen far offshore from boats. ▶ Sharply bicolored, blackish above, white below. The Baja race, a rare fall stray to California waters, has more white on face.

CRAVERI'S MURRELET   *Synthliboramphus craveri*

Nesting on Mexican islands, a few Craveri's visit the far-offshore waters of southern California in fall. Pronounced "kra-VAIR-eez." ▶ Very much like Xantus's. Craveri's has slightly longer, thinner bill, tends to show a dark wedge extending forward at side of chest, a bit more black reaching chin. Underside of wings mostly dusky, not white (this is hard to see).

SMALL WESTERN AUKS

Cassin's Auklet 8½"

Ancient Murrelet 10"
winter
summer

Marbled Murrelet 9½"
winter
summer

Kittlitz's Murrelet 9"
summer
winter
summer

Xantus's Murrelet 9½"
southern race (rare)

Craveri's Murrelet 9½"

SMALL NORTHERN AUKS

The Dovekie is a winter bird of the northeast; others on this page are most readily seen in summer at nesting colonies on Alaskan islands. Although these birds are quite noisy around their nesting sites, they are mostly silent elsewhere.

DOVEKIE *Alle alle*

This smallest auk in the Atlantic nests in Greenland, wanders widely in Canadian Arctic waters. During some winters may move south as far as New England or even farther, but usually stays well offshore; storms may drive flocks close to land. In addition to range shown on map, very small numbers are in Bering Sea, Alaska. ▶ Much smaller than other eastern auks, with tiny, stubby bill. In breeding plumage, shows sharp cutoff between black and white on chest. In winter, white from throat and chest curves up behind black on face.

PARAKEET AUKLET *Aethia psittacula*

Common in summer around many Alaskan islands, but usually in small groups, not large flocks. Swims and dives like other auks, using its odd-shaped bill to grasp small jellyfish and other creatures. Winter range is not well known, may move south far out at sea. ▶ Thick red bill, single white stripe on face. Gray throat and chest blends into *white belly*. Throat is paler in winter.

LEAST AUKLET *Aethia pusilla*

Common on some Bering Sea islands, often seen perched on rockpiles where they hide their nests. May gather in large, densely packed flocks, flying low over ocean. ▶ Tiny, with very small bill, usually a thin streak of white behind eye. Pattern of underparts is highly variable in summer, from white to spotted to heavily mottled gray-brown. In winter, all white below.

CRESTED AUKLET *Aethia cristatella*

Around some islands in the Bering Sea (including Pribilofs, St. Lawrence, Aleutians) this auklet is abundant, seen flying in large flocks, swimming on ocean, perched on cliffs. ▶ Slaty gray overall, with thick red bill, *floppy crest*, single white face stripe. In winter plumage, crest is shorter, bill is duller. Parakeet Auklet is similar but has white belly. On Aleutian Islands, see next species.

WHISKERED AUKLET *Aethia pygmaea*

Only in Aleutian Islands, Alaska, and localized even there (may be seen in waters near Dutch Harbor). Feeds in tide rips offshore, nests among island rocks. ▶ Like Crested Auklet but smaller, with *three* prominent white face plumes, longer thin crest on forehead.

SMALL NORTHERN AUKS

Dovekie
8¼"

summer

winter

Parakeet
Auklet
10"

Least
Auklet
6¼"

Crested Auklet
10"

Whiskered
Auklet
7½"

65

LOONS

(family Gaviidae) are expert divers, swimming powerfully underwater, but they are almost helpless on land. Their takeoff from the water is usually labored, but they are strong and swift in flight.

COMMON LOON   *Gavia immer*

At forest lakes across Canada and adjacent regions, the loon's wild yodeling is a typical sound on summer nights. The species winters mostly on coastal waters, a few on large lakes. ▶ Unmistakable in elegant summer plumage. Resembles other loons in winter; note thick bill, wedges of *dark and light pattern* at base of neck, pale areas around eye. Young birds in first winter have pale scaly back pattern.

YELLOW-BILLED LOON   *Gavia adamsii*

This big wilderness diver is local and uncommon in Alaska and western Canada. Rare south of Canada in winter, a few scattered on west coast and on large lakes inland. ▶ Bigger than Common Loon, with very *heavy pale bill,* the lower mandible *angling up* toward the tip. Often swims with bill pointed up slightly. In winter, has *upper ridge of bill mostly pale* (many winter Commons have pale bill but with upper ridge dark). Yellow-billed often looks paler overall, with darker ear spot.

RED-THROATED LOON   *Gavia stellata*

The smallest loon, nesting on Arctic ponds, wintering along coasts. A regular migrant on Great Lakes, but otherwise not often seen inland. ▶ *Thin bill* is slightly *upturned at tip* and often held angled up. Looks plainer than other loons in summer, lacking white checkering (red on throat is hard to see). Quite pale in winter with extensive *white on face* (usually), smooth gray back (showing fine white dots at close range).

PACIFIC LOON   *Gavia pacifica*

Nests on Arctic lakes as far east as Hudson Bay, but winters almost entirely along Pacific Coast. Scarce migrant and wintering bird inland. ▶ In summer, has gray head, white checkering on black back. In winter, like small Common Loon but has thinner bill, *more even division between dark and light* on side of neck. Less white around eye than Common or Red-throated.

ARCTIC LOON   *Gavia arctica*

Western Alaska only, and rare even there, in summer along coast, islands, lakes. (Widespread in Eurasia.) ▶ Very similar to Pacific Loon. A bit larger, with *white patch above waterline* on rear flanks, slightly bolder stripes on neck. At close range, Alaska race shows green gloss on throat (usually purple on Pacific Loon).

LOONS

first winter

Common Loon
32"

winter adult

summer

Yellow-billed Loon
34"

first winter

summer (on nest)

Red-throated Loon
25"

winter

summer

Pacific Loon
27"

first winter

winter adult

summer

summer

Arctic Loon
(rare, Alaska)
28"

67

CORMORANTS

(family Phalacrocoracidae) are snaky-necked, long-tailed divers with hook-tipped bills. They swim low in the water with heads angled up, and may perch with wings spread to dry. Often seen in flocks, flying in lines or V-formation. Usually silent except near nests. Cormorants are sometimes mistaken for loons (page 67), but have different bill shape, much longer tails, and different posture in flight (see comparison opposite).

DOUBLE-CRESTED CORMORANT   *Phalacrocorax auritus*

The most widespread and common cormorant, especially inland. Numbers have increased greatly since 1970s. Nesting colonies may be in trees near water, on cliff ledges, or on the ground on islands. ▶ Adults are blackish all over with *orange* bare skin on the face and throat, extending up to lores (in front of eye). (Compare the shape of this throat pouch to that of other cormorants, below and on next page.) In breeding plumage, western birds have white head tufts, lacking on eastern birds. Immatures are brownish, paler on foreneck and chest, often fading to whitish there. In flight, the neck is held with a slight crook or bend just behind the head (most cormorants look straight-necked in flight).

GREAT CORMORANT   *Phalacrocorax carbo*

Widespread in the Old World, this big diver reaches northeastern North America, where its numbers have increased in recent decades. Large flocks may be seen just offshore, but only a few wander inland. ▶ Large and bulky, with relatively short tail, big head, thick bill. Adult has broad *white band across throat* behind bare yellow face skin; in breeding season, shows white patches on flanks. Immature brownish at first; resembles Double-crested but usually has *neck and chest brown*, contrasting with *white belly*. Throat pouch dull yellow, not orange.

NEOTROPIC CORMORANT   *Phalacrocorax brasilianus*

Found all over the American tropics, this species reaches our area commonly in Texas, locally elsewhere in southwest. Often on the same lakes and ponds as Double-crested Cormorant. Formerly called Olivaceous Cormorant. ▶ Smaller than Double-crested (hard to judge except when they're together), with distinctly *longer tail*. Bare throat pouch is duller, yellowish instead of orange, and back edge of this bare skin is pointed (looks more rounded on Double-crested). In breeding plumage, adult has sharp white border setting off yellow throat pouch.

CORMORANTS

for comparison:
Pacific Loons
in flight

Double-crested
Cormorants, to
show flight silhouette

Double-crested
Cormorant
32"

wing-drying
posture

adult

immature

adult

Great
Cormorant
36"

Neotropic
Cormorant
26"

immature

adult

immature

69

These three cormorants are limited to the west coast. Anhingas **(family Anhingidae)** are specialties of southeastern swamps; they resemble cormorants but with a pointed bill and a long fan-shaped tail.

BRANDT'S CORMORANT   *Phalacrocorax penicillatus*

Very common along the west coast, mostly south of Alaska. Often seen in large flocks, flying in long lines low over the water. Almost never goes inland even a short distance, but may go well out to sea. Nests on islands and coasts, often in large colonies. ▶ Bulky and dark, usually looking quite plain. Bare skin of throat pouch turns bright blue in breeding season, but this is hard to see; more noticeable is pale *buff band* across throat. Immatures are mostly plain dark brown, somewhat paler below.

PELAGIC CORMORANT   *Phalacrocorax pelagicus*

This small diver is found the length of the west coast, but does not go inland. Less sociable than most cormorants, it may be seen singly or in small flocks, and usually nests in small colonies on steep cliffs. ▶ Smaller than other Pacific cormorants, with smaller head, thinner bill. Adults look very glossy overall; dark red on face is hard to see. In breeding plumage, develops patches of white flank feathers. Immatures are very plain dark brown, best identified by shape.

RED-FACED CORMORANT   *Phalacrocorax urile*

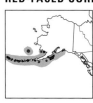

Alaska only. This cormorant is a permanent resident of some Alaskan islands (readily seen on the Pribilofs), nesting on cliff ledges with other seabirds. ▶ Red skin on face contrasts with *yellow* at base of bill. Wings often look brownish, duller than body plumage. In summer, red on face is brighter, and white patch develops on flank feathers. (Pelagic Cormorant also has red face and white flank patch, but has dark bill, wings the same color as its body.)

ANHINGA   *Anhinga anhinga*

A unique bird of southern swampland. Swims and dives, sometimes swimming with only head and neck above water (hence the nickname "snakebird"). On warm days may soar to great heights. Nests in colonies with egrets and other birds, building stick nest in low trees above water. ▶ Suggests a cormorant but has a narrow *dagger-pointed bill,* long fan-shaped tail, white markings on upper side of wings. Female has buff head and neck, male is mostly black.

CORMORANTS, ANHINGA

immature

Brandt's Cormorant 35"

non-breeding adult

breeding adult

Red-faced Cormorant 31"

summer

non-breeding adult

breeding adult

Pelagic Cormorant 26"

Anhinga 35"

female

male

Anhinga soaring, swimming, and in wing-drying posture

The birds on this page are all very large, and all are often seen in flight. Pelicans **(family Pelecanidae)** and frigatebirds **(family Fregatidae)** are very distinctive. For gannets and boobies **(family Sulidae)**, see next page.

AMERICAN WHITE PELICAN   *Pelecanus erythrorhynchos*

A massive bird, with nine-foot wingspan. Inhabits both coasts and large lakes. Flocks often soar high, circling in unison. On water, flocks may hunt together, lining up to drive fish into shallows. Unlike Brown Pelican, does not dive from the air for fish. ▶ Almost unmistakable. In high flight, looks all white with black flight feathers in wings; compare to Wood Stork and Whooping Crane (p. 152). Early in breeding season, adults develop raised vertical plate on bill, shed later in year.

BROWN PELICAN   *Pelecanus occidentalis*

Brown Pelicans flap and glide low over the surf or plunge from high in the air to capture fish in their huge bills. Mostly rare inland, but a few wander into the southwest every summer, and large numbers may visit Salton Sea, California. Endangered at one time by effects of pesticides, these pelicans have made a good comeback since use of DDT was outlawed. ▶ Distinctive shape. Adult gray-brown with pale head (back of neck turns chestnut in breeding season). Juvenile all brown at first, changing gradually to adult plumage.

NORTHERN GANNET   *Morus bassanus*

The biggest seabird of the cold North Atlantic, nesting in colonies on rock cliffs of Canadian islands. Widespread in winter, as far south as Gulf of Mexico. Stays at sea but may be seen from shore, flying high with several flaps followed by long glide, making steep dives to catch fish. ▶ Huge size, long pointed wings, spearlike bill, pointed tail. Adult *white with black wingtips*. Juvenile all gray-brown with white speckles at first, gradually changing to adult plumage over three or four years.

MAGNIFICENT FRIGATEBIRD   *Fregata magnificens*

Over calm tropical seas, frigatebirds soar for days with hardly a beat of their long wings. Fairly common on parts of Florida coast, scarce elsewhere, and a rare visitor inland. Often steals food from other birds after spectacular aerial chases. ▶ Long, narrow, angular wings; long tail; long hooked bill. Adult male all black with red throat pouch, sometimes inflated in display; female has white chest, juvenile has white head. Nothing else is really similar (Swallow-tailed Kite, p. 114, is *much* smaller, has blue-gray back).

HUGE WATERBIRDS

immature

adult

American White Pelican
62" w 108"
(w = wingspan)

immature

plunge-
diving

adult

Brown Pelican
50" w 84"

adult

adults

Northern Gannet
38" w 72"

immatures

female

adult
male

immature

adult female

Magnificent Frigatebird
40" w 90"

73

BOOBIES AND TROPICBIRDS

These tropical seabirds are mostly rare in North America. Boobies (so named by sailors because they seem stupidly tame) are related to gannets, on the previous page. Like tropicbirds **(family Phaethontidae)**, they feed by diving from the air to catch fish in their pointed bills.

MASKED BOOBY   *Sula dactylatra*

A regular visitor to North American waters, usually far offshore in Gulf of Mexico; rare off southern Atlantic Coast. Small numbers nest at the Dry Tortugas, Florida. ▶ Adult like Northern Gannet (previous page), which invades these tropical waters from late fall to spring, but the booby has black mask, yellow bill, *black tail, more black in wing*. Immatures also can look a lot like molting young Gannets, but have more white on underwing; also note *pale collar*.

BROWN BOOBY   *Sula leucogaster*

At sea off southern Florida, especially around the Dry Tortugas, these boobies are often seen perched on channel markers or flying with strong, swift wingbeats. Very rare elsewhere off southeastern coast; rarely wanders from western Mexico to lakes of Arizona and California. ▶ Typical booby shape with heavy pointed bill, pointed tail, long wings. Adults solid brown with sharply contrasting white belly, yellow bill. Immatures have brown mottling on belly, and youngest may be evenly brown all over.

BLUE-FOOTED BOOBY   *Sula nebouxii*

Native to tropical Pacific, this booby is a rare summer visitor to Salton Sea, California, and very rare elsewhere in southwest. ▶ Typical booby shape with heavy pointed bill, pointed tail, long wings. Looks dull at a distance, dark on wings, whitish below. White scaling on brown back; head finely streaked on adults, dingy on young birds. Feet *blue,* brightest on adults.

RED-FOOTED BOOBY   *Sula sula*

Very rare visitor to Dry Tortugas; a few have been recorded elsewhere off southern coasts. Widespread in tropical seas. ▶ Smaller than other boobies. Adults occur in white and brown color morphs (brown birds often white-tailed). White morph suggests pattern of Masked Booby, but has white tail. Immatures are brown. Feet *red* (adults) or pink (immatures).

WHITE-TAILED TROPICBIRD   *Phaethon lepturus*

Common in Bermuda but a rare visitor to North American waters. Sometimes seen around Dry Tortugas, Florida, or at sea off southeast coast. May be driven inland by hurricanes. ▶ White with long tail streamers (sometimes missing), black eye mark and wingtip, *black stripe* on inner part of wing. Bill yellow or orange. Juvenile short-tailed, with black bars on back.

RED-BILLED TROPICBIRD   *Phaethon aethereus*

Rare visitor to waters far off coast of southern California, very rare off southeastern U.S. ▶ White with long tail streamers (sometimes missing), black barring on back, red bill. Lacks black wing stripe of White-tail, and has more black on wingtip. Royal Tern (p. 90) is sometimes mistaken for a tropicbird.

74 AERIAL WATERBIRDS

BOOBIES, TROPICBIRDS

juvenile

Masked Booby
33"

adult

adult

Brown Booby
30"

immature

adult

Red-footed Booby
28"

white morph

Blue-footed Booby
32"

brown morph

Red-billed Tropicbird

White-tailed Tropicbird

20" (+ 20"tail)

16" (+ 16" tail)

75

GULLS

Gulls **(part of family Laridae)** are often called seagulls, but most don't go out to sea — they stick to the coast. Many are seen far inland, around lakes, rivers, and marshes in the center of the continent. Most are scavengers at least in part, and they may gather at landfills in large numbers.

Gulls are mostly large and easy to approach but are challenging because they vary so much. To identify them successfully, we often need to think about ages and seasons. Adults are smooth gray on the back and wings and have all-white tails (except Heermann's Gull). Their head pattern changes with season: some have black hoods in spring but become mostly white-headed by fall, while most gulls that are white-headed in spring develop dark head streaking in winter.

summer   winter   summer   winter

Laughing Gull   **Herring Gull**

Much more striking is the variation in young birds. Small gull species may reach adult plumage in only two years, but larger ones take three or four years, their plumage patterns changing throughout this time. A flock of gulls can show a dizzying array of different patterns, even if the birds all belong to the same species! These illustrations show some plumages worn by Herring Gulls. It takes them three and one-half years to go from all-brown juveniles to gray and white adults.

Gulls can be hugely confusing. Even experts are puzzled by some individuals. If you are just learning the gulls, focus on the clean-plumaged adults first; then look for birds of the same size and shape, to see if you can pick out immatures of the same species.

Field marks to check on adult gulls: Comparative size is very helpful if you see several species together, and bill shape is a good clue for gulls of any age. The other points below are affected by age, so try to make sure you're looking at a full adult (clean unmarked tail, no brown in wings).

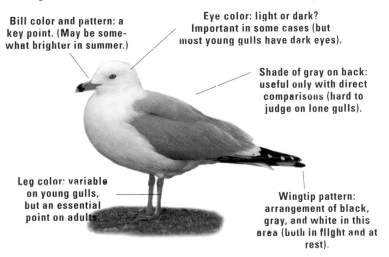

Bill color and pattern: a key point. (May be somewhat brighter in summer.)

Eye color: light or dark? Important in some cases (but most young gulls have dark eyes).

Shade of gray on back: useful only with direct comparisons (hard to judge on lone gulls).

Leg color: variable on young gulls, but an essential point on adults.

Wingtip pattern: arrangement of black, gray, and white in this area (both in flight and at rest).

Voices: Gulls are often noisy, but their sounds are seldom helpful in sorting out the most similar species, so I don't describe voice for most of them.

Hybrids: Far more than most wild birds, gull species often interbreed (especially the larger ones), so hybrids are sometimes seen. (Glaucous-winged x Western Gulls are actually common on parts of the west coast.) A gull that looks truly confusing could be a hybrid of some sort.

The same aspects that make gulls tough at first can make them interesting and fun when you have more experience. Experts even enjoy figuring out the precise ages of confusing immature gulls. However, no compact field guide can include enough information to allow you to age gulls accurately, and to attempt it here would be misleading. If you want to pursue this challenge, the best book currently is *Gulls: A Guide to Identification*, by P. J. Grant (2nd edition, 1986), or try the excellent gull videos in the Advanced Birding video series by Jon L. Dunn.

All of these, as adults, have white spots (or "mirrors") in black wingtips.

HERRING GULL   *Larus argentatus*

The most numerous large gull over most of the continent (except on west coast, where others are equally common). Concentrates at coast, large lakes, landfills, fishing docks. ▶ Adult has white spots in black wingtips, pale eyes, *pink legs*. Rather *heavy* bill is yellow with red spot. Immature all dark brown with blackish bill at first. Reaches adult plumage in fourth winter. See additional pictures of young birds on previous page.

RING-BILLED GULL   *Larus delawarensis*

Very common and widespread; the most numerous medium-sized gull in most areas. Gathers on beaches, ponds, rivers; large flocks rest in parking lots. A good bird to learn for comparison to others. ▶ Adult has *neat black ring* on yellow bill, white spots in black wingtips, yellow or greenish yellow legs, pale eyes. (Note: some Herring Gulls in winter have dusky bill rings.) Immature much paler and grayer than youngest Herring or California Gulls, with black-tipped pink bill. Reaches adult plumage in third winter.

CALIFORNIA GULL   *Larus californicus*

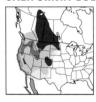

Widespread in the west in summer, at marshes and prairie lakes. Most go to Pacific Coast in winter, some stay in interior; very rare in east. ▶ Between Herring and Ring-bill in size. Adult slightly darker gray on back than either, with *dark eyes*, greenish yellow legs, black and red spots on yellow bill. In flight, shows large white spots in black wingtips. Immatures all dark brown at first, like Herring but smaller, and with thinner bill that is sharply pink at base. Changes with seasons; reaches adult plumage in fourth winter.

MEW GULL   *Larus canus*

This gull hugs the west coast in winter, spreads out over western Canada and Alaska in summer, often perching atop spruces near forest lakes. European race ("Common Gull") strays to Newfoundland in winter, sometimes elsewhere. ▶ More petite than similar gulls. Adult has *thin unmarked yellow bill*, big white spots in wingtip, darker gray back than Ring-bill, yellowish legs. Round head and dark eye create "gentle" look. See Black-legged Kittiwake (p. 86) (different wingtip pattern). Immature pale brown at first; later much like young Ring-bill but with thinner bill, more black in tail. Reaches adult plumage in third winter.

COMMON GULLS
(flying birds, immatures not to scale)

immatures

winter adult

summer adult

Herring Gull
25" w 58"
(w = wingspan)

winter adults

Ring-billed Gull
19" w 48"

immatures

summer adult

winter adult

immatures

California Gull
21" w 54"

summer adult

immatures

winter adult

Mew Gull
17" w 43"

summer adult

WESTERN GULL   *Larus occidentalis*

Abundant in coastal California and Oregon; the standard big gull on beaches and in open areas near the shore. Almost never goes more than a few miles inland. Nests in colonies, mostly on offshore islands. ▶ Size of Herring Gull (previous page) but looks bulkier, and bill often looks more swollen and drooping toward tip. Adults have back and wings *dark gray to blackish,* wingtips black and white, *legs pink.* Young birds all dark brown at first, similar to youngest Herring Gulls, but note bill shape and paler rump; gradually change to adult plumage by fourth winter. North of Monterey, adults are slightly paler gray above. In Washington, often interbreeds with Glaucous-winged Gull (next page), and hybrids occur all along the coast in winter.

GREAT BLACK-BACKED GULL   *Larus marinus*

Our biggest gull (almost eagle-sized), very common in the northeast, mainly along the coast. Has been expanding range in recent decades, but still rare on Gulf Coast in winter. ▶ Huge, heavy-billed. Adult is the only *black-backed, pink-legged gull* likely away from west coast (but outside usual northeastern range, such a bird might be a rare visitor such as Slaty-backed). Immatures show strong checkered pattern above at first, very pale on head and below; after two years, they start to develop black on back.

LESSER BLACK-BACKED GULL   *Larus fuscus*

A visitor from Europe, regular in small numbers in northeast in winter, rare south to Gulf Coast, very rare in west. ▶ Adult like Herring Gull (previous page) but with back and wings *darker* gray, *legs yellow.* Immatures very much like young Herring Gulls until back color begins to show.

YELLOW-FOOTED GULL   *Larus livens*

Only on Salton Sea, southern California. A regular visitor from the Gulf of California, western Mexico; numbers on the Salton Sea peak in late summer, and a few linger through winter and spring. ▶ Very much like Western Gull, but bill even thicker; legs of adults *bright yellow.* Immatures dingy brown, with pinkish legs at first. Best known by range (Western Gull is very seldom found at Salton Sea).

SLATY-BACKED GULL   *Larus schistisagus*

An Asian bird seen regularly in western Alaska in summer. Extremely rare visitor elsewhere in North America in winter. ▶ The only blackish-backed gull likely in western Alaska (but note that some Herring Gulls in western Alaska are slightly darker-backed than those elsewhere). Pink legs, noticeable pattern of white in wingtips.

immatures

DARK-BACKED GULLS
(immatures not to scale)

adults

Western Gull
26" w 58"
(w = wingspan)

adults

immatures

Great
Black-backed Gull
30" w 65"

immature

Lesser
Black-backed Gull
23" w 54"

adult
(winter)

Slaty-backed
Gull
(Alaska)
25" w 58"

immature

adult

Yellow-footed Gull
27" w 60"

GLAUCOUS-WINGED GULL   *Larus glaucescens*

The abundant big gull of the northern Pacific Coast, from Washington to southern Alaska; spreads south to California in winter. ▶ Bulky large gull with thick bill and pink legs, but wingtips patterned with gray, not black. Immature has wingtips pale gray-brown, not blackish as on the immatures of previous two pages. Often interbreeds with Western Gull on Washington coast, and hybrids are commonly seen.

GLAUCOUS GULL   *Larus hyperboreus*

The only big gull in most areas of high Arctic. A few come far south in winter, even reaching southern California, Great Plains, Gulf Coast. ▶ Very large; adult has pale gray back, white wingtips. Immatures vary from pale brown to white, always with very pale wingtips; heavy bill is sharply bicolored, pink and black. Note: immatures of other gulls (such as Herring) may become so worn and sun-bleached in summer that they suggest ragged Glaucous Gulls.

ICELAND GULL   *Larus glaucoides*

In the northeast in winter, usually seen in small numbers, mainly on the coast. Nests in northeast Canada and Greenland (not Iceland). ▶ Pale gray back, pink legs. Birds illustrated here are "Kumlien's" form, nesting in eastern Canada. Adults have variable wingtips, usually marked with gray, sometimes pure white; eyes usually dull yellow, sometimes brown. Immatures vary from pale brown to whitish, with very pale wingtips. Smaller than Glaucous Gull, with much smaller, thinner bill that is all blackish at first.

THAYER'S GULL   *Larus thayeri*

Fairly common in winter along coast in Pacific Northwest, some south along California coast; farther east, mostly rare and controversial. ▶ Adult suggests Herring Gull (p. 78) but smaller, with shorter bill, *dark eyes;* dark in wingtip more limited, may be gray instead of black. Immatures also suggest Herring, but wingtips paler. Some Western x Glaucous-winged hybrids (above) have similar patterns but are much thicker-billed. At all ages, the palest Thayer's Gulls are essentially identical to the darkest Iceland Gulls and can hardly be identified out of range. Some scientists call these all one species, grading from dark Thayer's in the west to lighter Iceland in the east.

GULLS WITH PALE WINGTIPS

immatures

Glaucous-winged Gull
26" w 58"
(w = wingspan)

adults

Western X Glaucous-winged hybrid

adult

Glaucous Gull
28" w 60"

adult

immatures

adult

Iceland Gull
23" w 54"

adults

first-winter
(variable)

first-winter
(variable)

adults

Thayer's Gull
23" w 54"

83

—but only in breeding plumage, in spring and early summer.

LAUGHING GULL *Larus atricilla*

Abundant along the southern Atlantic and Gulf coasts, north to New England in summer. Nests in colonies in salt marshes. Generally rare inland except on Salton Sea, California, and small numbers on Great Lakes. ▶ Adult has *dark gray back* fading into *mostly black wingtips*. Bill and legs dark (often with strong red tinge). Immatures with scaly brown pattern at first, gray-backed by first winter; note bill shape, dark legs. ♪ **Voice**: well named, with laughing call, classic sound of southeast coast.

FRANKLIN'S GULL *Larus pipixcan*

A heartland gull, nesting in northern prairie marshes, migrating through southern plains; rare stray to either coast. Winters on west coast of South America. ▶ Adult suggests Laughing Gull but *wingtips mostly white,* crossed by ragged black bar. Fall immature has cleaner look than young Laughing, with neat dusky scarf on head. Some subadults have black hood, dark wingtips; note smaller bill than Laughing Gull.

BONAPARTE'S GULL *Larus philadelphia*

Our smallest common gull, summering around lakes in northern forest, wintering mainly near coast. Less a scavenger than most large gulls and does not usually flock with them; less likely to gather at landfills. ▶ Thin black bill, black hood in summer. Best known by flight pattern, with big white triangle in outer part of wing. Immature also has much white in outer wing, edged in black. Looks delicate and buoyant in flight.

BLACK-HEADED GULL *Larus ridibundus*

An Old World gull, locally common in winter in Newfoundland (where a few nest) and the Maritimes, rare in northeastern U.S. and Alaska, very rare elsewhere. Lone strays may associate with flocks of Bonaparte's Gulls. ▶ Adult has white triangle in outer wing like Bonaparte's, but underside of wingtip is *extensively black* (Bonaparte's is almost entirely white there). Black-headed has thicker bill, usually red (not black); immature's bill has pale base. Noticeably larger than Bonaparte's when seen together.

LITTLE GULL *Larus minutus*

This tiny gull lives mainly in the Old World, but a few nest in the Great Lakes region and winter along Atlantic Coast, rarely straying elsewhere. May travel with flocks of Bonaparte's Gulls. ▶ Adult has *black underwings.* Upper side of wingtip has no black on adults, entirely pale gray with big white tips on feathers. Immature has dark cap, dark "M" pattern on back and wings. Note tiny size, thin bill.

HOODED GULLS

winter adult

immatures

summer adults

Laughing Gull
17" w 40"
(w = wingspan)

immature

Franklin's Gull
15" w 36"

spring adults

fall adult

immatures

Bonaparte's Gull
13" w 32"

winter adults

summer adult

Black-headed Gull
16" w 40"

winter

immature

summer adult

immatures

Little Gull
11" w 24"

winter adult

summer adult

85

BLACK-LEGGED KITTIWAKE   *Rissa tridactyla*

This actually is a "sea gull," usually far out at sea. Sometimes seen from shore in winter, especially during storms. Nests in colonies on rock cliffs of northern islands. ▶ Unmarked yellow bill, pale gray back and wings, *wingtips sharply cutoff black* without white spots (as if dipped in ink). Immature has black bar across nape, black pattern on pale wings. ♪ **Voice**: noisy around nesting colonies; nasal *ki-ti-waahk*.

RED-LEGGED KITTIWAKE   *Rissa brevirostris*

Alaska only, Bering Sea, nesting on Pribilof and Aleutian Islands. Even there, usually outnumbered by its black-legged relative. ▶ Much like Black-legged Kittiwake but has shorter bill, steeper forehead, much *darker wings* (so that black tips contrast less), red legs and feet. Immatures like young Black-legged but lack black tail band, have darker forepart of wings.

SABINE'S GULL   *Xema sabini*

Beautiful small gull nesting on Arctic tundra, migrating offshore to winter on southern oceans. Migrants may be seen on boat trips off west coast, but rare off east coast. A few juveniles show up on lakes far inland every fall. ▶ Striking *wing pattern* in flight is best mark (but see immature Kittiwake). Adults have black hoods in summer; fall juveniles brownish and scaly on back.

ROSS'S GULL   *Rhodostethia rosea*

Very rare, mostly Siberian. In Alaska, seen at Pt. Barrow in fall, sometimes elsewhere in spring. Has nested several times at Churchill, Manitoba. Scattered winter records in southern Canada and U.S. ▶ Short bill, wedge-shaped tail. Adult in summer has *black neck ring*, strong *pink tinge* on body; both mostly missing in winter. In flight, adult shows dark gray underwings. Immature has wedge-shaped tail, wing pattern like Kittiwake.

IVORY GULL   *Pagophila eburnea*

An extreme northerner, spending all year around openings in pack ice of Arctic Ocean. A scavenger, feeding at seal carcasses left by polar bears. Rarely wanders to southern Canada or northern states in winter. ▶ Adult pure white with black legs, yellow tip on black bill. Immatures have black spots on wings and tail, black on face.

HEERMANN'S GULL   *Larus heermanni*

From nesting sites in western Mexico, this gull moves up the coast to northern California, sometimes farther. Very rarely seen inland. ▶ Adult has *gray body, black tail*, red bill. Head white in breeding plumage, mottled at other seasons. Immature smooth dark brown or gray-brown (without the heavy mottling of other dark young gulls); bill pinkish at base, *legs black*.

summer adults

CLASSY GULLS

immature

Black-legged Kittiwake
17" w 36"
(w = wingspan)

winter

juvenile

summer adults

Sabine's Gull
14" w 33"

Red-legged Kittiwake
15" w 33"

summer adults

summer

Ross's Gull
13" w 33"

immature

Ivory Gull
17" w 37"

adult

Heermann's Gull
19" w 50"

spring adults

immature

winter adult

87

TERNS

are in same family as gulls but are mostly smaller, more graceful in flight. Most plunge-dive from the air into the water to catch minnows in their bills. The four on this page can all look quite similar. Birds shown here are adults unless stated otherwise; younger birds resemble winter adults.

FORSTER'S TERN *Sterna forsteri*

Scarce in the northeast, but often more common than the Common Tern in the west and south. Nests in marshes, seen around any body of water during migration. ▶ Like others on this page, has long forked tail, black cap in breeding season. Summer adults have *pale silvery upperside of wingtips;* base of bill orange. Young and winter adults mostly white-headed with bold *black ear patches,* not connecting across nape as on other terns. ♪**Voice:** harsh *kyaar,* other notes.

COMMON TERN *Sterna hirundo*

Nests in colonies on islands or beaches, laying eggs in simple scrape on open ground. Intruders are likely to be dive-bombed by noisy, aggressive terns, who may even strike with their bills. ▶ Like Forster's Tern but bill is slightly slimmer, redder (less orange) at base in summer. Upperside of wingtip *partly a contrasting darker gray.* In winter (mostly absent from our area) has solid black from eyes back across nape, not separated patches. Juveniles and fall adults have black shoulder bar. ♪**Voice:** harsh drawn-out *keeaaar,* other notes.

ARCTIC TERN *Sterna paradisaea*

The only tern in most areas of the far north. Nests in colonies at tundra lakes and coastal beaches. South of the breeding grounds it migrates mostly far out at sea, going to Southern Hemisphere, and is seldom seen from land. ▶ Longer-tailed and smaller-headed than Common Tern, with narrower black edge on underside of wing; *quite gray below,* with white stripe on face. Relatively short-legged. Bill *solid red* in summer. Upperside of wingtip uniformly gray, without darker area of Common. ♪**Voice:** harsh *kee-yar,* other notes.

ROSEATE TERN *Sterna dougallii*

Atlantic Coast only (mainly northeast and Florida), uncommon and declining. An endangered species. Light and buoyant in flight, with quick shallow wingbeats. ▶ Noticeably *long bill* is usually *mostly black,* even in summer; develops obvious red at base during peak of breeding season. Very *long tail streamers* in summer; wings very pale above. ♪**Voice:** distinctive soft *chivvyit,* also harsh notes.

MEDIUM-SIZED TERNS

winter

summer

Forster's Tern
14½" w 30"
(w = wingspan)

juvenile

summer

summer

juvenile

summer

summer

Common Tern
14" w 30"

juvenile

summer

summer

Arctic Tern
15½" w 31"

summer

summer

Roseate Tern
15" w 29"

juvenile

89

These are all bigger than the "typical" terns on the previous page. Immatures resemble adults but have extra dark markings on wings, tail, and back. Young birds may stay with parents for several months.

CASPIAN TERN *Sterna caspia*

As big as a gull, this tern is wide-ranging but usually seen in small numbers. Like most terns, it flies high, hovers, then plunges into water to capture fish in its bill. The only large tern normally seen at inland waters. ▶ Large size, *thick red bill;* short crest gives square-headed look. Forehead is clouded with streaks in winter and on immatures (not clear white as on many Royal Terns). In flight, shows *blackish underside of wingtips.* ♪ **Voice:** rough, guttural *kahhrrrrr.* Immature has thin whistle, often heard as young bird follows its parent.

ROYAL TERN *Sterna maxima*

A characteristic bird of beaches, barrier islands, and coastal marsh in the southeast. Less numerous northward on Atlantic Coast (mostly late summer), and appears on southern California coast mainly in winter. Very rare inland. ▶ A bit slimmer than Caspian, with wispy crest, fairly thick *carrot orange bill.* Underside of wingtips much paler. Forehead is *white* most of year (becomes black for part of breeding season). On Pacific Coast, see Elegant Tern. ♪ **Voice:** bleating *keeey-y-yeer.*

ELEGANT TERN *Sterna elegans*

A specialty of southern California. Wanders along coast to northern California, mostly in late summer. In warm-water years, flocks may go farther north. Strictly coastal, almost never seen inland. ▶ Very similar to Royal Tern. Smaller (apparent only when they are together). Has *much slimmer bill* that often looks slightly droopy. In "winter" plumage (worn for most of year), black from nape *usually* extends forward to include the eye on Elegant, not on Royal Tern. ♪ **Voice:** sharp *kee-rrik.* Abruptly two-noted, unlike Royal's call.

SANDWICH TERN *Sterna sandvicensis*

Along the southern Atlantic and Gulf coasts, this bird acts like the Royal Tern's kid brother: tagging along with it, even nesting in the same colonies, but usually less common. ▶ Contrasting *yellow tip* on *long* black bill is diagnostic but hard to see (and is faint on some young birds). Wispy crest; forehead is white from late summer through winter. Shape and flight style intermediate between Royal Tern and smaller "typical" terns. ♪ **Voice:** sharp *kee-rrick,* abruptly two-noted.

LARGE TERNS

summer adults

winter

Caspian Tern
21" w 50"
(w = wingspan)

winter

Royal Tern
20" w 42"

adult in molt

adult in full breeding plumage

winter

Elegant Tern
17" w 34"

adult in molt

adult in full breeding plumage

Sandwich Tern
15" w 33"

summer adults

winter

91

SOOTY TERN *Sterna fuscata*

Widespread in tropical oceans. Tens of thousands of Sooties nest on the Dry Tortugas, west of Key West, Florida. Elsewhere off the southern Atlantic and Gulf coasts they usually stay far offshore, where they feed by swooping down to take small fish from the sea surface. Sometimes driven to shore by hurricanes. ▶ Large, strongly patterned. *Blackish above* and bright white below, with *white forehead.* Immature mostly dark sooty brown, with white spots on back. ♪ **Voice:** noisy around nesting colonies; loud *wide-a-wake.*

BRIDLED TERN *Sterna anaethetus*

Seldom seen from land in North America, but fairly common over the Gulf Stream far offshore, from Florida to the Carolinas. Also far out in Gulf of Mexico. Rarely nests on Florida Keys. Sometimes driven to shore, even inland and well north, by hurricanes. ▶ Like Sooty Tern but slimmer, a little paler on back, with a *whitish collar* across the hindneck. Shows more white in outer tail feathers and on underside of wingtip.

ALEUTIAN TERN *Sterna aleutica*

Alaska only, locally along coast and Aleutian Islands. Uncommon; often nests with colonies of Arctic Terns (p. 80), but is usually outnumbered by them. Winter range, unknown until recently, is apparently in the tropical West Pacific. ▶ Gray with black bill, sharp white forehead patch. Some young Arctic Terns have dark bills and white foreheads; note *dark trailing edge* on inner part of Aleutian's wing. Voice differs. ♪ **Voice:** distinctive, whistled *wheeyee,* odd sparrowlike chirping.

BROWN NODDY *Anous stolidus*

Widespread in tropical seas, noddies seem the reverse of most terns: dark with white caps, tails wedge-tipped (not forked), oddly gentle and quiet around nesting colonies. Brown Noddies nest on Dry Tortugas, west of Key West, and are seen at sea elsewhere off Florida; may be driven to land in the southeast by hurricanes. ▶ White-capped adults easily recognized; immatures show less white, mainly on forehead.

BLACK NODDY *Anous minutus*

Among the Brown Noddies on the Dry Tortugas, one or two Black Noddies appear in most years. ▶ Very similar to Brown Noddy but smaller, slightly darker, with distinctly thinner and longer-looking bill. Edge of white cap may seem more sharply defined.

HOT AND COLD TERNS

Sooty Tern
16" w 32"
(w = wingspan)

adults

juvenile

Aleutian Tern
14" w 29"

Bridled Tern
15" w 30"

Brown Noddy
15" w 32"

Black Noddy (rare)
14" w 30"

Brown Noddies look very dark in flight

BLACK TERN *Chlidonias niger*

A beautiful small tern, nesting in freshwater marshes, wintering at sea in the tropics. Numbers have declined seriously in many areas, probably owing to loss of nesting habitat. ▶ Summer adult has head and body *mostly black,* wings and tail silvery gray. Immatures and winter adults less distinctive, mostly white below, but still darker on back than other small terns, with dark mark at shoulder. Adults molting out of breeding plumage in late summer look patchy black and white.

WHITE-WINGED TERN *Chlidonias leucopterus*

An Old World tern. One or two show up almost annually in North America, mostly on east coast with flocks of Black Terns. ▶ Summer adult like Black Tern but *whiter* on upperside of wings and has contrasting *whitish tail;* underside of wing shows *black wing linings* (pale gray on Black Tern). Immatures and fall adults very much like Black Tern.

LEAST TERN *Sterna antillarum*

Our smallest tern, strictly a summer resident, wintering well to the south. Nests on beaches and on river sandbars of interior; endangered in many areas because of disturbance to nesting places. ▶ Small size, narrow wings, deep quick wingbeats in flight. Adult has yellow bill with black tip, sharp white patch on forehead. Younger birds black-billed. ♪**Voice:** very vocal; high sharp notes, including *zzrreep* and *kvick, kvick.*

GULL-BILLED TERN *Sterna nilotica*

Subtly unusual in shape and actions, this pale tern nests on beaches and barrier islands but does most of its feeding by catching flying insects in midair over marshes, fields. ▶ Thick black bill, relatively long legs, overall pale look. In flight, looks broad-winged and buoyant. Summer adult has black cap, but young and winter adults very white-headed. Compare to Forster's and other terns on p. 88 (different feeding actions).

BLACK SKIMMER *Rynchops niger*

A bizarre relative of the terns. Feeds by flying low, trailing its long lower mandible in the water, then snapping its bill shut when it detects a minnow. Flocks rest on beaches, fly with slow beats of long wings. ▶ Black above, white below, with lower mandible much longer than upper. Long wings make resting bird look like long, low, black triangle. Juveniles browner above but still unmistakable. ♪**Voice:** short, barking *wurf, wurf.*

juvenile

winter

summer
adults

molting
adult

Black Tern
10" w 24"
(w = wingspan)

**White-
winged
Tern**
(rare)
9½" w 23"

juvenile

Least Tern
8½" w 20"

summer
adults

immature

Gull-billed Tern
14" w 34"

summer
adults

summer
adult

Skimmer
skimming

Black Skimmer
18" w 44"

adult

juvenile

95

are predatory relatives of gulls, often chasing other seabirds to make them drop their catch. Except in the Arctic, where jaegers nest, they mostly stay out at sea. Adult jaegers (pronounced YAY-grrs) can be identified by central tail feathers, but younger birds are *very* difficult.

PARASITIC JAEGER   *Stercorarius parasiticus*

All jaegers are oceanic in most seasons, but this one is sometimes seen from shore, especially on west coast, chasing gulls out over the waves. Nests on open tundra. Rare stray inland farther south, mainly in fall. ▶ Adult has fairly *short, pointed central tail feathers.* Varies from dark gray to whitish below, usually with dark chest band; often less barred, grayer-headed than Pomarine Jaeger. Juvenile in first fall dark brown with buff bars. Later immature stages variable. ♪ **Voice:** all jaegers mostly silent at sea, make whistles, harsh notes on tundra.

LONG-TAILED JAEGER   *Stercorarius longicaudus*

The smallest jaeger and the one that stays farthest offshore for most of year. Widespread on tundra in summer, including central Alaska, but a very rare stray inland farther south. ▶ Adult has *very long, pointed central tail feathers.* Plumage less variable than other jaegers, with white chest, neat black cap, blue-gray back. Juvenile in first fall grayish brown, with whitish barring. Later immature stages quite variable.

POMARINE JAEGER   *Stercorarius pomarinus*

The largest jaeger. Nests in high Arctic, usually stays well offshore farther south; unlikely to be seen from shore. Very rare stray inland in any season. ▶ Adult has *wide, blunt-tipped central tail feathers.* Pattern of underparts highly variable: white, dark, heavily barred, often with *dark chest band.* Looks *heavy-billed,* very black on head. Juvenile in first fall usually dark brown with buff barring. Later immature stages quite variable.

SOUTH POLAR SKUA   *Stercorarius maccormicki*

Nests only in Antarctic region, but occurs far off both our coasts in warmer months — uncommon in Pacific, uncommon to rare in Atlantic. ▶ Bulky, powerful, with wide wings, thick neck. Brown with *white wing flash* (more obvious than in jaegers). Dark back contrasts with *pale nape;* head and underparts often paler also. Young Pomarine Jaeger can resemble skua.

GREAT SKUA   *Stercorarius skua*

Nests in Iceland and islands off northwest Europe, wanders to waters far off the coasts of northeast Canada in summer, eastern U.S. in winter. Predatory and piratical, harassing other seabirds. ▶ Very much like South Polar Skua, but head and body typically all dark with heavy *pale stripes.*

JAEGERS AND SKUAS

Parasitic Jaeger
w 42″
(w = wingspan)

juvenile

immature

adults

adult

juvenile

Long-tailed Jaeger
w 38″

adult

adult
on nest

immature

adult

Pomarine Jaeger
w 48″

adults

South Polar Skua
w 52″
(not to scale)

Great Skua
w 55″
(not to scale)

97

are remote from everyday experience for most of us. These birds may spend months or even years completely out of sight of land, coming to shore (mostly islands) only to raise their young.

At some coastal points, we may be able to watch seabirds offshore with the aid of a telescope. Where deep water comes close to the coast, seabirds may come close too (as at Monterey Bay, California, where thousands of Sooty Shearwaters are sometimes within binocular range). But in general we don't see these birds well unless we go offshore.

Whale-watching trips are sometimes productive for birds as well (and the guides sometimes know the seabirds). There are also organized pelagic trips for birders (pelagic means "of the ocean"), usually one-day trips out to deep water. These almost always have expert birders along to help with identifying the difficult species.

Such help is worth having, because many seabirds *are* difficult. Especially among the smaller shearwaters (pp. 100–105) and storm-petrels (p. 106), subtleties of shape and flight style are the main field marks. Adding to the challenge are many remote possibilities—seabirds that are both very rare in our waters and very hard to recognize. This guide omits the rarest visitors to focus on those that you have a reasonable chance of seeing.

Albatrosses **(family Diomedeidae)** are the largest true seabirds, able to glide and circle low over the waves for hours with hardly a flap of their long wings. Most species live in southern oceans, but two are common in the North Pacific.

BLACK-FOOTED ALBATROSS *Phoebastria nigripes*

Nesting mainly in Hawaii but ranging widely at sea, this gentle giant occurs off our west coast in all seasons, most commonly in late spring and summer. Sometimes these birds gather near fishing boats far offshore. ▶ Much larger than any of the other true seabirds seen commonly off the west coast, with very long narrow wings, heavy bill, and slow wingbeats interspersed with long glides. In windy conditions, may not have to flap at all. Dusky brown, with white around base of bill and sometimes at base of tail; bill and feet dark.

LAYSAN ALBATROSS *Phoebastria immutabilis*

Very common far out in the Pacific but usually rare close to shore; being seen more often in recent years, however. Occurs off our west coast most frequently in winter, off southern Alaska in summer. ▶ Back and upper wings dark, body mostly white. Has dark marks on center of white underwing and U-shaped white pattern across rump. Note: at least six other albatross species have reached North American waters rarely, most of them white-bodied like Laysan. The species recorded most often have been Short-tailed Albatross (*Phoebastria albatrus*) in the west and Yellow-nosed Albatross (*Thalassarche chlororhynchos*) in the east.

TRUE SEABIRDS

Head of Audubon's Shearwater, showing the tubular nostrils typical of true seabirds

Shearwaters are shaped like narrow-winged gulls but fly very differently, with fast wingbeats followed by stiff-winged glides

Storm-petrels are tiny seabirds that flutter low over the waves

Black-footed Albatross 28" w 80"

Laysan Albatross 31" w 82" (w = wingspan)

99

Shearwaters, fulmars, and petrels (**family Procellariidae**) have narrow wings and distinctive flight, with quick flaps and stiff-winged glide, often scaling with one wing up and the other pointed down at the water.

SOOTY SHEARWATER   *Puffinus griseus*

Often the most abundant bird off our Pacific Coast (and fairly common in the Atlantic), the Sooty nests only on islands deep in the Southern Hemisphere, making a great cyclic migration around the world's oceans. Some are present off California all year, but peak numbers (in the millions) are in late summer. ▶ Best recognized by shape and typical shearwater flight action, flapping and gliding in calm weather, gliding and scaling more in wind. Dark all over with tapering forehead and thin black bill, and with *ragged white area* on underside of wing. See next two species.

SHORT-TAILED SHEARWATER   *Puffinus tenuirostris*

Nesting on islands near Australia, this shearwater migrates through the North Pacific and the Bering Sea. Often common in Alaskan waters in summer. Farther south, occurs off California mostly in late fall and winter. ▶ Much like Sooty Shearwater, not always identifiable. Tends to have shorter bill, rounder head, steeper forehead. Underside of wings often *uniform,* medium gray to pale gray, without white flash of Sooty.

FLESH-FOOTED SHEARWATER   *Puffinus carneipes*

Another visitor from southern oceans, the Flesh-foot is rare but regular off the Pacific Coast, most likely to be seen in fall with large flocks of other shearwaters. ▶ Bigger than Sooty Shearwater, with slower, more loping wingbeats. Looks more uniformly dark brown, without underwing flash. Thick bill is *pale pink at base,* and feet are the same color.

NORTHERN FULMAR   *Fulmarus glacialis*

Related to shearwaters, but unlike them it nests on cliffs of northern islands. Ranges widely at sea, sometimes following fishing boats for scraps. May be increasing off northeast coast. Numbers moving south off west coast vary from winter to winter; sometimes common, and may show up around harbors, piers. ▶ Like a stocky, big-headed shearwater with a very thick yellow bill. Overall color is highly variable. Has dark and light morphs as well as many intermediates. Pattern of light birds might suggest a gull, but note the fulmar's stubby bill, very different flight style (quick flaps and stiff-winged glide, with wings held flat and straight).

Sooty Shearwater
18" w 41"
(w = wingspan)

Flesh-footed
Shearwater
20" w 43"

Short tailed
Shearwater
17" w 40"

Northern Fulmar
19" w 42"

101

In addition to these light-bellied species, Sooty Shearwater and Northern Fulmar (previous page) are common off the Atlantic Coast.

CORY'S SHEARWATER   *Calonectris diomedea*

Rather common far off Atlantic Coast, mostly from late spring to mid-fall; rare in Gulf of Mexico. In New England, sometimes seen from shore during storms in early fall. ▶ Large and long-winged, with slower wing-beats than other eastern shearwaters. Brownish gray above and whitish below, but colors smudge together, *without* strong contrast. Base of bill *yellow*.

GREATER SHEARWATER   *Puffinus gravis*

This shearwater moves through offshore waters of the east during the warmer months, especially in spring, and is numerous off eastern Canada in summer. It nests on islands in the South Atlantic. ▶ Contrasting pattern with sharp black cap, dark brown back set off by narrow whitish band across rump and usually across nape. White below with black marks under base of wing, blurry dark patch on belly.

MANX SHEARWATER   *Puffinus puffinus*

Mainly seen far off the northeast coast as a visitor from islands off Great Britain; a few also breed in Newfoundland. Scarce in winter off southern Atlantic Coast, and very rare off California. ▶ Sharply contrasting, blackish above, white below and on wing linings. Face is dark; white from throat notches up behind the dark ear patch. Flies with fast wingbeats, short glides.

AUDUBON'S SHEARWATER   *Puffinus lherminieri*

Nesting on Caribbean islands, this small shearwater is common far off our southeastern coast from spring through fall, scarcer toward the north. ▶ Dusky brown above, white below. Like Manx Shearwater but has distinctly *longer tail,* more dark under tail, somewhat less white under wing. White may come up higher on face. Flies with fast wingbeats and short glides.

BLACK-CAPPED PETREL   *Pterodroma hasitata*

A mysterious bird until recent decades, this deep-water petrel has proven to be regular over the Gulf Stream off our southeast coast. It nests in holes in steep cliffs on Caribbean islands. ▶ Flies fast, with deceptively slow wingbeats, long glides, high arcs. Pattern suggests Greater Shearwater, but Black-cap has smaller black cap, usually more white on collar and rump, longer tail, black bar on underwing.

ATLANTIC SHEARWATERS

Greater Shearwater on the water

Cory's Shearwater 18" w 46"

Greater Shearwater 19" w 44" (w = wingspan)

Manx Shearwater 13" w 33"

Audubon's Shearwater 12" w 28"

Black-capped Petrel 16" w 37"

These are the light-bellied species of our Pacific waters. See also the dark shearwaters and Northern Fulmar on p. 100.

PINK-FOOTED SHEARWATER   *Puffinus creatopus*

The most common light-bellied shearwater off the west coast (but not seen from shore as often as Black-vented Shearwater), mostly present in summer and fall. Nests on islands off western South America. ▶ Gray-brown above, whitish below. Larger, with slower wingbeats than other light-bellied shearwaters in west. *Pink base of bill* is easier to see than pink feet.

BULLER'S SHEARWATER   *Puffinus bulleri*

This graceful flier nests on small islands near New Zealand, visits waters off our west coast mostly from late summer through fall. Formerly called New Zealand Shearwater. ▶ Beautiful clean pattern, bright white below with *underwings almost entirely white,* gray above with black pattern (like a wide, flat M) across wings, sharp black cap. Much more contrast than other western shearwaters. Looks long-tailed and long-winged, flies with long buoyant glides.

BLACK-VENTED SHEARWATER   *Puffinus opisthomelas*

Not a world traveler like some shearwaters: nests on islands off northwest Mexico and moves north along California coast, moving farther and in larger numbers in warm-water years. Stays close to coast and is often visible from shore. ▶ Small, with faster wingbeats than other western shearwaters. Very dingy around head and throat, dark under base of tail. Manx Shearwater (previous page), very rare off west coast, similar in size and flight but whiter below, especially under base of tail.

DEEP-WATER PETRELS

Several species of true petrels (not to be confused with storm-petrels, on next page) have been found as rare visitors to North American waters. Black-capped Petrel (previous page) is the only one seen regularly within 100 miles of the coast. These birds (in the genus *Pterodroma*) are long-winged, very fast-flying relatives of the shearwaters, mostly staying very far out at sea. **Cook's Petrel** (*Pterodroma cookii*), shown opposite, may be regular between 100 and 200 miles off the California coast, out of range for ordinary birding boat trips. Mottled Petrel (*Pterodroma inexpectata*), not shown, may be regular in waters off southern Alaska; similar to Cook's but has distinct gray belly patch, black mark on underside of wing. Several other species have been found rarely in North American waters, mainly off North Carolina or California, but their status is still being worked out.

PACIFIC SHEARWATERS

Pink-footed
Shearwater
19" w 43"
(w = wingspan)

Buller's Shearwater
16" w 39"

Cook's Petrel
(rare)
11" w 27"
(not to scale)

Black-vented Shearwater
14" w 34"

105

Tiny seabirds that flutter low over the waves. Storm Petrels (**family Hydrobatidae**) nest in burrows on islands, visit their nests only at night, and are seldom seen from land. Most are hard to identify, known by subtle difference in flight style.

WILSON'S STORM-PETREL *Oceanites oceanicus*

Sometimes common in summer off Atlantic Coast, where it may be seen during deep-water fishing or whale-watching trips; quite rare off Pacific Coast. Nests on islands far south of Equator. ▶ Black, with obvious white rump patch, short *squared-off* tail. Flies with quick, shallow wingbeats, like a Purple Martin. May patter feet on water while hovering; feet may extend past tail tip in level flight. Yellow webs between toes (hard to see).

LEACH'S STORM-PETREL *Oceanodroma leucorhoa*

Far offshore from all coasts (but rare off southern Atlantic and Gulf) in summer, nesting on some islands. ▶ Fairly long angled wings, *forked* tail. The only white-rumped storm-petrel usually seen off Pacific Coast (but some there have dark rumps). In Atlantic, larger and longer-winged than Wilson's, with much more erratic flight, bounding about like a nighthawk.

BAND-RUMPED STORM-PETREL *Oceanodroma castro*

Uncommon in summer far offshore from southern Atlantic and Gulf coasts. ▶ Suggests Leach's, but rump band is more even-edged. Different flight, less erratic, with shallow wingbeats and stiff-winged glides.

ASHY STORM-PETREL *Oceanodroma homochroa*

Pacific Coast only. Nests on Farallones and other islands off California; concentrates well offshore on Monterey Bay in fall. ▶ All dark but not as black as next species; has brown or gray tinge. Wingbeats *shallower* than those of Black Storm-Petrel, wings raised only to about horizontal.

BLACK STORM-PETREL *Oceanodroma melania*

Pacific Coast only. Common off southern California in warm seasons, north to Monterey Bay. ▶ Largest western storm-petrel. All black; tail rather long, forked. Flies with relatively slow, *deep* wingbeats.

LEAST STORM-PETREL *Oceanodroma microsoma*

Nests on islands off western Mexico; a few wander north off California coast, especially in warm-water years. ▶ Tiny and all black, with relatively *short*, *wedge-shaped* tail. Wingbeats are deep and rather fast.

FORK-TAILED STORM-PETREL *Oceanodroma furcata*

Pacific Coast only. Numerous off Alaska and western Canada (although some reach south to California), nesting on offshore islands. Flies with quick shallow wingbeats. ▶ *Gray*, with blackish on wings and around eye. Compare to Ashy Storm-Petrel (can look pale), also phalaropes (p. 190).

WHITE-FACED STORM-PETREL *Pelagodroma marina*

Rare off Atlantic Coast, mostly over Gulf Stream. ▶ Gray-brown above, *white below* and on eyebrow, with long legs. Odd flight, gliding on stiff wings, rocking back and forth, touching feet down to water.

STORM-PETRELS

Wilson's Storm-Petrel 7" w 15" (w = wingspan)

foot-pattering

Leach's Storm-Petrel 8 1/2" w 18"

Ashy Storm-Petrel 8" w 17"

Band-rumped Storm-Petrel 9" w 17"

in nest burrow

Black Storm-Petrel 9" w 19"

Least Storm-Petrel 6" w 13"

White-faced Storm-Petrel 7 1/2" w 17"

Fork-tailed Storm-Petrel 8 1/2" w 18"

107

BIRDS OF PREY

Included here are hawks, which hunt by day, and owls, most of which hunt by night. Hawks and owls are not closely related to each other, but both groups have been admired by humans for thousands of years.

Birds of prey, also known as raptors, play an essential role in the balance of nature. At one time, many hawks and owls were shot by people who were ignorant of the value of these magnificent creatures. Today, all birds of prey are strictly protected by law.

Hawks are mostly solitary hunters. Ordinarily you will see only a few in a given day. At some places, however—mainly along the coast, lake shores, or mountain ridges—large numbers of hawks may be seen in spring or fall migration. Hawkwatching at such lookouts has become very popular.

Many hawk species vary in color, with different plumages at different ages, or with a variety of different color morphs. This can make them harder to identify. Hawks are often easier to recognize when they're in flight than when they're perched, because you can see so much more on a flying bird: the pattern of its wings and tail, its style of flight, and especially its overall shape. Experts may be able to identify every species of hawk by details of its shape and actions, and beginning hawkwatchers will find shape extremely helpful in placing a hawk in the right group, as outlined below.

IDENTIFYING THE MAJOR GROUPS OF RAPTORS: These groups include all of the most widespread species. In warmer climates, you might see some other distinctive hawks, such as kites (p. 122) or Crested Caracara (p. 116).

BUTEOS (beginning on p. 110) are chunky hawks with broad wings and short, wide tails. They may soar for hours at a time with hardly a flap of their wings, and they often perch in the open. Over most of North America, the Red-tailed Hawk is the Buteo that is seen most frequently.

ACCIPITERS (p. 124) are slim hawks with relatively short rounded wings and long tails. They often hide inside the woods, where they pursue prey (including small birds) with stealth and agility. When out in the open, they usually fly with several quick wingbeats followed by a glide, although they do sometimes soar.

NORTHERN HARRIER (p. 120) lives in very open country and usually flies low, gliding on uptilted wings. Known by its long wings, long tail, and contrasting white rump patch.

FALCONS (beginning on p. 126) have angular, pointed wings and rather long tails. Found in open country, they pursue prey with rapid flight or with power-dives from above. In most areas, the American Kestrel is the most frequently seen falcon.

OSPREY (p. 118) is likely to be seen soaring or hovering over the water before plunging feet-first to catch a fish. Recognized by its long narrow wings, with a crook in the wrist, and its contrasting pattern of dark and white.

EAGLES (p. 118) are massive hawks, seen perched in the open or soaring on very long, broad wings. Golden Eagles are mostly in very open and dry country (mainly in the west), while Bald Eagles are most often seen near water.

VULTURES (p. 120) are scavengers that may look like hawks, but are not related to them. Recognized by their huge size, naked (unfeathered) heads, and habit of soaring for hours as they search for carrion.

OWLS (beginning on p. 130) are mostly active at night and may go unseen even where common. Some owls, especially among the smaller species, are very similar and can be recognized most easily by voice. Songbirds may sometimes lead you to roosting owls in daylight by their excited "mobbing" behavior.

BUTEOS OF OPEN COUNTRY

These are the first of the true hawks and eagles (**family Accipitridae**). Buteos are hawks with relatively broad wings and short tails, often seen soaring overhead. Most buteos and similar hawks are easier to identify in flight, when their tail and wing patterns can be seen most readily.

RED-TAILED HAWK *Buteo jamaicensis*

The common hawk perched along roads and soaring over open country throughout North America. Builds bulky nest in tree, sometimes on cliff, power pole, giant cactus. Migrates late in fall, early in spring. ▶ On most adults, tail reddish above, whitish below (color shows through in flight overhead). Juvenile's tail *brown* above, with dark bars. East of the Mississippi, most Red-tails have white chest, *dark "belly-band" of streaks*. Western Red-tails are much more variable, from pale to rust-brown to blackish. (Some, known as "Harlan's Hawks," are usually dark-bodied and have tail whitish with dark marbling.) On all but the darkest birds, note *whitish patches on back*. In flight overhead, leading edge of inner wing looks contrastingly dark. Study flight silhouette of "typical" Red-tails for comparison to other hawks. ♪**Voice**: squealing *keeeyahh*.

ROUGH-LEGGED HAWK *Buteo lagopus*

A cold-weather hawk, nesting on cliffs in high Arctic, moving south rather late in fall. Favors tundra in summer, farmland and prairies in winter. May be seen hovering on rapidly beating wings. ▶ In flight, tail shows white at base, dark banding at tip; blackish patch at wrist of wing contrasts with paler flight feathers. Body plumage quite variable; typical juvenile shows black belly contrasting with streaked buffy chest. Dark-morph birds are hard to identify when perched, but show distinct pattern on wings and tail in flight. ♪**Voice**: near nest, a clear descending cry, *keeeeyr*.

FERRUGINOUS HAWK *Buteo regalis*

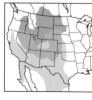

Our largest buteo, usually uncommon on western grasslands. Sometimes seen sitting on the ground in open fields. ▶ Variable. Typical adult pale, with rufous shoulders and thigh feathers; whitish tail washed with rufous toward tip. Juvenile usually lacks rufous on thighs. Some pale Red-tails have very similar markings, but note different structure: Ferruginous has wide head, long wings broad at base but tapering toward tips, wings held up in shallow V while soaring. Dark morph can suggest dark Rough-legged Hawk, but lacks dark tail-bands. ♪**Voice**: near nest, a high *keeyah*.

SOARING HAWKS

juvenile

typical adults

Red-tailed Hawk
19" w 50"
(w = wingspan)

variations
(not to scale)

juvenile

Rough-legged Hawk
21" w 53"

variations

dark and light morphs

typical adult

Ferruginous Hawk
23" w 56"

dark-morph adult

juvenile

adult

111

See also the Accipiters, the ultimate forest hawks, on p. 116.

BROAD-WINGED HAWK *Buteo platypterus*

A crow-sized buteo, summering mostly in northeastern forest, wintering in the tropics. Migrates in large flocks, especially in fall, and may concentrate along ridges and near coastlines. ▶ Chunky and compact, soars with wings held flat and tapering to a point. Adult is only eastern buteo with *broad tail-bands*, has dark back, reddish chest. Juvenile has narrow tail-bands (last one thicker), dark blotches on side of white chest. On all, wings are pale or whitish below with dark tips and trailing edges. A rare dark-bodied morph (not shown) occurs mainly in western part of range. ♪ **Voice:** thin piercing whistle, *eeh-eeeeeee*, all on one pitch.

RED-SHOULDERED HAWK *Buteo lineatus*

A forest hawk, usually uncommon in the northeast, can be common in Florida and California. Noisy, often heard before it is seen. ▶ Larger than Broad-wing, with longer wings and tail. Often flies with several quick flaps and a glide, suggesting the Accipiters (p. 124). Adult striking: narrow black and white bands on flight feathers of wings and tail, reddish shoulders and chest. West coast birds redder, Florida ones paler, grayer-headed. Juveniles in east are browner, with narrower bars on tail. On all, note *pale crescent* near wingtip in flight. ♪ **Voice:** repeated cries, *keeyar, keeyar, keeyar.*

GRAY HAWK *Asturina nitida*

Scarce and local along Arizona rivers in summer, and in south Texas at all seasons. Favors wooded areas, flying among the trees, more agile than some buteos. ▶ Adult *gray*, finely barred below, with bold *black and white bands on tail*. Juvenile less distinctive: brown above, streaked below. Suggests juvenile Broad-winged Hawk but has more striking face pattern, fine bars (not spots) on thighs. ♪ **Voice:** repeated loud whistle, *ohWAAah*, higher in middle. Also clear descending *keeeyah.*

HOOK-BILLED KITE *Chondrohierax uncinatus*

South Texas only, a few pairs in woodlands along the Rio Grande. Sluggish, perching inside forest, but may soar above trees on warm days. Feeds mostly on tree snails. ▶ *Large hooked bill, pale eyes.* In flight, wings rounded at tips, narrow at base, outer part of wings heavily barred. Overall color varies: adult male mostly gray; female has rusty bars below, rusty collar, brown back, dark cap; juvenile brown on back, barred below.

WOODLAND HAWKS

adults

juvenile

Broad-winged Hawk
16" w 34"
(w = wingspan)

juvenile

adult

adults

eastern
juvenile

**Red-shouldered
Hawk**
17" w 40"

California
juvenile

adult

adult

female

young
male

Gray Hawk
17" w 36"

**Hook-billed
Kite**
(rare)
18" w 36"

adults

male

female

juvenile

113

SWAINSON'S HAWK   *Buteo swainsoni*

This slim buteo is common over western grasslands, but only in summer. Although it can take rodents, reptiles, and birds, this hawk often feeds on large insects. Most migrate to southern South America for the winter. Big flocks of migrants are seen as far east as Texas in spring and fall. A few individuals stray to Atlantic Coast in fall, Florida in winter. ► Slim, with small head and bill, long wings and tail. When soaring, wings are held above horizontal, and wingtips look rather pointed. Typical adult has bright *white wing-linings* contrasting with dark flight feathers; narrow brown chest-band between white throat and white belly. Also many variations: can be barred or rusty below, or mostly dark brown. Juveniles usually have heavy streaks at sides of chest, strong face pattern. Winter reports of Swainson's are usually based on Red-tailed or Rough-legged Hawks. Color patterns of all these buteos are variable; study flight silhouettes to clinch identifications. ♪ **Voice**: thin *kyeeeer*, higher than Red-tail's call.

WHITE-TAILED HAWK   *Buteo albicaudatus*

Southeastern Texas only, uncommon on coastal prairies, ranch country. (Also widespread in grasslands of the tropics.) May be seen perched atop high power poles or low shrubs, or soaring ponderously over prairie. ► Bulky, with very *short tail*, broad wings that taper to a point. Soars with wings held up in shallow V. Adult shows striking pattern, especially in flight, when white tail (with black band) and white rump may be visible at great distance. Also note *rusty shoulders,* smooth gray back, contrasting white wing-linings. Juvenile very dark at first, usually with whitish patches on face and chest; tail pale gray.

SHORT-TAILED HAWK   *Buteo brachyurus*

This tropical buteo is an uncommon resident in Florida. Often soaring very high, it may go unnoticed at times; seldom seen perched. Recently a few have summered in mountains of southeast Arizona, and strays have reached Texas. ► A rather small and compact buteo with a big-headed look (despite name, does not look especially short-tailed). Two color morphs, differing in color of underparts and wing-linings: black or white. Both morphs are blackish on back and head and have the flight feathers of wings and tail gray with darker bars. Light morph has noticeable *black hooded effect.*

SOARING HAWKS

typical adults

color variations

Swainson's Hawk
19" w 51"
(w = wingspan)

juveniles

White-tailed Hawk
20" w 51"

adults

juvenile

Short-tailed Hawk
16" w 36"

light- and dark-morph adults

115

HAWKS OF THE SUBTROPICS

These birds are not closely related (the caracara belongs to the falcon family—see p. 126), but all are large soaring birds of warm climates.

HARRIS'S HAWK · *Parabuteo unicinctus*

A striking hawk of desert and brush country, mainly in Texas and Arizona. Unlike most hawks, usually seen in family groups, and may hunt cooperatively. Perches boldly in the open on poles, cactus. ▶ Dark body contrasts with bright rufous shoulders, wing-linings, thighs. Tail black, with white at base and tip. Juvenile is streaked brown below, has narrow tail-bands. Some dark-morph Swainson's Hawks (previous page) have similar color pattern. ♪ Voice: hoarse, harsh *khhhaaaaa*.

ZONE-TAILED HAWK · *Buteo albonotatus*

Uncommon in summer in the southwest, where it wanders widely over all habitats. Nests in tall trees along rivers, canyons. Sometimes overlooked in flight because of its remarkable resemblance to the common Turkey Vulture. A few may winter in Arizona, southern California. ▶ Flying at a distance, looks much like Turkey Vulture (p. 120): blackish body, two-toned wings, soars with wings held in shallow V. With closer view, shows a few white tail-bands, narrow barring on wings, slightly different shape from vulture. Juvenile may lack obvious white tail-bands. ♪ Voice: squealing whistle.

COMMON BLACK-HAWK · *Buteogallus anthracinus*

Scarce and local in summer in tall cottonwoods along southwestern rivers. Spends little time soaring; often perches very low near the water's edge, hunting frogs, minnows. ▶ Bulky, with very broad wings, short tail. Note long yellow legs, *single* obvious *white tail-band*. Zone-tailed Hawk (more tail-bands) has strikingly different shape, especially in flight. Juvenile black-hawk is brown and buff, with patterned face, many narrow tail-bands; may not look as short-tailed as adult. ♪ Voice: near nest, whistled *yeep-yeep-yeep* . . .

CRESTED CARACARA · *Caracara cheriway*

A tropical member of the falcon family (see p. 126), but shaped like a hawk and feeds like a scavenger. Caracaras often join vultures to feed at carrion and may fly along highways looking for road-killed animals. Locally common in Texas, but scarce in Arizona and Florida. ▶ Colorful face, black crest, black belly. In flight, dark body and wings contrast with pattern of four *pale areas:* chest, base of tail, and patches near each wingtip. Juvenile is browner.

SUBTROPICAL HAWKS

Zone-tailed Hawk
20" w 51"
(w = wingspan)

adults

Harris's Hawk
21" w 46"

adults

juvenile

Common Black-Hawk
20" w 50"

adults

juvenile

Crested Caracara
23" w 50"

117

OSPREY AND EAGLES

OSPREY *Pandion haliaetus*

The "fish hawk," common in some coastal areas, mostly uncommon inland. Soars high above water or hovers and then plunges, feet-first, to grab a fish in its talons. Bulky stick nest usually built atop a bare tree or pole. The Osprey was seriously endangered in the 1970s by effects of DDT and other pesticides; has recovered since DDT use was outlawed. ▶ In flight, the long wings are held above horizontal, with a distinct *bend at wrist*. Soaring at a distance, suggests a large gull more than a hawk. Sharp pattern below (with black wrist patches), dark back, *black face stripe.* Juvenile has pale scaling on back. Adult female may show more streaks on chest. ♪**Voice:** calls often, loud clear *keyew keyew keyew . . .*

BALD EAGLE *Haliaeetus leucocephalus*

National symbol of the United States, the Bald Eagle was seriously endangered in the 1970s, but has been making a gradual comeback since. Might be seen almost anywhere, but is numerous in a few areas, including parts of Florida, Alaska, and (in winter) around some lakes and rivers in midwest. Although it can be a superb hunter, often it feeds on carrion (including dead fish), and sometimes it steals fish from Ospreys. Numbers of Bald Eagles may gather where big concentrations of fish (as at spawning runs) make for easy pickings. ▶ Adults unmistakable. Immatures take four years to reach adult plumage; youngest juveniles have dark brown heads and bodies, some whitish mottling in wings and tail; older immatures may have much white on body. ♪**Voice:** rather weak, harsh chatter.

GOLDEN EAGLE *Aquila chrysaetos*

This magnificent hunter favors wilderness areas. Usually rare in the east, somewhat more numerous in open country of the west. Regularly takes prey as large as jackrabbits and marmots; also feeds on carrion. Usually solitary or in pairs, not gathering in groups as the Bald Eagle sometimes does. ▶ Very large, mostly dark brown. Long broad wings held flat while soaring. Adult solid brown with golden feathers on nape, faint pale bands on tail. Immature has white patch in center of wing, white base of tail. Compared to young Bald Eagle, Golden looks a bit longer-tailed, smaller-headed, with slightly smaller bill. Young Balds show at least a little white mottling on body or wing-linings (visible in flight) in areas where lacking on Goldens. ♪**Voice:** usually silent. Sometimes clear yelping whistles.

OSPREY AND EAGLES

Osprey
23" w 63"
(w = wingspan)

adults

Osprey
nest

immature

Bald Eagle
31" w 80"

adults

immature

adult

adults

**Golden
Eagle**
30" w 80"

immature

119

Harriers fly low in open country. New World vultures **(family Cathartidae),** related to storks (p. 152), look like birds of prey. They soar for hours at a time, seeking carrion. Nests are well hidden in caves, hollow logs, etc.

NORTHERN HARRIER   *Circus cyaneus*

A long-winged, long-tailed hawk that hunts by flying low over open fields and marshes, looking and listening for prey. Takes many rodents, also some birds. Perches low or on ground, seldom on tall poles or trees; usually flies low except when migrating. Formerly called "Marsh Hawk." ▶ Best known by shape and by low, slow flight, wings angled up in shallow V. Contrasting *white rump* is conspicuous. Adult males gray with black wingtips. Female and juvenile brown; juvenile is rusty orange below, female whiter with more streaks. ♪ **Voice:** mostly silent. Sometimes a thin whistle.

TURKEY VULTURE   *Cathartes aura*

Very common in warmer climates, soaring all day over open country, forests, deserts. Many may roost together in tall trees at night. Flocks also come together in migration, or to feed at carcasses. ▶ Very large with *long wings, long tail, small head.* Soars with wings held in *shallow V;* when flapping on takeoff, wingbeats are deep, ponderous. *Two-toned* look to underwing, black wing-linings against gray flight feathers. Juvenile has gray head, not red; compare to Black Vulture.

BLACK VULTURE   *Coragyps atratus*

Very common in parts of the south, but less widespread than its red-headed cousin. Spends less time soaring, except on the hottest days. ▶ Very different shape from Turkey Vulture: stocky, *short-tailed,* with bigger head, broad wings. Soars with wings held flat, and its glides are often punctuated by several quick flaps. *Whitish patch near wingtips* shows up in flight. Head always dark gray. Young Turkey Vulture is also dark-headed, but when perched, note Turkey Vulture's browner tinge, different head/bill shape.

CALIFORNIA CONDOR   *Gymnogyps californianus*

This huge vulture, a holdover from prehistoric times, almost became extinct in the 1980s. The last few wild individuals in southern California were captured in 1987 for captive breeding. Some condors raised in captivity have been released into the wild again in California and northern Arizona. ▶ Huge. Soars ponderously on broad, flat wings. Adult has orange head, white wing-linings; immature all dark at first. Other soaring birds (eagles, vultures) are longer-tailed, not nearly as large.

HARRIER AND VULTURES

adult males

adult females

juveniles

Northern Harrier
18" w 44"
(w = wingspan)

Turkey Vulture
26" w 67"

adult

juvenile

California Condor
(rare)
46" w 109"
(not to scale)

Black Vulture
25" w 59"

KITES

A diverse set of hawks, not all closely related (see also Hook-billed Kite, p. 112). Most species are graceful fliers; man-made paper kites were named after these birds, not the other way around.

MISSISSIPPI KITE *Ictinia mississippiensis*

Uncommon in southeast but now common in summer on southern Great Plains, where tall trees (especially cottonwoods) stand next to open country. Winters in South America. May hunt and migrate in flocks. Buoyant and graceful in the air, gliding and diving as it pursues flying insects. Strays north of mapped range, mainly in late spring. ▶ Mostly gray, with paler head, black tail. *Whitish patch* on upperside of inner wing may be conspicuous as bird maneuvers in flight. Juvenile mostly brown and streaky, with pale bars on tail. Any age might suggest Peregrine Falcon (p. 128), but flight behavior is different. ♪ **Voice:** thin whistle.

WHITE-TAILED KITE *Elanus leucurus*

Widespread in open country, fairly common in California and Texas. Often seen perched on a lone treetop or hovering on rapidly beating wings before dropping to the ground to grab a rodent. Expanding its range; strays might appear beyond mapped area. Formerly called Black-shouldered Kite. ▶ Gray and white, with *black on shoulders* and under bend of wing. May suggest a gull more than another hawk. Juvenile has brown markings on chest and back, but basic pattern is recognizable. ♪ **Voice:** whistled *keer, keer.*

SWALLOW-TAILED KITE *Elanoides forficatus*

A beautiful hawk, swooping and gliding gracefully over pine woods, cypress swamps. Summer resident in the southeast, sometimes fairly common in Florida, scarce elsewhere. Arrives very early in spring, departs in early fall, spending winter in tropics. A few strays show up well north of mapped range. ▶ Almost unmistakable. Frigatebirds (p. 72) are *much* larger, long-billed, lack white wing-linings. ♪ **Voice:** thin high whistle.

SNAIL KITE *Rostrhamus sociabilis*

Florida only (also in American tropics). Uncommon and local in sawgrass marshes, mostly south-central part of peninsula. Flies slowly and low over marsh, seeking its main food, large Pomacea snails. ▶ Broad wingtips, deeply hooked bill, orange-red legs and face. Male has slaty black, with much white at base of tail. Female browner, with white marks on face and streaks below, barring on wing feathers. ♪ **Voice:** short cackle.

KITES

juvenile

adults

Mississippi Kite
14" w 32"
(w = wingspan)

adult

White-tailed
Kite
15" w 39"

juvenile

adult

Swallow-tailed Kite
22" w 51"

Snail Kite
17" w 42"

males

females

123

are short-winged, long-tailed hawks, built for agility and bursts of speed as they thread their way through dense cover. Except when migrating, they are usually secretive, staying inside the woods. They eat many smaller birds, catching them by surprise. Our three species can be very hard to tell apart: their size differences can be difficult to judge in the wild, and females of all three are much larger than males.

SHARP-SHINNED HAWK *Accipiter striatus*

The smallest of our Accipiters is also usually the most common, especially in the east. It favors dense woods but sometimes comes into suburbs, where it may nab small birds near feeders. ▶ Adults blue-gray above, pale reddish below; young brown above, striped below. Small size is sometimes apparent (but female Sharp-shin can be almost as big as male Cooper's). Tip of tail usually looks *squared off* (but can look rounded, especially when spread); also looks small-headed and has pencil-thin legs. Juvenile Sharp-shin may show more blurry streaking below than young Cooper's. Also compare to American Kestrel and Merlin (next page). ♪ **Voice:** in alarm near nest, a harsh *kee-kee-kee-kee . . .*

COOPER'S HAWK *Accipiter cooperii*

This mid-sized Accipiter can be very elusive in heavily wooded country, but elsewhere it may come out in the open, especially in west and southwest. May perch on telephone poles in open situations (Sharp-shin rarely does). ▶ Adults blue-gray above, pale reddish below; young brown above, striped below. Bigger than Sharp-shin with relatively bigger head, longer tail, thicker legs. Tip of tail *more rounded* (can be hard to judge), often shows wider white tip than Sharp-shin. Adult Cooper's may show more contrasting dark cap, and juvenile may show sharper dark streaking on white chest. ♪ **Voice:** in alarm near nest, a harsh, nasal *keh-keh-keh-keh . . .*

NORTHERN GOSHAWK *Accipiter gentilis*

A powerful hunter, generally scarce and not often seen, lurking in forests of the north and the mountains. Pursues prey as large as rabbits and grouse, hunting mostly inside the forest. Some move south in late fall and may invade to central U.S. in some winters. ▶ Adult distinctive if seen well, *gray-barred* below, with *black face*, sharp *white eyebrow*. (Note that some female Cooper's can look quite gray.) Compare also to Gyrfalcon, p. 128. Juvenile much like young Cooper's Hawk, but fluffy white undertail coverts have large *dark spots;* bars on tail form more obvious zigzag pattern. ♪ **Voice:** in alarm near nest, high-pitched *kek kek kek kek . . .*

ACCIPITERS

Sharp-shinned Hawk
9"–13" w 20"–26"
(w = wingspan)

adults

juveniles

adult

Cooper's Hawk
14"–19" w 28"–34"

juvenile

adults

adult

Juvenile

Northern Goshawk
18"–24"
w 38"–45"

juveniles

adults

(family Falconidae) have fairly long tails and pointed wingtips. They hunt in open country, pursuing prey in fast flight or power-diving out of the sky.

AMERICAN KESTREL   *Falco sparverius*

Our smallest falcon is common and widespread. In most regions, it is seen far more often than the other falcons. Favors open country, farms, fields, deserts, sometimes towns. Typically seen perched on wires along roadsides. When hunting, often hovers in one spot on rapidly beating wings. Feeds mostly on large insects but also takes rodents, small birds, etc. Nests in holes in trees (or holes in giant cactus in southwest), or will use large birdhouses. ▶ Relatively small and long-tailed, with two sharp face stripes. Female all red-brown above with narrow dark bars, including on tail. Male has red-brown tail with black tip, red-brown back contrasting with blue-gray wings. ♪**Voice:** shrill *killy-killy-killy.*

MERLIN   *Falco columbarius*

A compact, dashing falcon, very fast and direct in flight. Usually uncommon, seen as scattered singles, but sometimes seen in fair numbers, as along coastlines during migration. In recent decades, has become a fairly common year-round resident around some towns on northern prairies and nearby regions. ▶ Relatively short-tailed. Female and immature brown above, male blue-gray above, all are streaked below. *Dark tail* is crossed by narrow *whitish bands.* In pale prairie form, male is almost sky blue above, while pale brown females can suggest small version of Prairie Falcon (next page). A scarce blackish form lives along northwest coast, seldom wanders elsewhere. Most widespread form is intermediate in color. Sharp-shinned Hawk (previous page) has similar markings but has wingtip rounded (not pointed), no white bands on tail. ♪**Voice:** rapid harsh chatter, *ki-ki-ki-ki* . . .

APLOMADO FALCON   *Falco femoralis*

Very rare, near Mexican border. Formerly resident in dry grasslands of the southwest, mostly disappeared before middle of 20th century. Recently a few have reappeared in west Texas and have even nested in New Mexico. A major attempt to re-introduce the species to south Texas has been ongoing since the 1980s. ▶ Black side patches almost meet on lower breast; belly and thighs rufous. Long blackish tail has narrow white bars. Juvenile is browner. Juvenile Prairie Falcon (next page) sometimes shows extensive black side patches, but lacks rufous thighs and white trailing edge on inner part of wing. Juvenile Swainson's Hawk (p. 114) also can look surprisingly similar to Aplomado.

FALCONS

female

male

male

female

American Kestrel
10" w 22"
(w = wingspan)

females

Merlin
11" w 24"

male

male

pale prairie form
of Merlin

Aplomado Falcon
(rare)
16" w 35"
(not to scale)

(not to scale)

northwestern
"black" form
of Merlin

127

PEREGRINE FALCON *Falco peregrinus*

Found almost worldwide but usually uncommon, this superb hunter was once threatened with extinction in North America; it has made a fairly good comeback since use of the pesticide DDT was outlawed. Occurs in many habitats, but often along coastlines, especially in migration. Usually nests on cliffs, but also may nest on ledges of tall buildings in cities. ▶ Large and powerful, with typical pointed-winged falcon silhouette. Flies with strong shallow wingbeats; when diving on prey, may reach speeds of well over 100 mph. Usually looks quite dark (although Arctic birds are paler), with *dark hooded effect.* Adults blue-gray above, narrowly barred below; juveniles browner, streaked below. ♪**Voice**: near nest, a harsh *kyah kyah kyah . . .*

PRAIRIE FALCON *Falco mexicanus*

In the wide-open west, this falcon is fairly common over dry grasslands, sagebrush flats, deserts. Shaped much like the Peregrine, it differs in hunting behavior: rather than diving out of the sky, it often pursues its prey (including small birds, ground squirrels) in very rapid maneuverable flight, close to the ground. Usually nests on cliff ledges. In winter, may roost on buildings in cities. ▶ Brown overall, with narrow dark whisker mark. Paler than Peregrine (especially on tail and underparts), and lacks the dark hooded effect. Best known in flight by heavy *black mark under base of wing.* (A trace of this sometimes shows on perched birds.) Compare to female Merlin of the prairie race (previous page), which can look as pale. ♪**Voice**: usually silent. Noisy around nest, a complaining *kyaah, kyaah . . .*

GYRFALCON *Falco rusticolus*

The world's largest falcon, a hunter of barren open terrain in the far north. Nests on cliffs along Arctic rivers, ranging widely over surrounding treeless country in pursuit of ptarmigan and other large birds. A few Gyrs drift south in winter; south of Canada they are only rare visitors, mostly seen along coast or in very open country. ▶ Most in North America are gray, but dark and white morphs also occur. Very large and broadwinged, but can be confused with the other two large falcons. All but the darkest Gyrs lack hooded effect of Peregrine; all lack the black wingpits of Prairie Falcon. Compare also to Goshawk (p. 124). ♪**Voice**: usually silent. Near nest, a harsh *kyeh, kyeh . . .*

LARGE FALCONS

adult

juvenile

juvenile

Peregrine Falcon
17" w 41"
(w = wingspan)

adult

Prairie Falcon
17" w 40"

Gyrfalcon
22" w 47"

white morph
(not to scale)

dark morph

gray morph
(not to scale)

OWLS

(family Strigidae) and Barn Owls **(family Tytonidae)** have upright posture, short necks, and big heads with eyes facing forward. More often heard than seen, most are active at night. Very acute hearing, keen eyesight in dim light, and their own silence in flight make them supreme nocturnal hunters. Roosting owls sometimes can be located in daylight by the excited "mobbing" behavior of smaller birds.

GREAT HORNED OWL   *Bubo virginianus*

Found almost everywhere, including forest, swamps, deserts. A powerful predator, taking prey as large as rabbits, snakes, even skunks. Hunts mostly at night; often harassed by crows in daylight. ▶ Large size, "ear" tufts, white throat, *horizontal bars* on belly. Downy young (like those of other owls) are whitish at first. ♪ **Voice:** deep hoots; usual pattern is *hoo, hoo-hoo . . . hoo . . . hoooh.* Also other hoots, shrieks. Young birds make hoarse, rasping whine.

LONG-EARED OWL   *Asio otus*

Widespread but uncommon, the Long-ear is often quiet, easily overlooked. Hunts only at night. Groups are sometimes found roosting in pines or other dense trees in winter. When alarmed, may draw itself up to thin, tall posture with "ear" tufts erect. ▶ Like smaller, slimmer version of Great Horned Owl, but has *stripes* (not horizontal bars) on belly, black around eyes. ♪ **Voice:** relatively silent. Sometimes gives low moaning hoots.

SHORT-EARED OWL   *Asio flammeus*

An open-country owl, at times common over marshes, fields, tundra. Sometimes hunts by day, coursing low over the ground in buoyant, floppy flight; several may hunt over the same fields. ▶ Pale buffy look, streaked chest, black around eyes. Short "ear" tufts are seldom obvious. In flight, shows *black mark* at wrist, *buff patch* in outer wing; paler on belly than Long-eared Owl. ♪ **Voice:** usually quiet; sometimes a sharp, wheezy bark.

BARN OWL   *Tyto alba*

Widespread in North America (and the world), but scarce over much of its range. Hunts by night, seeking rodents; by day, it lurks inside barns, old buildings, dry wells, caves, dense trees. ▶ Pale overall, with odd heart-shaped face, *dark eyes.* Compare to much larger Snowy Owl (p. 134). Note that downy young owls of other species may be white and make hissing noises. ♪ **Voice:** dry rasping hiss, metallic clicking noises. In flight, a hoarse shriek that cuts off abruptly at the end.

Great Horned Owl
nest and young

Great Horned
Owl
23"

adults

Short-eared
Owl
15"

Long-eared
Owl
15"

nestling

Barn Owl
16"

131

are active and vocal at night. These five species all nest in cavities in trees (or holes in giant cactus). They feed mostly on insects and other invertebrates, although screech-owls also capture many rodents.

EASTERN SCREECH-OWL   *Megascops asio*

Common (but often overlooked) in areas with large trees; lives undetected in many parks, suburbs. Color varies: gray morph is most widespread and common, but red morph is frequent in southeast, and many in Florida are intermediate or brown. ▶ "Ear" tufts may be raised or flattened, changing appearance of head shape. ♪**Voice**: descending wail or whinny, with quavering sound. Also long low trill on one pitch.

WESTERN SCREECH-OWL   *Megascops kennicottii*

In open woods, deserts, suburbs, often fairly common but overlooked. ▶ Gray (sometimes brown in northwest). Much like Eastern Screech-Owl; where they meet (western plains), base of bill yellow-green on Eastern, *blackish* on Western. Best known by sound. ♪**Voice**: short low hoots speeding up to short trill, *hoh hoh hoh hoh huhuhuhuh*. Also short trill followed by longer trill.

WHISKERED SCREECH-OWL   *Megascops trichopsis*

Near the Mexican border, in oak woods of mountains and canyons, overlaps with Western Screech-Owl and reaches higher elevations. ▶ Like Western but smaller, with smaller feet, coarse plumage pattern, yellow-green base of bill. Best known by sound. ♪**Voice**: Fast series of about 8 short low hoots, trailing off at end. Also choppy "Morse code," *dudu doot doot, dudu doot doot,* etc.

FLAMMULATED OWL   *Otus flammeolus*

An elusive little owl of western pine forests. Sometimes common in summer but easily overlooked, with small size, quiet voice, and good camouflage against tree bark. ▶ The only *small* owl with *dark eyes*. Short "ear" tufts, heavily mottled plumage, often with rusty marks on shoulders. ♪**Voice**: soft, low-pitched *boop,* sometimes varied to *bu-boop*. Calls most often late at night.

ELF OWL   *Micrathene whitneyi*

The smallest owl (sparrow-sized), common in deserts and canyons in summer, nesting in holes in saguaro cactus and in sycamores and other trees. Now scarce in Texas and California. Active only at night. ▶ Tiny size, no "ear" tufts, short tail. Blurry streaks below, white eyebrows, white stripe above wing. ♪**Voice**: yelping *chy-ewp* and a chuckling, chattering series of notes.

SMALL OWLS

brown morph

red morph

Eastern Screech-Owl
8½"

gray morph

juvenile screech-owl

Western Screech-Owl
8½"

Whiskered Screech-Owl
7½"

Flammulated Owl
6½"

Elf Owl
5½"

BARRED OWL *Strix varia*

Southern swamps sometimes echo with the rich hoots of Barred Owls. Elsewhere this species is less common, but widespread, in dense forest. Expanding its range in the northwest. Mostly nocturnal, sometimes active on cloudy days. ▶ *Dark eyes,* no "ear" tufts. Horizontal *bars* on chest, vertical *stripes* on belly. ♪ **Voice:** baritone hoots, series of 8–9: *Who cooks for you, who cooks for you-allll,* last note drawn out. Also other hoots, screams.

SPOTTED OWL *Strix occidentalis*

Uncommon and local. Favors old-growth forest in Pacific states, wooded canyons in southwest. Active only at night; roosts in dense trees by day. ▶ *Dark eyes,* no "ear" tufts. Much like Barred Owl but a bit smaller, with different pattern below (brown with white spots). ♪ **Voice:** deep, barking *huh . . . hoo-hooh . . . hooooah.* Also various other hoots, yelps, thin rising whine.

GREAT GRAY OWL *Strix nebulosa*

A big phantom of northern forest (and high mountain forests in west). Usually hard to find. May hunt by day, especially in winter; despite its large size, it eats mostly rodents. In some winters, a few Great Grays invade open country of southern Canada and northeastern states. ▶ Huge size, longish tail, *dark rings* on face, yellow eyes. Two *white neck marks* may be conspicuous. ♪ **Voice:** deep hoots, not often heard.

SNOWY OWL *Bubo scandiacus*

A powerful Arctic predator, summering on northern tundra. Hunts by day. A few drift south in winter; sometimes they invade well south of Canadian border, drawing attention as they perch in open fields, around airports, even rooftops in cities. ▶ Bulky and round-headed, with yellow eyes. Variable black barring: young females heavily marked, old males almost pure white. White owls seen in other climates are usually Barn Owls (p. 130) or downy young of other owl species.

NORTHERN HAWK OWL *Surnia ulula*

A scarce, hawklike owl of northern forest. Hunts by day or night. May be seen perched at the very tip of a spruce, or flying fast and low from one tree to another. Rarely moves south of boreal forest in winter. ▶ *Long tail,* heavily *barred* underparts, black rim around face. Posture less vertical than that of most owls. ♪ **Voice:** sharp chattering. Sometimes a low hooting trill.

OWLS

Barred
Owl
21"

Spotted
Owl
18"

Snowy Owl
24"

Great Gray
Owl
27"

adult

nestling

fledgling

adult

Northern Hawk Owl
16"

135

of various types. These all lack "ear" tufts. Burrowing Owl nests in holes in the ground, the others mostly nest in holes in trees.

NORTHERN SAW-WHET OWL *Aegolius acadicus*

This small owl likes dense cover, summering mostly in conifer forest of north and mountains. In winter, may favor planted evergreens. Discovered on its day-time roost, may act remarkably tame. ▶ No "ear" tufts, overall warm brown, *reddish streaks* on white chest. Juveniles in summer are *chocolate brown* with tawny buff belly, white eyebrows. In far north, see Boreal Owl (rare). ♪**Voice**: long series of single toots, mostly late at night. Also hoarse note like saw against whetstone.

BOREAL OWL *Aegolius funereus*

A scarce, elusive owl of the north and the high moun-tains. Very rarely wanders south of the boreal forest, but if found, may act quite tame. ▶ Bigger and grayer than Saw-whet Owl, with noticeable *black rim* around pale face, bill *yellow* (not dark). Juveniles in summer are very dark below, with white eyebrows, pale bill. ♪**Voice**: fast series of short hollow notes, *hoh-hoh-hoh-hoh-hoh-hoh-hoh* . . . , rising slightly. Also hoarse *chyah.*

BURROWING OWL *Athene cunicularia*

Once a common and well-known ground owl of open country, now declining in numbers. Nests in under-ground burrows. Hunts mostly at night, but often seen perching on ground or fenceposts by day. Sometimes hovers on rapidly beating wings. ▶ *Long legs,* barred underparts, terrestrial habits. Juveniles plainer below. See Short-eared Owl (p. 130), also often on ground. ♪**Voice**: hollow *coo-hooooo;* squeaky chuckling chatter.

NORTHERN PYGMY-OWL *Glaucidium gnoma*

Tiny but tough, may capture rodents or birds almost as large as itself. Often active by day. Widespread in mountain forest but not common anywhere, usually hard to find. ▶ Small, with *pale* bars on *long tail.* Sharp streaks on white belly. Two bold spots (like false eyes) on back of head. Overall color varies from grayish to warm brown. ♪**Voice**: fairly slow series of short whistles (given either singly or doubled), easy to imitate.

FERRUGINOUS PYGMY-OWL *Glaucidium brasilianum*

Scarce and localized in dry woods of southern Texas, very rare in deserts of south-central Arizona. ▶ Like Northern Pygmy-Owl but has black bars on *reddish tail*, narrow streaks (not spots) on crown; found at *lower elevations* in southwest. ♪**Voice**: fairly rapid series of short, sharp whistles.

juvenile

SMALL OWLS

Boreal
Owl
10"

juvenile

Northern
Saw-whet Owl
8"

adult

adult

"eye" spots on
back of head

color
variation

Burrowing
Owl
9½"

Northern
Pygmy-Owl
7"

juvenile

adults

Ferruginous
Pygmy-Owl
7"

WOODLAND GROUSE

Everyone knows chickens, but not everyone knows that the domestic chicken is descended from a wary wild bird of south Asian forests, Red Junglefowl. Like the birds below, it belongs to the **family Phasianidae**. These are all short-billed, strong-legged birds that spend much time on the ground. The forest grouse below all can be surprisingly tame.

RUFFED GROUSE   *Bonasa umbellus*

Fairly common in deciduous or mixed woods. Usually seen on ground, also perches high in trees. In spring courtship display, male struts on log with tail spread and neck ruffs puffed up and rapidly drums the air with his wings. ▶ Short crest; long, fan-shaped tail with wide *blackish band near tip*. Has two color morphs, most obvious in tail color (gray or reddish). Black neck ruffs not usually apparent except during displays. Wide bars of dark and white on sides (below wings) may be conspicuous. ♪**Voice:** loud *chuck* and soft clucks. Most frequent sound is deep wing-thumping of male.

SPRUCE GROUSE   *Falcipennis canadensis*

Although it is fairly common across the great northern forest, this grouse can be hard to find because it is too tame, sitting motionless while a birder walks right past. In courtship display, male struts with spread tail, drums with wings. ▶ Male looks gray, with white edging on black throat and chest, red "combs" above each eye. In most regions, note the *rusty tip on black tail*. Female may look reddish or grayish overall. Similar to Ruffed Grouse but has shorter, darker tail, black and white bars on belly; lacks broad bars on sides. Note: in a form found in northern Rockies called "Franklin's Grouse" (not shown), male lacks rusty tail tip and has white spots above base of tail. ♪**Voice:** clucking notes. Displaying males may give deep hoots.

BLUE GROUSE   *Dendragapus obscurus*

A big dark grouse of western forest. Not always in deep woods; favors areas near large clearings. In courtship display (sometimes performed high in trees), male spreads tail, struts, gives deep hoots. ▶ Over most of range, known by broad *gray tip on dark tail* (in northern Rockies, tail is all dark). Male is gray, darker and more uniform than other grouse. White feathers around bare reddish or yellow neck patches are visible only in display. Female mottled brown and gray, with *belly mostly gray*, lacking the black and white barring of Spruce or Ruffed Grouse. ♪**Voice:** clucks and cackles. Male in display gives series of loud deep hoots.

WOODLAND GROUSE

Ruffed Grouse
17½"

male in display

gray morph

red morph

Spruce Grouse
16"

female with chick

male

immature

Blue Grouse
19"

male (n. Rockies) in display

female

male

139

BARREN-GROUND GROUSE

Ptarmigan (the "p" is silent) are ptough grouse, adapted to extreme Arctic conditions. Camouflaged at all seasons, they molt from white winter plumage to mottled summer plumage (but still with white wings). Feathers on their feet add insulation and act as snowshoes, helping them to walk on the snow's surface. Snowcocks are native to high mountains of Asia.

WILLOW PTARMIGAN   *Lagopus lagopus*

The most numerous grouse of the far north, common on open tundra, willow thickets. Gathers in small flocks during the winter. Rarely strays south of mapped range. ▶ White with black tail feathers in winter. More variable in summer, changing during the season. Male in late spring may have white body, chestnut head and neck; later he is mostly reddish brown with white wings. Female is better camouflaged, duller mottled brown through summer. Compare to other ptarmigan species. ♪ **Voice**: various clucks and cackles. Male has low barking chatter, *go-back-go-back.*

ROCK PTARMIGAN   *Lagopus muta*

Although it overlaps broadly with Willow Ptarmigan's range, the Rock Ptarmigan is usually in more barren open places, higher ridges. ▶ Female Rock and Willow Ptarmigan are very hard to tell apart, but Rock is smaller, with *smaller bill.* Male Rock molts later than other ptarmigan; in early summer, may still be mostly white, while females are brown and male Willow has chestnut head and neck. In winter, male Rock has *black line* from eye to bill. ♪ **Voice**: varied clucks and cackles. Male has deep growl, *krrh kr-krrrrrrr.*

WHITE-TAILED PTARMIGAN   *Lagopus leucura*

The mountain ptarmigan; found from Alaskan ridges to the highest peaks of New Mexico. Usually hard to find, walking quietly on tundra, sitting motionless (relying on camouflage) when approached. ▶ Similar to other ptarmigan, but smaller. Has *white tail feathers,* not black (but this is hard to see except in flight). In Alaska and northwest Canada, usually lives at higher elevations than its relatives, and this is the only ptarmigan found south of Canada in the west. ♪ **Voice**: clucks and cackles. Male gives high *kr-kreeee, kurree.*

HIMALAYAN SNOWCOCK   *Tetraogallus himalayensis*

This huge Asian grouse was introduced as a game bird in the Ruby Mountains of northeastern Nevada and seems to be well established there, at high elevations above timberline. Elusive, hard to spot as small groups walk on barren slopes. ▶ Unmistakable in its limited U.S. range: *very large,* with chestnut stripes around pale face and throat. ♪ **Voice**: clucking notes.

BARREN-GROUND GROUSE

females
(summer)

Willow Ptarmigan
15"

male
(spring)

winter

male
(winter)

female
(summer)

male
(summer)

Rock Ptarmigan
14"

male
(spring)

Himalayan Snowcock
(not to scale)
28"

White-tailed Ptarmigan
12½"

winter

male
(summer)

141

GREATER SAGE-GROUSE　*Centrocercus urophasianus*

Tied to the great sagebrush flats of western plateaus, this superb grouse is now disappearing along with its habitat. Males gather in spring and perform spectacular courtship displays to attract females, puffing out bare yellow chest sacs and making loud popping sounds. ▶ Male's white breast contrasts with black bib, black belly. Long spiky tail. Female plainer, known by large size, rather long tail, contrasting *dark belly patch.*

GUNNISON SAGE-GROUSE　*Centrocercus minimus*

Differences from Greater Sage-Grouse were not recognized until the 1990s. Now known to be a distinct species, found mainly in Gunnison Basin of southwest Colorado, locally into Utah. ▶ Smaller than Greater Sage-Grouse. Male has more obvious pale bars on tail feathers, longer tuft on back of head. Best identified by range (the two sage-grouse species do not overlap).

GREATER PRAIRIE-CHICKEN　*Tympanuchus cupido*

Once abundant, now a disappearing part of our prairie heritage. Where they persist (mostly native grassland), males gather in spring on traditional booming grounds to perform courtship dances to attract females, posturing and stamping and making moaning sounds. Isolated race formerly found on Atlantic Coast ("Heath Hen") is extinct, and "Attwater's" race in Texas is seriously endangered. ▶ Brown, heavily *barred* below. In flight, shows *short black tail.* See next two species.

LESSER PRAIRIE-CHICKEN　*Tympanuchus pallidicinctus*

A pallid prairie-chicken, adapted to dry short-grass plains with scattered scrub oak patches. Once numerous, now fading like the old west; probably endangered. Its courtship displays are similar to those of Greater Prairie-Chicken. ▶ Best recognized by range (no overlap with Greater). Paler overall, slightly smaller. In display, male shows purplish neck sacs, not yellow.

SHARP-TAILED GROUSE　*Tympanuchus phasianellus*

This grouse favors areas where prairie is mixed with scattered groves of trees, and it often perches up in trees in cold weather, feeding on buds. Males gather in spring and dance to attract females, posturing with tail up, making mellow cooing sounds. ▶ Similar to prairie-chickens, but has underparts mostly *spotted,* not barred. In flight, shows longer tail with *white outer feathers* (prairie-chickens have short black tails).

PRAIRIE GROUSE

Greater Sage-Grouse
28" (male), 23" (female)

female

male

displaying male
(not to scale)

displaying males

**Gunnison
Sage-Grouse**
22" (male),
19" (female)
(not to scale)

displaying
male

Greater Prairie-Chicken
17½"

female

male

**Lesser
Prairie-Chicken**
16"

Sharp-tailed Grouse
17"

displaying
male

143

QUAIL AND PARTRIDGES

Gray Partridge and Chukar are related to the grouse and other birds on previous pages. The other two here belong to a distinct family, the New World quail (**Odontophoridae**), which continues on the next page.

NORTHERN BOBWHITE   *Colinus virginianus*

The familiar little quail of the southeast. In spring, males whistle their name from fenceposts, low branches. In other seasons, small flocks (coveys) run on the ground, hide in dense grass of brushy fields, open woods. In many areas, populations have declined seriously in recent decades. ▶ Contrasting *pale eyebrow and throat,* buff on female, white on male. Reddish brown body, very short tail. See other chunky birds of fields, such as meadowlarks (p. 334). Male of endangered Sonoran race, **"Masked Bobwhite"** (being reintroduced in Arizona), has black face, rusty chest. ♪ **Voice**: whistled *bobwhoit!* or *er-bob-whoit!* Covey call, whistled *quoy-kee.*

MONTEZUMA QUAIL   *Cyrtonyx montezumae*

In foothills of the southwest, these quail favor tall grass among scattered oaks. Uncommon and quiet, easily overlooked. If approached, they often sit motionless, relying on camouflage, then burst into flight almost underfoot. Also called Harlequin Quail or Mearns's Quail. ▶ Small, chunky, with puffy head. Male's clownish pattern unmistakable. Female more subtly marked in pale brown but has recognizable head shape and pattern. ♪ **Voice**: ghostly, descending trill, *wheeerrrrr.*

GRAY PARTRIDGE   *Perdix perdix*

Brought from Europe and released here as a game bird, and has thrived in some areas, especially farm country of northern prairies. It walks on the ground in open fields, usually in coveys or pairs, often hidden in tall grass. ▶ Mostly gray below, with *orange face and throat.* Chestnut patch on belly (reduced on female). In flight, short tail shows *rusty outer feathers.* ♪ **Voice**: metallic grating *kyerr-r-reck.* When flushed, sharp chipping.

CHUKAR   *Alectoris chukar*

Native to southern Asia and the Middle East, brought to North America as a game bird. Does well in some parts of the west, especially in dry, rocky canyons with dense brush. Lives in coveys at most seasons. ▶ Bold black bars on flanks, *black outline around pale throat,* red bill and legs. Unlike any other North American bird, but some other Old World partridges are very similar (and are sometimes released here as game birds). ♪ **Voice**: in spring, a hoarse cackling *chuk chuk chukar.*

QUAIL AND PARTRIDGES

male
"Masked
Bobwhite"

Northern Bobwhite
10"

female

male

female

Montezuma
Quail
9"

male

male

Gray
Partridge
12½"

female

Chukar
14"

145

Baby quail leave the nest shortly after hatching, following their parents around. Their wings develop rapidly, and they can fly before they are full-grown. (The same is true in the grouse and pheasant family, except that the young are usually tended by only their mothers, not both parents.)

CALIFORNIA QUAIL *Callipepla californica*

In brushy woods and lowland chaparral of the far west, pairs and coveys of these elegant little chickens walk on the ground, nodding their heads at each step. They can even survive in suburbs and city parks if there is enough ground cover. ▶ Curving topknot, white stripes on *gray-brown sides*, heavily *scaled pattern* on belly. Mountain Quail is mostly at higher elevations, has broad white bars on reddish sides. In desert country, see Gambel's Quail. ♪**Voice:** loud *chi-CAH-go;* clucking notes. In spring, males give loud descending *waow*.

GAMBEL'S QUAIL *Callipepla gambelii*

The desert quail, common in the land of cactus and mesquite. Also comes into the edges of cities. Like other quail, travels in flocks (coveys) for most of year, in pairs during nesting season. ▶ Curving topknot, white stripes on *chestnut-red sides*. Male has reddish cap, *black patch* in center of yellow belly. Female is redder on sides than female California Quail, with less scaly pattern on belly. ♪**Voice:** loud *chi-CAH-go* or *chi-CAH-guh-go;* varied clucking notes. In spring, males perch high, give loud descending *waow*.

MOUNTAIN QUAIL *Oreortyx pictus*

In brushy foothills and mountains of the Pacific states, this quail is sometimes common but usually elusive, hiding in dense chaparral, manzanita thickets. ▶ Two long thin plumes on head (often combining into one) stand straight up. Blue-gray head and chest, chestnut face, broad *white bars on chestnut sides*. ♪**Voice:** in spring, male gives loud *quawock* with rich ringing quality, audible from a distance, repeated at long intervals.

SCALED QUAIL *Callipepla squamata*

This gray quail is common in dry open grassland of the southwest, but avoids true desert areas that lack good ground cover of grass. ▶ Blue-gray overall, with *fluffy white crest* ("cottontop" is one nickname). Dark edges on gray body feathers create *scaled look*. Sexes very similar, but female may have shorter crest. ♪**Voice:** loud *pock pock,* first note slightly stronger; also a loud *pwock* and varied clucking notes.

WESTERN QUAIL

California Quail 10"

female

male

quail pair with chicks

Gambel's Quail 11"

female

male

Scaled Quail 10"

Mountain Quail 11"

147

Pheasants and turkeys are classified in the same family as the grouse, but the chachalaca belongs to the **family Cracidae**, the curassows and guans of the American tropics. The roadrunner has a similar shape but is totally unrelated, belonging to the cuckoo family (see p. 200).

RING-NECKED PHEASANT   *Phasianus colchicus*

Native to Asia, introduced to North America as a game bird. It thrives in some areas, especially farmland, prairie, brushy woods. ▶ Male unmistakable, colorful with long tail, white neck ring. Mottled brown female known by size, long tail, pale belly; see Prairie Grouse on p. 142. "Green Pheasant" (not shown), sometimes considered a separate species, found locally on east coast; both sexes are darker, and males lack white neck ring. ♪ **Voice:** males give harsh crowing, *khaaa-angk.*

GREATER ROADRUNNER   *Geococcyx californianus*

This famous ground-running cuckoo is most common in southwestern desert, but small numbers range east to the Ozarks and north to central California. It can fly, but usually chooses not to; bursts of speedy running allow it to catch large insects, lizards, snakes, rodents, small birds. ▶ Unmistakable. Streaky pattern, long tail with white spots. Shaggy crest may be raised or lowered. ♪ **Voice:** mostly quiet, but makes sharp bill-rattling. Song is a slow, descending series of cooing notes.

PLAIN CHACHALACA   *Ortalis vetula*

A Texas specialty (also introduced on Sapelo Island, Georgia). Runs on the ground and clambers about high in trees. Shy and elusive in the tropics, but has become tame in some Texas parks and towns. Flocks make loud clattering from treetops, especially at dawn. ▶ Large, long-tailed, small-headed. Dull olive brown, grayer on head, buff on belly. May show red on throat. Wide black tail feathers have white tips. ♪ **Voice:** gritty cackling, *cha-cha-lac, cha-cha-lac,* in loud chorus by flocks.

WILD TURKEY   *Meleagris gallopavo*

The wild ancestor of the domestic turkey is a wary, elegant bird and a strong flier. May be seen high in trees, although it feeds on the ground. Once hunted out of many regions, it has made a good comeback and has been introduced into places beyond the original range. Still increasing in eastern states. ▶ Huge, with naked head and long wide tail. Looks trimmer and stronger than the barnyard variety. Females and young are smaller and duller than adult males. ♪ **Voice:** loud gobbling, often heard at dawn. Also low clucks.

LARGE LONG-TAILED BIRDS

female

Ring-necked Pheasant
21" (female), 33" (male)

male

Plain Chachalaca
22"

Greater Roadrunner
23"

Wild Turkey
37" (female), 46" (male)

male in display

female

male

Ibises and spoonbills **(family Threskiornithidae)** and flamingos **(family Phoenicopteridae)** are wading birds with highly distinctive bill shapes. Members of both families fly with their long necks fully outstretched.

GLOSSY IBIS *Plegadis falcinellus*

In marshes of Florida and the Atlantic Coast, flocks of these sickle-billed birds probe in mud for insects or other creatures. Sometimes called "curlew," but real curlews (p. 188) belong to the sandpiper family. ▶ Very dark, with curved bill. In good light, adult shows chestnut body, green and purple and pink gloss on wings. In breeding season, slaty face skin has narrow pale blue border. Otherwise almost identical to next species.

WHITE-FACED IBIS *Plegadis chihi*

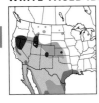

Fairly common in western marshes in warmer seasons. ▶ Very similar to Glossy Ibis, usually best identified by range. (They overlap on western Gulf Coast, and each may wander into range of the other.) In breeding plumage, has border of *white feathers* around *red face* skin (Glossy has dark gray face skin with pale blue edge, no white feathering), often has reddish legs. Immatures not safely identified; winter adults of the two species almost identical, although White-faced has red eyes.

WHITE IBIS *Eudocimus albus*

In parts of the southeast, flocks of White Ibises wade in the shallows, probing or sweeping with their bills. Colonies nest in low waterside trees. A few birds wander far north and west of mapped range. ▶ Adult unmistakable, white with *red bill and legs,* black wingtips. Young bird mostly brown with white belly at first, recognized by pink curved bill; becomes patchy as it matures.

ROSEATE SPOONBILL *Platalea ajaja*

Mostly in Florida and coastal Texas, these odd, beautiful birds swing their spatulate bills from side to side as they wade in shallow water. Typically seen in small groups, often with other wading birds. Rarely wanders well to north and into southwest. ▶ Adults known by bright pink tones, naked greenish heads. Young birds much paler, with feathered white heads.

GREATER FLAMINGO *Phoenicopterus ruber*

Flamingos escaped from captivity may be seen almost anywhere on rare occasions. Wild birds from the Bahamas are rare visitors to Everglades National Park, Florida. ▶ Much longer neck and legs than Roseate Spoonbill, different bill shape. Immatures paler, grayer. Note: escaped flamingos of other species are also seen at times.

WADERS WITH ODD BILLS

Glossy Ibis 23"
winter
breeding adult

White-faced Ibis 23"
winter
breeding adult

subadult

adult

immature

adult

White Ibis 25"

Roseate Spoonbill 32"
immature
adults

Greater Flamingo 46" (not to scale)

151

Four of our biggest waders are grouped here. Herons, introduced on page 154, are sometimes mistaken for cranes (family **Gruidae**) or storks (family **Ciconiidae**). Unlike herons, cranes and storks fly with their necks fully outstretched, often soaring high in flocks.

GREAT BLUE HERON   *Ardea herodias*

Our most widespread and familiar heron, also the largest. Often solitary, except around nesting colonies; lone birds may be seen flapping slowly overhead, even miles from water. Stands patiently at waterside, waiting to spear fish or other creatures. ▶ Huge and gray, with massive bill, *black crown stripe* on whitish head. Other grayish herons have different head pattern; Sandhill Crane has different body shape. Two distinct forms of Great Blue are restricted to Florida: **"Great White Heron"** (all white with yellow bill, pale legs) and **"Wurdemann's Heron"** (white-headed), mostly in the Keys.

SANDHILL CRANE   *Grus canadensis*

Highly social and quite localized, may occur in large flocks in some places and be absent elsewhere. Sandhill Cranes nest around marshes, but in migration and winter may feed on waste grain in open fields. ▶ Adult all gray with red patch on head, sometimes brown staining on body feathers; juvenile has brownish head. Different shape from Great Blue Heron, with shorter bill, *bushy tuft of feathers* over rump. ♪ **Voice**: guttural crowing rattle, often heard from flocks high overhead.

WHOOPING CRANE   *Grus americana*

This magnificent crane almost became extinct in the 1940s, and is still rare and endangered. Small numbers migrate from western Canada to winter on Texas coast (Rockport area). Attempts are being made to introduce them elsewhere, including Wisconsin (migratory flock) and Florida (non-migratory). ▶ Larger than egrets (next page), different shape. Adult has bare red skin on head, juvenile has brown on head and back. Black wing pattern shows in flight; compare to Wood Stork, also American White Pelican (p. 72). ♪ **Voice**: rich bugling.

WOOD STORK   *Mycteria americana*

Our only native stork. Year-round in Florida; visits elsewhere in southeast in summer, very locally in southwest. Walks in shallow water, head down, feeling for prey with its bill. Nests in colonies in treetops. Flocks sometimes soar high. ▶ *Naked gray head*, heavy bill. Juvenile has yellow bill and dusky head. In flight, wing pattern suggests American White Pelican (p. 72).

HUGE WADERS

"Wurdemann's Heron"

Great Blue Heron 47"

adults

"Great White Heron"

juvenile

other Great Blues (not to scale)

Sandhill Crane 42"

juvenile (not to scale)

Whooping Crane 52"

adult

adult

juvenile

Wood Stork 40"

adults

153

In the heron family **(Ardeidae)**, the terms "heron" and "egret" are applied loosely, although most egrets are white. These birds are usually seen wading or standing in shallow water, waiting to spear small fish. Voices of most herons are harsh squawks, not described below. Herons and egrets usually place their bulky stick nests close together in trees or shrubs; several kinds may nest together in mixed colonies.

GREAT EGRET *Ardea alba*

This elegant wader is our most widespread white egret, often seen standing like a statue along the edges of lakes and marshes. Egret populations were decimated by hunting for their feathers by about 1900; their recovery was largely thanks to efforts by the Audubon Society, newly formed at that time. ▶ Large, long-necked, and white, with *yellow bill, black legs.* In Florida, **"Great White Heron"** is even larger, but has pale legs. Cattle Egret is much smaller, with much shorter bill and legs.

SNOWY EGRET *Egretta thula*

A dainty egret that dances in the shallows, often shuffling its feet or dashing about actively as it pursues minnows and tadpoles. Many egrets develop long filmy feathers (called "aigrettes") in breeding plumage; those of the Snowy are especially long and lacy. ▶ Legs mostly *black,* with bright *yellow feet* ("golden slippers"). Bill black, with *yellow on lores* (in front of eye). Immatures may have legs mostly greenish at first, base of bill gray; see immature Little Blue Heron (next page).

CATTLE EGRET *Bubulcus ibis*

Forsaking the watery haunts of most herons, Cattle Egrets stalk about in open fields, hunting grasshoppers and other large insects. Often they forage near farm animals that may flush insects from the grass. For nesting and roosting sites, however, they usually pick trees near water. Cattle Egrets spread from Africa to South America, then reached North America in the 1950s. ▶ More compact and chunkier than other white herons. *Yellow bill* is noticeably *short.* Legs vary from yellow or pink in breeding season to dusky or black in winter. In breeding plumage, shows patches of buff feathers.

OTHER WHITE HERONS AND EGRETS

The **"Great White Heron,"** a race of the Great Blue Heron (page 152), is found locally in Florida, especially the Keys and the Everglades. Bigger than Great Egret, with more massive bill, and has *pale legs.* See next page for the white immature stages of Little Blue Heron and the white morph of Reddish Egret, either of which might be confused with Snowy Egret.

WHITE EGRETS

plumes
raised

Snowy
Egret
24"

adults

peak breeding
season color

Cattle
Egret
19"

winter

breeding
season

Great
Egret
39"

adults

BILLS & HEADS COMPARED

Great
Egret

Cattle
Egret

Snowy
Egret

"Great
White
Heron"
47"
(see text)

immature
Little Blue
Heron
(next page)

white morph
Reddish Egret
(next page)

LITTLE BLUE HERON   *Egretta caerulea*

A trim heron, very similar in size and shape to Snowy Egret (previous page). Little Blues are common in the southeast, mostly rare in the west. Often seen wading slowly or standing motionless with neck fully outstretched, head held high but pointed down, looking straight down at the water. ▶ Adults solidly dark blue-gray, tinged more red-violet on head and neck; bill *blue with black tip.* Smaller and more compact than dark morph of Reddish Egret, with shorter bill and legs, different bill color. Immature all white at first; very much like young Snowy Egret but usually *gray* (not yellow) on bare skin near eye, legs dull greenish. Dusky wingtips may be visible in flight. Usually feeds more slowly and methodically than Snowy Egret. When molting to adult plumage, may be patchy white and blue ("calico" phase).

TRICOLORED HERON   *Egretta tricolor*

A slender, graceful heron of the southeast, mostly in coastal marshes, swamps. Sometimes wanders far inland and to the west. Formerly called Louisiana Heron. ▶ Dark blue upperparts contrast with *white belly* and *white stripe up foreneck.* Base of bill and bare face skin are yellowish at most seasons, bright blue in breeding season. Slender shape makes this species look even longer-billed and longer-necked than most herons. Immature has reddish brown replacing blue on neck and has reddish brown markings on wings.

REDDISH EGRET   *Egretta rufescens*

Restricted to salt water in the southeast, this lanky heron is seldom seen away from the coast. In tidal lagoons it often runs and lurches about, stopping abruptly and spreading its wings or turning to jab at a fish. ▶ Long-legged, with *long, straight, heavy bill* and usually with shaggy neck feathers. Two color morphs: dark morph (all slaty and reddish brown) and scarcer white morph. Unlike Little Blue Heron, these are not age-related: the birds are dark or light for life. Base of bill *bright pink* on breeding adults, dusky at other seasons and on immatures (immatures also lack shaggy neck feathers). Compare dark morph to Little Blue Heron. White morph in non-breeding plumage (especially immatures) can suggest Snowy Egret (previous page), but they lack yellow on feet and before eye.

HERONS

immature

adults

Little Blue Heron
24"

molting immature

non-breeding adult

Reddish Egret feeding tactics

immature

breeding adult

Tricolored Heron
26"

dark morph adult breeding

dark morph immature

Reddish Egret
30"

white morph adult non-breeding

white morph adult breeding

157

NIGHT-HERONS, BITTERN, LIMPKIN

Night-Herons and American Bittern are heavy-bodied and short-legged and tend to be more secretive than other herons. The Limpkin, placed in its own family **(Aramidae)**, is an odd snail-eater of the tropics.

BLACK-CROWNED NIGHT-HERON   *Nycticorax nycticorax*

Stocky and short-necked, night-herons may stand about in a hunched posture in trees or marsh during the day, come out in the evening to begin feeding. Although they roost and nest in groups, they usually hunt alone. ▶ Adult unmistakable with black cap and back, gray wings. Juvenile very different, all brown with white spots at first; compare to young Yellow-crowned and to American Bittern. Later immature stages look more like brownish versions of adults. ♪**Voice:** hollow *wock!,* often heard overhead at night.

YELLOW-CROWNED NIGHT-HERON   *Nyctanassa violacea*

Mainly a southeastern bird, only a very rare visitor in the west. Hunts by day or night; in coastal regions, eats many crabs. ▶ Adult all gray, with black and white face pattern (pale yellow on crown not usually obvious). Juvenile very similar to young Black-crowned but has longer legs, *thicker all-black bill,* often a grayer look with smaller pale spots above. In flight, feet extend much farther past tip of tail. ♪**Voice:** hollow *wack!,* a bit higher than Black-crown's call.

AMERICAN BITTERN   *Botaurus lentiginosus*

A shy, solitary heron of dense marshes, often remaining out of sight. If alarmed, it may point its bill skyward, mimicking the vertical pattern of marsh grass. Has declined or disappeared in many areas with loss of wetland habitat. ▶ Warm brown overall, with strong stripes below. *Black neck mark* is obvious on adult, replaced by brown on juvenile. Compare to young night-herons. Least Bittern (page 160) shares marsh habitat but looks very different. ♪**Voice:** in breeding season, deep booming *ooomm-ka-chooom,* the sharp middle note (like hammer hitting metal) audible from far away.

LIMPKIN   *Aramus guarauna*

Not related to herons; probably closer to rails (next page). Stalks about in Florida marshes and swamps with odd limping gait, seeking large snails and other creatures. Looks gangly in flight, neck outstretched. May be active at night. ▶ Deep brown, with sharp white streaks on the neck, back, and shoulders. Long bill is slightly downcurved and paler at base. ♪**Voice:** a loud rolling wail, *kkrrrraaow,* often heard at night.

older immatures

Black-crowned
Night-Heron
25"

juvenile

adults

adult

juvenile

adult

Yellow-crowned
Night-Heron
25"

American
Bittern
26"

Limpkin
25"

159

Our two smallest herons are shown here with the first of the rail family **(Rallidae)**. Rails are secretive marsh birds, heard more often than seen.

GREEN HERON   *Butorides virescens*

Along wooded creeks, ponds, and marshes, the little Green Heron jerks its short tail up and down as it stalks the water's edge. If alarmed, it flies up with a sharp cry. Builds a stick nest in a tree, usually as isolated pairs, not in colonies. ▶ Small and dark, with *orange-yellow legs.* Chestnut neck, black crown feathers often raised in a bushy crest, dark back glossed with green or blue. Young bird duller and browner, with striped neck. ♪**Voice:** when alarmed, a sharp *skyowk!*

LEAST BITTERN   *Ixobrychus exilis*

A tiny, secretive heron that hides in dense marshes. Most often seen as it flies low over marsh. If disturbed, it freezes with bill pointed up, mimicking appearance of marsh grass. ▶ Buffy overall, with cap and back brown (female) or black (male). Big *buff patches* on inner part of wing are obvious both perched and in flight. Young Green Heron can look very brown, but lacks these wing patches. ♪**Voice:** short fast gobbling, *koo-hoo-hoo-hoo-hooh.* Also a harsh cackle, *kek-kek-kek-kek.*

CLAPPER RAIL   *Rallus longirostris*

This "marsh hen" hugs salt marshes of the Atlantic and Gulf coasts. Still fairly common, but has declined with loss of habitat. Scarce and local in west (California coast, Colorado River area). Secretive, but often noisy; seen walking on mud at marsh edge or swimming across channels. ▶ Chicken-sized, with long narrow bill, barring on flanks. Underparts buffy gray or dull cinnamon on Atlantic and Gulf coasts, brighter cinnamon in west. ♪**Voice:** clattering series, *kek-kek-kek-kek-kek-kek,* often speeding up and then slowing down.

KING RAIL   *Rallus elegans*

A big, colorful rail of fresh marshes in the east. Uncommon in most areas, and has lost much of its original habitat with draining of wetlands. ▶ More richly colored than eastern Clapper Rail. Flanks *more sharply barred* black and white; back feathers have warm buff edges; much *reddish on wings.* Habitat is a good clue (King in fresh water, Clapper in salt water), but they meet and sometimes interbreed in brackish marshes. Virginia Rail (next page) much smaller, with gray cheeks. ♪**Voice:** sharp *kek kek kek kek,* usually shorter and more even series than Clapper Rail.

SMALL HERONS, LARGE RAILS

juvenile

Green Heron
19"

adults

male

Least
Bittern
13"

west
coast
adult

female

Clapper
Rail
15"

adults

King
Rail
16"

SORA *Porzana carolina*

Widespread and fairly common, and seen more often than most rails. Favors large freshwater marshes for nesting, but during migration and winter may be in salt marsh or in narrow marshy edges of small ponds. When it walks on open mud at edge of marsh, often flicks its short tail nervously. ▶ Chunky and *short-billed.* Adult has *black face* contrasting with rich brown back, gray chest, yellow bill. Juvenile lacks black face and is buffier below, sometimes mistaken for the rare Yellow Rail. ♪ **Voice:** clear whistle that rises at end, *surrrr-eeeee.* Also sharp *keek* and sharp descending whinny, *keehehehehehehehehee.*

VIRGINIA RAIL *Rallus limicola*

The other common rail of inland marshes. Not seen as often as the Sora, although the two are often in the same places. ▶ *Long-billed.* Rich rusty cinnamon below, with contrasting *gray cheeks,* sharp black and white bars on flanks, reddish on wings. King Rail (previous page) is much larger, has tan or brownish cheeks. Compare also to western races of Clapper Rail (previous page). Juvenile Virginia Rail is blackish at first. ♪ **Voice:** sharp metallic *kik kidik kidik kidik;* also harsh descending *wenk-wenk-wenk-wenk-wenk.*

YELLOW RAIL *Coturnicops noveboracensis*

Among North American birds, this is the most difficult to see. Nests on northern prairies and winters in southeast, in wet meadows, shallow marsh, rice fields. Never comes out in the open by choice. ▶ Small and short-billed; dark above, buffy below. Suggests juvenile Sora but smaller, blacker above, with narrow *white bars* on back. In flight, shows *white patch* on inner part of wing (unlike other rails). ♪ **Voice:** dry mechanical *tictick tictictick tictick tictictick,* mostly late at night.

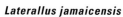

BLACK RAIL *Laterallus jamaicensis*

A dark little gnome, scarce and seldom seen. On coast, often in spartina marshes; inland, in various shallow marshes with very dense stands of short grass. Quite secretive, may go undetected because it calls mostly very late at night. ▶ Sparrow-sized, short-billed. Slaty all over with *chestnut nape,* white spots on back, red eyes. Note: small downy young of some other rails are black and are often mistaken for Black Rails. ♪ **Voice:** harsh, squeaky *kee-kee-grrr,* second note highest. Also a low *grrrr grrr grrr.*

SMALL RAILS

first autumn

Sora
9"

adult

juvenile

Virginia
Rail
9½"

juvenile

adults

Yellow
Rail
7"

Black Rail
6"

163

Many birds are found on the shore, but when birders say "shorebirds," they mean the sandpipers, plovers, and related families. These provide much excitement for observers: at some times and places, it is possible to find up to 30 species of shorebirds in a day. However, they also provide challenges, because many shorebirds are difficult to identify.

PLOVERS (family Charadriidae) have short, straight bills, short necks, and a rather round-headed look. They often run a few paces and then stop. **STILTS AND AVOCETS (family Recurvirostridae)** have thin bills and very long, thin legs. They usually feed by wading in shallow water. **OYSTERCATCHERS (family Haematopodidae)** are big, stocky birds with bladelike bills, usually seen on beaches or rocky shores.

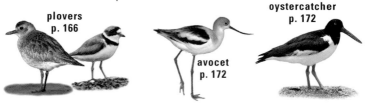

plovers
p. 166

avocet
p. 172

oystercatcher
p. 172

Most shorebirds belong to the **SANDPIPER family (Scolopacidae)**. These can be as small as sparrows or as big as ducks; their bills may be short or long, straight or curved. Some types of sandpipers are shown below:

yellowlegs
p. 182

curlew
p. 188

"peeps"
p. 176

phalarope
p. 190

dowitcher
p. 184

godwit
p. 186

Habitat varies: despite the name, shorebirds aren't always on the shore. Many nest on tundra of the high Arctic. At other seasons they gather on mudflats: tidal flats on the coast, edges of ponds or rivers inland. Huge numbers migrate through the Great Plains, stopping at shallow wetlands. Even if you are far from the coast, if you can find ponds with muddy edges, you can probably find migrating shorebirds.

Some shorebirds choose odd habitats. A few species live in open fields, seldom visiting the water's edge, while woodcocks (p. 184) live in forest.

Timing of shorebird migration might not be what you expect. Shorebirds often migrate late in spring and early in fall. Northbound birds may still be passing through our middle latitudes in the first week of June, while some returning southbound birds may show up by early July. For some, their "fall" migration may be at its peak in August, even if we think of that as summer. Keep this in mind when looking at the range maps: some shorebirds might be found on their "winter" ranges practically all year.

Seasonal change in color is striking for some shorebirds. The adults may be in their **winter plumage** for more than half the year — from late summer well into spring. But then many species molt into a colorful **breeding plumage,** just before heading to their nesting grounds. By the time these adults come back south in late summer, their colors may be fading, or molting back to winter plumage. But the young birds, or **juveniles,** often migrate south in a distinctly different plumage, looking crisp and fresh compared to the adults.

Western Sandpiper:

juvenile

winter
plumage

breeding
plumage

Voices of many sandpipers and plovers may include trilled or whistled songs on nesting territory, often given in a fluttering display flight. Most of these songs are not described here; instead, I focus on callnotes that they use all year. In some cases these calls are very useful for telling similar species apart.

Identifying shorebirds can be an absorbing challenge. Here are some key clues to consider. **Size** is almost useless for recognizing a lone shorebird, because apparent size can be so misleading. But often you'll see several species together; if you can identify one with certainty, comparative sizes may help you figure out the others. **Bill shape** is often very important, even among species that are very similar otherwise; try to see it as clearly as you can. **Overall shape** is also quite helpful. Look at whether the bird is slim or stout, whether its neck and legs are short or long, whether its wingtips extend past the end of the short tail. **Feeding behavior** is often an excellent clue. Some shorebirds run about actively, picking at the surface, while others stand in one spot and probe the mud.

Don't become discouraged if you can't name all the shorebirds right away. It may take many field trips to learn them all, but even without knowing their names, you can enjoy the grace and energy of these subtle birds.

Plovers **(family Charadriidae)** may be on shorelines or barren fields. They run a few paces, then stop to pick at the ground with their short bills.

KILLDEER   *Charadrius vociferus*

A big noisy plover of open country almost everywhere except far north. Lake shores and rivers, also plowed fields, pastures, large lawns, often far from water. When disturbed near nest, Killdeers can do a very convincing broken-wing act, flopping along the ground to lure intruders away. ▶ *Two* black chest bands; white collar. Rather *long tail* is *mostly orange*. Downy young may have only a single black band; compare to small plovers on next page. ♪ **Voice:** very vocal, calling at any disturbance. Clear plaintive *kil-deeah* and *dee-dee-dee . . .*

BLACK-BELLIED PLOVER   *Pluvialis squatarola*

This stocky plover haunts the outer beaches. Nests only in Arctic, but some occur at all seasons on southern coastlines. Mostly scarce migrant in interior. ▶ Short *thick* bill. Compare to golden-plovers. In winter, *mottled back and chest* (not smooth, like plovers on next page). In flight, note *black "wingpits,"* whitish rump and tail. Some sandpipers also short-billed and gray in winter (see Sanderling and Red Knot, p. 174). ♪ **Voice:** mournful whistle dropping in middle, *wheeyoo-wee.*

AMERICAN GOLDEN-PLOVER   *Pluvialis dominica*

A long-distance migrant, nesting on Arctic tundra. Spring flocks pass mostly through Great Plains, pausing on pastures, flooded fields. In fall, most fly direct from eastern Canada to South America, but some stop on east coast and elsewhere. ▶ Slimmer than Black-bellied Plover, with smaller bill. In late spring and summer, has more black below and more golden brown look above. In other plumages, usually browner with more obvious pale eyebrow. In flight, golden-plovers are much plainer; lack the black "wingpits" and are plain brown above. ♪ **Voice:** rich whistled *quee-doh.*

PACIFIC GOLDEN-PLOVER   *Pluvialis fulva*

In western Alaska in summer, this Asian bird overlaps with its American cousin. Small numbers also migrate along Pacific Coast, with a few wintering in California. ▶ Very similar to American Golden-Plover, not always identifiable. In breeding plumage, Pacific shows *more white below,* in stripe extending along sides. Fall and winter birds usually look brighter, more golden, and have shorter wingtips than Americans. ♪ **Voice:** clear rich whistle, *chu-weet* or *chu-wee-doh.*

LARGE PLOVERS

adult in distraction display

downy young

Killdeer
10½"

adults

molting adult

juvenile

winter adult

Black-bellied Plover
11½"

summer adult

winter adult

fall juvenile

summer female

Pacific Golden-Plover
9¾"

summer male

American Golden-Plover
10¼"

summer male

SEMIPALMATED PLOVER   *Charadrius semipalmatus*

Usually the most common of the small plovers. Nesting in far north and wintering on southern beaches, the Semi is found everywhere during spring and fall migration, on mudflats of coast, lakes, rivers. ▶ *Dark* brown back, *single* dark chest band. Legs usually *orange*. Darker above than Snowy or Piping Plovers, much smaller bill than Wilson's. See downy young Killdeer (previous page). ♪**Voice:** clear, whistled *chuweep*, rising.

WILSON'S PLOVER   *Charadrius wilsonia*

Fairly common on southeastern beaches, especially in summer, but seldom seen in large numbers. Almost never wanders inland. ▶ *Large black bill* is best mark; longer and heavier than on other small plovers. Also note dull legs, dark brown back, rather wide chest band (brown on female and winter male, black on breeding male). ♪**Voice:** sharp, slightly metallic *pwoik*.

PIPING PLOVER   *Charadrius melodus*

Nests on Atlantic beaches and on salt flats around lakes and rivers on northern prairies. Populations are declining in both areas; an endangered species. Winters on southeast coast, on beaches and mudflats with other plovers. ▶ *Pale back* (color of dry sand), very *short stubby bill*. Legs are *orange* (brightest in breeding season). Black chest band in summer may be complete or broken; in winter, replaced by dusky patches at sides of chest. ♪**Voice:** whistled *peep* or *peep-loh*.

SNOWY PLOVER   *Charadrius alexandrinus*

Found year-round on dry sand beaches of Pacific and Gulf coasts; also in summer around salt lakes and alkali flats in western interior. On coast, threatened by loss of safe nesting sites on beaches. ▶ Suggests Piping Plover but has *thinner, longer bill;* dull *gray or black legs.* Western Snowies not quite as pale above. Black chest band always incomplete. ♪**Voice:** soft *trrr* and *tu-wee*.

MOUNTAIN PLOVER   *Charadrius montanus*

Neither a mountain bird nor a "shore" bird, this drab plover haunts dry short-grass plains in summer. In winter, flocks gather in plowed fields, barren flats far from water. Uncommon and declining. ▶ Pale and plain. Black head marks in summer, but no dark chest bands. Habitat is often best field mark. Smoother gray above, whiter below, paler legs than Golden or Black-bellied Plovers (previous page). ♪**Voice:** low *trrr*.

SMALL PLOVERS

winter adult

fall juvenile

summer adult

Semipalmated Plover 7¼"

Wilson's Plover 7¾"

female or winter male

summer adult

summer male

winter

Piping Plover 7¼"

summer adult

summer male

summer

winter

Mountain Plover 9"

Snowy Plover 6¼"

female or winter male

169

NORTHERN LAPWING   *Vanellus vanellus*
In Europe and Asia this big plover is common in farmland, pastures, open fields. In North America it is a very rare visitor to the northeast (especially eastern Canada), with most records in winter. ▶ Striking pattern with greenish back, black chest, *long thin crest.* In flight, shows white tips on broad, rounded wings. ♪**Voice:** plaintive whistled *twee-ip.*

EUROPEAN GOLDEN-PLOVER   *Pluvialis apricaria*
Newfoundland only. A rare spring visitor to Newfoundland after strong storms over the North Atlantic. Has been seen a few times in nearby areas of eastern Canada. Similar birds seen elsewhere are undoubtedly American or Pacific Golden-Plovers (p. 166). ▶ Very much like other golden-plovers but slightly larger, chunkier, with thicker neck. In breeding plumage, amount of black on underparts varies, but always restricted and surrounded by white. In flight, underside of wings white (grayer in other golden-plovers). ♪**Voice:** mournful whistled *tlooo-weee.*

COMMON RINGED PLOVER   *Charadrius hiaticula*
Nests locally in high Arctic Canada (eastern Ellesmere Island, northern Baffin Island), also rarely in western Alaska on St. Lawrence Island. Migrates to wintering grounds in the Old World. Similar birds found elsewhere in North America are undoubtedly Semipalmated Plovers (previous page). ▶ Almost identical to Semipalmated. Tends to have slightly broader black chest band, more obvious white eyebrow, slightly longer bill. Difference in voice may be noticed by very experienced birders. ♪**Voice:** mellow whistled *too-wee,* somewhat lower than *chu-weep* of Semipalmated.

LESSER SAND-PLOVER   *Charadrius mongolus*
Rare migrant and summer visitor to western Alaska (has nested there). Migrants have been found rarely elsewhere, mostly on Pacific Coast but also farther east, on beaches and mudflats with other typical plovers. Formerly called Mongolian Plover. ▶ Broad *cinnamon band across chest* (often duller on females) is distinctive in spring and summer. Fall and winter birds confusingly plain, may suggest Mountain Plover (previous page) but usually have darker legs, different habitat. ♪**Voice:** short, dry trill, *trididit.*

EURASIAN DOTTEREL   *Charadrius morinellus*
This gentle, tame little plover is a very rare summer visitor to western Alaska (mostly Seward Peninsula and St. Lawrence Island) and may sometimes nest there. Fall migrants have been found a few times along Pacific Coast. Favors tundra in summer, dry fields at other seasons. ▶ In breeding plumage, has narrow *white band* across gray chest; belly cinnamon and black; bold white eyebrow. Females brighter than males. Young birds and winter adults lack bright colors but show hint of summer pattern on chest, face. ♪**Voice:** usually quiet, sometimes soft whistles or trills.

RARE NORTHERN PLOVERS

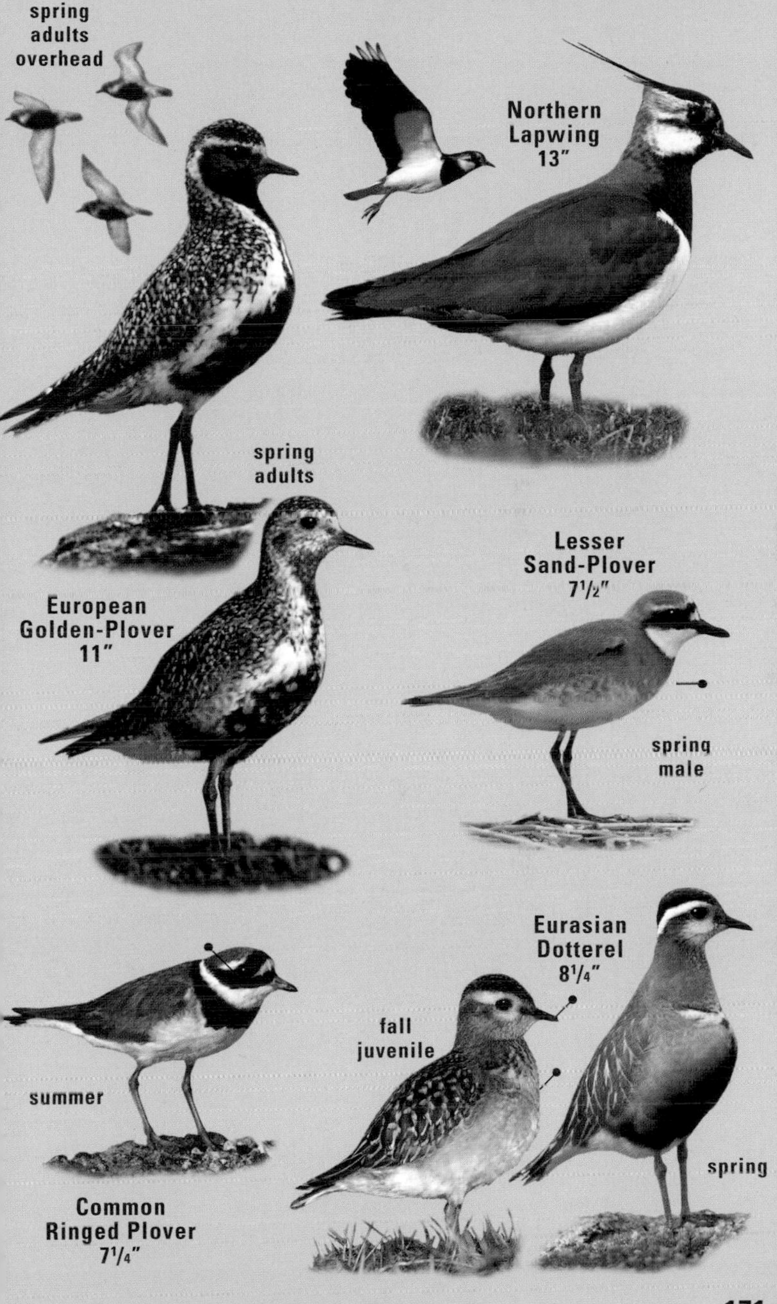
spring
adults
overhead
Northern
Lapwing
13″
spring
adults
European
Golden-Plover
11″
Lesser
Sand-Plover
7½″
spring
male
Eurasian
Dotterel
8¼″
fall
juvenile
summer
spring
Common
Ringed Plover
7¼″

Stilts and avocets (**family Recurvirostridae**) have incredibly thin legs, thin bills. They wade in shallow marshes and lakes. Oystercatchers (**family Haematopodidae**) haunt coastal rocks and beaches, using their bladelike bills to pry or hammer open the shells of mollusks.

BLACK-NECKED STILT *Himantopus mexicanus*

Flocks of well-named stilts wade in the shallows, picking delicately at tiny creatures on the water's surface. Excitable and noisy, especially near nesting areas on bare open ground near water; intruders near the nests may be mobbed by yapping stilts. Increasing numbers in recent years; a rare migrant east and north of mapped range. ▶ Sharp black-and-white pattern, *coral-pink legs*. In flight, wings solid black above. Female browner than male on center of back; juvenile has pale scaling above. ♪**Voice**: loud, sharp, grating *yek yek yek yek*.

AMERICAN AVOCET *Recurvirostra americana*

Wading in shallow marshes and lakes, the avocet sweeps its bill from side to side, with the tip just below the water's surface. Small groups nest on open flats near the water, laying their eggs on bare open soil, and protest loudly if intruders approach. ▶ Blue-gray legs, *upcurved bill* (more strongly curved in female). Bold black-and-white pattern on back and wings. Head and neck pale cinnamon in summer, gray in winter. ♪**Voice**: shrill *kleeap*, often repeated.

AMERICAN OYSTERCATCHER *Haematopus palliatus*

This stocky shorebird hugs the beaches and tidal flats of the Atlantic and Gulf Coasts and almost never wanders inland. Usually seen in pairs or family groups in summer, it may gather into flocks of dozens or more in winter. Resident on Pacific Coast of Mexico, very rarely reaches California. ▶ Bold pattern with black head and neck, dark back, white belly; *oversized red bill* is best mark. Shows broad white wing stripe in flight. Juvenile has brown scaling on back, dark tip on bill. ♪**Voice**: loud, clear *wheeep* with quality of human whistle.

BLACK OYSTERCATCHER *Haematopus bachmani*

Along the Pacific Coast, this bird haunts wave-washed rocks and is seldom found where the coast lacks rocky areas. Usually seen in pairs. While most other young shorebirds find their own food as soon as they hatch, oystercatcher parents feed their young. ▶ All black (browner on back) with *oversized red bill*, yellow eyes. Juvenile has dark tip on bill. ♪**Voice**: loud, clear *wheeep* with quality of human whistle.

LARGE SHOREBIRDS

juvenile

Black-necked Stilt 14"

summer

American Avocet 18"

winter

adult

American Oystercatcher 18 1/2"

juvenile

adults

Black Oystercatcher 17 1/2"

173

SANDPIPERS

(family Scolopacidae) can be as small as sparrows or as big as ducks. Here are three common medium-small species. These can be found along all our coastlines for most of the year, and less commonly as migrants through the interior, but they nest only on tundra of the high Arctic.

SANDERLING *Calidris alba*

The small pale sandpiper that runs up and down the beach, chasing the waves. While most sandpipers are actually "mudpipers," this one really does inhabit sandy beaches, usually in small flocks. ▶ Very pale and plain in "winter" plumage (worn for most of year), with straight, *stout, black bill*, blackish legs. Black *smudge at shoulder* may be obvious or hidden. In flight, shows bold white wing stripe. Has larger bill, plainer face than small pale plovers on p. 168. Also see winter Western Sandpiper (next page). In breeding plumage (worn only briefly, late spring to late summer), rich *reddish brown* on head and foreparts. Very rare Red-necked Stint (next page) is smaller, with thinner bill. ♪**Voice:** hard *kwip,* often repeated.

DUNLIN *Calidris alpina*

Named for its dun-colored winter plumage, this sandpiper occurs all along our coastlines in winter. Forages on mudflats, walking slowly, picking or probing with bill. In flight, big flocks twist and turn through the air in unison. In spring, just before migrating to Arctic tundra, Dunlins molt into colorful breeding plumage. ▶ Note *bill shape:* heavy at base, drooped at tip. Winter plumage (worn at least half the year) dull brownish gray on head, chest, back. Western Sandpiper (next page) paler, especially on chest, and smaller. Purple and Rock Sandpipers (p. 180) darker, chunkier, with paler legs. Breeding plumage distinct, but in western Alaska see Rock Sandpiper. ♪**Voice:** rasping *crreez.*

RED KNOT *Calidris canutus*

Along the coast during migration seasons and winter, this stout sandpiper is widespread but spotty: present in large flocks in a few places, small numbers elsewhere. Favors open tidal flats, sandy beaches. Only a rare migrant through interior. ▶ Winter plumage lacks obvious marks. Larger than most plain gray sandpipers; note *stout, straight black bill,* short neck, *short legs.* Dowitchers (p. 184) and Willet (p. 186) much longer-billed. In breeding plumage, face and underparts washed with robin red. Fall juveniles show scaly pattern on gray back. ♪**Voice:** soft *krrup.* Often silent.

SANDPIPERS

spring adults

winter adults

fall juvenile

Sanderling
8″

winter

fall juvenile

Dunlin
8½″

spring adults

late fall

early spring

fall juvenile

Red Knot
10½″

winter adult

spring adult

175

The smallest shorebirds, called "peeps" in North America, "stints" in Europe. The first three below are common on mudflats in migration season — Semipalmated mainly in the east, Western mainly in the west, and Least everywhere, including small marshy ponds inland.

LEAST SANDPIPER *Calidris minutilla*

May be outnumbered by other peeps on the coast, but inland the Least is the one seen most often, on muddy edges of rivers, ponds, marshes. Usually in flocks. Nests at marshes of far north. ▶ Very small, with *very thin bill* that turns *down* slightly at tip. Legs yellow or greenish, but color is often hard to see (and legs may be mud-covered). Overall *more brown* than other small peeps (brightest on juveniles in fall, dullest on winter birds), with brown wash across chest. ♪ **Voice:** thin drawn-out *creeeep,* often given in flight.

SEMIPALMATED SANDPIPER *Calidris pusilla*

In spring and fall, the "Semi" often swarms on mudflats of the eastern two-thirds of North America. It nests on Arctic tundra, winters on tropical shores. Name refers to slight toe webbing (not a field mark). ▶ Small, plain. Short *straight bill* looks *blunt at tip.* Season for season, grayer (less brown) than Least Sandpiper, paler on the chest. Legs *black or gray* (not yellowish), but this is often hard to see. Western Sandpiper (below) much more similar at times. Winter plumages almost identical; such birds in our area in winter are almost all Westerns. ♪ **Voice:** low *chrk* (lacks *ee* sound of others).

WESTERN SANDPIPER *Calidris mauri*

Nesting in Alaska, this peep spreads across the continent in migration. On east coast, rare in spring but may be common in fall; winters along southeast coast. Likes open flats, may wade more than Least or Semi. ▶ Bill usually *longer* than on Semipalmated, *drooped* at tip (but some overlap in bill shape). Spring adult has rusty marks above, black spots on sides. Fall juvenile like Semi but usually has *rusty stripe on scapulars,* whiter eyebrow. Winter adults gray above, pale below; see Dunlin and Sanderling (previous page). Not as brown as Least Sandpiper; has *dark* legs. ♪ **Voice:** thin *cheet.*

RED-NECKED STINT *Calidris ruficollis*

Asian bird, summering in very small numbers in Alaska. Very rarely strays to other parts of North America, even to east coast of U.S., on mudflats with other peeps. ▶ In summer, has *reddish face and throat.* Sanderling (previous page) in summer very similar, but larger, with stouter bill. Juvenile and winter very much like Semipalmated Sandpiper.

TINY SANDPIPERS

winter

Least
Sandpiper
6"

spring
adults

fall
juveniles

fall
adult

Semipalmated
Sandpiper
6¼"

spring
adults

fall
juvenile

fall
juvenile

Western
Sandpiper
6½"

spring
adults

winter
Western

Red-necked
Stint
6¼"

summer
adult

177

The first four here are similar to (and related to) the "peeps" on the previous page, but are slightly larger. All nest on tundra of high Arctic.

PECTORAL SANDPIPER   *Calidris melanotos*

Often a "grasspiper" in migration, favoring marshes, grassy mudflats, flooded fields. Winters in South America. ▶ Might suggest Least Sandpiper (previous page), mostly brown with yellowish legs, but much larger, with more stretched-out shape. *Sharp contrast* separates brown streaked breast from white belly. Heavily striped on back. Males larger than females. ♪ **Callnote:** low *krrrek*. **Song:** deep hooting in courtship display.

SHARP-TAILED SANDPIPER   *Calidris acuminata*

Rare fall visitor to Pacific Northwest; also occurs as rare migrant in western Alaska. An Asian relative of Pectoral Sandpiper. ▶ Most seen in North America are fall juveniles. Size and shape of Pectoral but bright *rich buff* on chest (with very few streaks), *reddish* on cap, more obvious eye-ring.

WHITE-RUMPED SANDPIPER   *Calidris fuscicollis*

Often overlooked among other shorebirds. An uncommon migrant through eastern and central regions. Often in flooded fields, marshy edges of mudflats. Winters in South America. ▶ *Long wingtips* extend past tip of tail. In spring, black streaks on chest and down sides, upperparts warmer brown. Fall juveniles chestnut on crown and back (see Western Sandpiper, previous page). Fall adults very plain above. *White rump* visible only in flight. ♪ **Voice:** distinctive thin, squeaky *jeeet*.

BAIRD'S SANDPIPER   *Calidris bairdii*

Another subtle species. Most migrate through center of continent. Often common on Great Plains, on grassy mudflats, flooded fields, sometimes dry pastures. Winters in South America. ▶ *Long wingtips* extend past tip of tail. Suggests White-rump but browner overall, with *brown wash* across chest (in flight, lacks white rump patch). Fall juvenile has buff brown head, scaly back. Least Sandpiper (previous page) smaller, with finer bill, paler legs. ♪ **Voice:** rolling *krrrit*.

BUFF-BREASTED SANDPIPER   *Tryngites subruficollis*

Seldom on mudflats, this odd sandpiper favors short-grass plains and plowed fields. Spring migration is mostly through Great Plains; in fall, small numbers also reach Atlantic Coast. ▶ *Smooth pale buff* on face and underparts, dark scaly back, yellow legs. Has dovelike or "gentle" expression, with dark eye on pale face, short bill, round head. Habitat is good clue.

SANDPIPERS

Pectoral Sandpiper 8½"

fall juvenile

adults

Sharp-tailed Sandpiper 8½"

fall juvenile

fall adult

White-rumped Sandpiper 7½"

fall juvenile

spring

fall juvenile

Buff-breasted Sandpiper 8"

Baird's Sandpiper 7½"

adult

adult

RUDDY TURNSTONE   *Arenaria interpres*

Common along coast during migration and winter, but seldom seen inland, except near Great Lakes. Favors rocky shores (like others on this page), also beaches, mudflats. Often uses pointed bill to flip pebbles as it seeks tiny creatures to eat. ▶ Chunky, with short *orange legs,* short bill. Unmistakable pattern in breeding plumage. In fall and winter, dull dark brown above, with dark chest pattern. ♪ **Voice:** sharp low rattle.

BLACK TURNSTONE   *Arenaria melanocephala*

Hugs the west coast at all times, almost never seen inland. Mostly on rocks, jetties, sometimes on mudflats, beaches. ▶ Blackish, with white belly. White face marks in breeding plumage. In winter, blacker than Ruddy Turnstone, legs usually duller. Both turnstones show strong pattern in flight. Darker than Surfbird or Rock Sandpiper, with different bill shape. ♪ **Voice:** thin rattle.

SURFBIRD   *Aphriza virgata*

On the Pacific shoreline in winter, this sandpiper uses its thick stubby bill to wrench barnacles and mollusks off of rocks just above the pounding surf. Nests in high mountains of Alaska, northwest Canada. ▶ Stout, short-necked. In winter, mostly dusky gray with white belly, dark spots along sides. *Bill shape* is best clue. Breeding plumage has black spots below, rusty above. In flight, shows white tail with black tip.

PURPLE SANDPIPER   *Calidris maritima*

In winter on the northern Atlantic Coast, these hardy birds scramble about on rocks and jetties just above the crashing waves. They arrive late in fall from high Arctic nesting grounds; very rare in winter on Great Lakes, Gulf Coast. ▶ Chunky with short yellowish legs, yellow base to rather long bill. Dark slaty in winter, unlike any other shorebird on Atlantic Coast. Breeding plumage browner, less distinctive, but note shape and habitat.

ROCK SANDPIPER   *Calidris ptilocnemis*

The western replacement for Purple Sandpiper, nesting in Alaska, wintering along coast south to Oregon (a few to California). ▶ In winter almost identical to Purple Sandpiper, identified by range. Summer adults might suggest Dunlin (p. 174) but larger, with dark gray patch on lower breast (not black patch on belly). Rock Sandpipers nesting on Pribilof Islands are larger and paler than those elsewhere in Alaska.

BIRDS OF ROCKY SHORES

summer

Ruddy Turnstone
9½"

summer

winter

winter

Black Turnstone
9¼"

summer

winter

Surfbird
10"

summer

Rock Sandpiper
9"

winter

winter

Purple Sandpiper
9"

summer

summer

181

These five often bob their tails or heads up and down. Yellowlegs may be in small flocks, but the other three usually forage as individuals.

SPOTTED SANDPIPER *Actitis macularius*

Teetering and bobbing as it walks, the Spotty is common along tiny creeks and ponds as well as edges of coastal mudflats. Usually seen singly, not in flocks. Flies with oddly shallow, stiff wingbeats. ▶ In breeding plumage, only sandpiper with *round black spots* below. Plainer in fall and winter; note *white wedge* up onto shoulder. Bobbing behavior and stiff flight are good clues. ♪ **Voice:** abrupt *peet-weet* and *weet, weet, weet . . .*

SOLITARY SANDPIPER *Tringa solitaria*

Haunts the edges of creeks, wooded ponds; usually uncommon and solitary. Summers in northern spruce bogs, where it lays its eggs in old nests of songbirds high in trees (most sandpipers nest on ground). ▶ Slender, with thin straight bill. May bob its head when excited. *Darker* than Spotted Sandpiper, more obvious white eye-ring. In flight, tail shows dark center, white outer edges. ♪ **Voice:** shrill *peet-weet*, sharper than Spotted's.

LESSER YELLOWLEGS *Tringa flavipes*

At fresh ponds and coastal marshes, yellowlegs wade in shallow waters, picking at surface. Lesser Yellowlegs is often in small flocks. ▶ Slender, with *bright yellow legs.* In flight shows dark wings, mostly white rump and tail. Very much like Greater Yellowlegs, but note voice and shorter, thinner, straighter bill. See also Stilt Sandpiper (next page). ♪ **Voice:** short, mellow *tu tu* or *tu-tu-tu.*

GREATER YELLOWLEGS *Tringa melanoleuca*

Wading in shallow waters, sometimes dashing about, yellowlegs look trim, alert. The species overlap widely; Greater is more likely to be seen in cold weather. ▶ Very much like Lesser Yellowlegs; size difference obvious only when together. Greater's bill is longer, *thicker* toward the base, may look *slightly upturned.* Voice is best clue. ♪ **Voice:** loud, striking whistle, *whee whee whew!*

WANDERING TATTLER *Heteroscelus incanus*

Usually seen on coastal rocks (like birds on previous page), singly or in small numbers. Nests along mountain streams in Alaska and northwest Canada, winters on coasts and islands of Pacific. ▶ Teetering behavior suggests Spotted Sandpiper, but larger, grayer, with gray chest in winter, *barred* underparts in summer. In flight, solid gray above, with no white in wings or tail. ♪ **Voice:** loud, rapid whistles, *tu-tu-tu-tu-tu-tu.*

SANDPIPERS

fall juvenile

Spotted Sandpiper
7½"

winter

summer

summer adult

Solitary Sandpiper
8½"

fall juvenile

fall juvenile

summer adult

Lesser Yellowlegs
10½"

summer adult

Greater Yellowlegs
14"

fall juvenile

winter adult

summer

Wandering Tattler
11"

winter

WILSON'S SNIPE *Gallinago delicata*

Lurks in marshes, damp fields, muddy edges of creeks, solitary and often unseen. If disturbed, may flush practically underfoot and make off in zigzag flight, with a harsh callnote. More flamboyant in summer, calling from bush tops, performing flight displays. ► *Long bill*, short legs, lengthwise *stripes on head* and back, bars on sides. ♪ **Voice:** on takeoff, harsh *zzkahh*. In high flight display in summer, fast hooting trill ("winnowing").

AMERICAN WOODCOCK *Scolopax minor*

Never a "shore" bird, this odd sandpiper hides in forest thickets by day, may come out to damp fields at night, to probe in the soil for earthworms. Starting very early in spring, males perform remarkable musical courtship flight at night. ► Round-bodied, short-legged, long-billed. Note orange-buff belly, *crosswise black bars* on crown. ♪ **Callnote:** nasal *pzeeent*. **Song:** in high, twisting display flight at night, wings make musical twittering.

LONG-BILLED DOWITCHER *Limnodromus scolopaceus*

Flocks of dowitchers stand in shallow water, bills straight down, patiently probing the mud. The two dowitcher species are *very* similar, often safely told only by voice. Long-billed favors fresh water, is usually the more common species inland. ► Chunky with short neck and long bill. In spring, patterned brown above, rich chestnut below. Winter birds all gray. ♪ **Voice:** varied. Distinctive is thin high *keekeekeek* on taking flight.

SHORT-BILLED DOWITCHER *Limnodromus griseus*

Chunky and sluggish, dowitchers stand in the shallows, probing up and down. ► *Very* similar to Long-billed (bill length unreliable). In breeding plumage, Short-bill may show more white on belly or be evenly pale orange below, not deep chestnut. Fall juvenile Short-bills more brightly marked. This is usually the common dowitcher in salt water. Voice is best clue. ♪ **Voice:** varied. Distinctive is mellow *tututu* on taking flight.

STILT SANDPIPER *Calidris himantopus*

Feeds like a dowitcher, probing in the shallows; shaped more like a yellowlegs (previous page). Migrates mostly through Great Plains in spring, more widespread in fall, but seldom seen in large numbers. ► In breeding plumage has chestnut ear patches, dark bars below. More subtle in other plumages; note feeding actions, slender shape, *drooped tip* on bill. ♪ **Voice:** low *tyew*.

PROBING SANDPIPERS

American
Woodcock
11"

Wilson's
Snipe
10¹/₂"

winter

Long-billed
Dowitcher
11¹/₂"

spring

Short-billed Dowitcher
11"

spring
(two variations)

winter

fall
juvenile

winter

Stilt Sandpiper
8¹/₂"

fall
juvenile

molting
adult

spring
adult

Willets are big sandpipers, often common in coastal regions. Godwits, among the largest sandpipers, are known by their slightly upcurved bills.

WILLET *Catoptrophorus semipalmatus*

Stodgy and plain, the Willet looks boring until it flies, showing off spectacular wings. Nests in marshes of Atlantic and Gulf Coasts and in western interior; winters along coasts in warmer climates. ▶ When standing, known by bulky body; *long, straight, heavy bill;* thick gray legs. Mottled and barred in breeding plumage, plain grayish in winter plumage. Western birds are slightly larger and paler. In flight, *wing pattern* diagnostic. ♪ **Voice:** noisy on nesting grounds, ringing *pill will willet.* Fairly quiet at other times.

MARBLED GODWIT *Limosa fedoa*

Flocks of godwits stand on flooded tidal flats in winter, probing the mud with their bills. Very common along the Pacific Coast, also fairly common locally in Texas and the southeast. In summer, they nest around marshes on the northern prairies. ▶ Very large, evenly warm brown, with dark barring (heavier in summer). *Long,* slightly *upcurved bill* has *pink at base.* In flight, shows bright *cinnamon in wings.* Long-billed Curlew (next page) has similar pattern but different bill shape. ♪ **Voice:** loud ringing *kawhick!*

HUDSONIAN GODWIT *Limosa haemastica*

Uncommon. Migrates mostly through Great Plains in spring, off Atlantic Coast in fall in long overwater flight to South America. ▶ Typical godwit bill with pink base. In breeding plumage, rich *chestnut below* with black barring (females somewhat paler). Fall adults and juveniles much grayer and plainer than Marbled Godwit. Flying birds in all plumages show striking *black on underside of wing* and contrasting *black tail, white rump.* ♪ **Voice:** high *kaweap.*

BAR-TAILED GODWIT *Limosa lapponica*

An Alaskan specialty, nesting on open tundra in western part of state. Winters in Old World; a few strays reach Pacific Northwest, rarely elsewhere. ▶ In breeding plumage, male bright cinnamon below; female much paler. Fall adults and juveniles show striped pattern above (not plain like Hudsonian); unlike Marbled Godwit, lacks cinnamon flash in wings. In flight, shows dark barring on pale tail. *Shorter-legged* than other godwits. ♪ **Voice:** loud *kaweck.*

WILLET AND GODWITS

Willet 15"

winter

summer

Marbled Godwit 18"

fall adult

fall juvenile

Hudsonian Godwit 16"

spring

fall juvenile

Bar-tailed Godwit 16"

spring male

187

CURLEWS AND UPLAND SANDPIPER

Curlews are large sandpipers known by long downcurved bills. Upland Sandpiper, a prairie bird, is related to curlews but differently shaped.

WHIMBREL   *Numenius phaeopus*

The most widespread curlew. Migrates in flocks along all coasts, but scarce in interior, except around Great Lakes and Salton Sea. Nests on Arctic tundra; migrants and wintering birds are found on mudflats, beaches, flooded fields. ▶ Larger than most shorebirds, with *downcurved bill*. Overall rather *plain gray-brown*, but has *strong black head stripes*. Very plain-looking in flight, with no contrasting colors in wings or tail. Eurasian Whimbrels with white or pale rumps sometimes seen in Alaska or on Atlantic Coast. ♪ **Voice**: fast whistled *wi-wi-wi-wi-wi*, often given in flight.

BRISTLE-THIGHED CURLEW   *Numenius tahitiensis*

Only in western Alaska, this rare curlew nests on hilly tundra. It winters on islands in tropical Pacific Ocean. Not well known; nesting grounds were not discovered until 1948. ▶ Very much like Whimbrel, but has bright *peachy cinnamon rump and tail*, visible in flight. When standing, shows somewhat more contrast on upperparts (but fall juvenile Whimbrels can be similar). *Voice* differs. Long bristles at base of legs hard to see. ♪ **Voice**: clear whistled *teeyu-wit*, very unlike Whimbrel's.

LONG-BILLED CURLEW   *Numenius americanus*

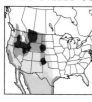

Our largest sandpiper is mostly a western bird, summering on dry grassland, wintering on coastal mudflats, fields, farmland. Forages by walking steadily, reaching ahead to pick or probe with the tip of its long bill. ▶ Remarkably *long curved bill* (length varies; some are not so extreme). Warmer brown than Whimbrel, and *lacks* strong head stripes. In flight, shows bright *cinnamon in wings*. ♪ **Voice**: loud whistled *curr-leea*.

UPLAND SANDPIPER   *Bartramia longicauda*

A bird of tall-grass plains, not the shore. On the prairies in summer, may be seen standing on a fencepost or flying overhead with oddly shallow, stiff wingbeats. Now scarce in the east, but still fairly common in summer on Great Plains; winters in Argentina. Formerly called Upland Plover. ▶ Best known by habitat and shape. *Long-tailed* for a sandpiper, with thin neck, short bill, small dovelike head. Large eye conspicuous on plain face. ♪ **Voice**: on breeding grounds, long, slow, breathy whistle, *wrrreeee wheeeyeeww*. Flight call a rapid rippling trill.

CURLEWS, UPLAND SANDPIPER

Whimbrel
17"

Bristle-thighed Curlew
(Alaska only)
17"

Long-billed Curlew
23"

Upland Sandpiper
12"

189

Phalaropes are odd sandpipers that usually forage by swimming, often spinning in one spot, picking at water's surface. Red and Red-necked spend most of the year out at sea. Male phalaropes, duller than females, incubate the eggs and care for the young. Jacanas represent a separate family (**Jacanidae**) of odd tropical shorebirds.

WILSON'S PHALAROPE   *Phalaropus tricolor*

Mainly a bird of prairie marshes and western lakes, often very common there, swimming and spinning on water or running about on shore. Winters mostly in Argentina. ▶ Spring female distinctive, with black and chestnut *neck stripes,* pearly crown. Male duller. Fall adults pale gray and white, with gray or yellowish legs; note actions plus thin, straight bill. Longer bill and fainter face patch than on other fall phalaropes. Juvenile looks scaly brown above at first; compare to sandpipers on p. 182. ♪**Voice:** soft *wurf.*

RED-NECKED PHALAROPE   *Phalaropus lobatus*

Summers in the far north, around ponds and tundra; winters at sea, mostly far to the south. As a fall migrant, fairly common in west, but seldom seen in the east except offshore and near Great Lakes. The smallest phalarope, looking dainty as it floats and spins lightly on the water. ▶ Spring female mostly gray with *red neck, white throat,* rich buff stripes on back. Male duller. Fall adults gray above, white below, with *stripes on back* and sharp black patch on face. Fall juveniles have similar pattern but show much more buff at first. ♪**Voice:** hard *pik.*

RED PHALAROPE   *Phalaropus fulicarius*

The most northerly phalarope in summer, and the most strictly oceanic at other seasons. Not usually seen from land except in the Arctic. A few stray migrants appear far inland, mostly in late fall. On ponds or at sea, swims and spins like other phalaropes. ▶ Spring female rich *chestnut-red below,* with white on face, yellow base of bill, buff back stripes. Male duller. Fall adults similar to Red-necked but *smoother gray on back* (without stripes), and have much *thicker bill.* Fall juveniles show more buff at first. ♪**Voice:** sharp *pik.*

NORTHERN JACANA   *Jacana spinosa*

Jacanas live on tropical ponds, where their long toes enable them to walk on floating plants such as lily pads. This species is a rare visitor to southern Texas, accidental in Arizona. ▶ Adults black with *bright chestnut* back and wings. Young birds brown above, white below, with white eyebrow. All ages show *bright yellow flight feathers* in spread wings.

PHALAROPES AND JACANA

fall

summer juvenile

spring female

fall

Wilson's Phalarope 9½"

spring male

fall juvenile

fall adult

spring male

Red-necked Phalarope 8"

spring female

fall juvenile

Red Phalarope 8½"

spring female

fall adult

Northern Jacana 9½"

wing pattern (all ages)

juvenile

adult

RUFF *Philomachus pugnax*

An odd Eurasian sandpiper, rare but regular in North America. Several are seen every year on both coasts and in Alaska, with fewer scattered through the interior. Found mostly on marshes, flooded fields, mudflats. ▶ Spring males highly variable and colorful, with neck ruffs and head tufts of chestnut, black, and white. In other plumages, best known by overall buff brown look, and by shape: stocky body, small round head, short bill. Legs vary from orange to greenish. Males are much larger than females.

CURLEW SANDPIPER *Calidris ferruginea*

Appears in very small numbers along Atlantic Coast every spring and fall. Also seen in small numbers in western and northern Alaska (has nested at Barrow), but extremely rare elsewhere in North America. Favors open mudflats frequented by other shorebirds. ▶ Shaped somewhat like Dunlin (p. 174) but with longer legs and more *smoothly curved bill.* Spring adults mostly rich reddish brown. Darker, more slender than Red Knot (p. 174).

WOOD SANDPIPER *Tringa glareola*

A regular migrant on westernmost Aleutian Islands (and has nested there) and a rare visitor elsewhere in western Alaska. Favors edges of marshy ponds. ▶ Suggests Solitary Sandpiper (p. 182) but not as dark, and has very obvious pale eyebrow. In flight, tail mostly white with narrow black bars (Solitary has center of tail dark). ♪ **Voice**: high thin *weet weet weet.*

GRAY-TAILED TATTLER *Heteroscelus brevipes*

Very small numbers appear in far western Alaska every spring. Often on mudflats, not on rocks like Wandering Tattler. ▶ Like Wandering Tattler (p. 182) but more lightly and finely marked in breeding plumage, with very narrow dark bars on sides and flanks that do not extend across the white belly. In fall and winter, almost identical to Wandering. ♪ **Voice**: rising whistled *too-weeap,* unlike rapid short whistles of Wandering.

COMMON SANDPIPER *Actitis hypoleucos*

Alaska only, a rare visitor to Bering Sea islands, more regular on outer Aleutians. ▶ Very similar to Spotted Sandpiper (p. 182) in winter plumage. Has *longer tail,* tends to look richer brown above. Similar birds seen away from western Alaska are undoubtedly Spotted Sandpipers.

SPOTTED REDSHANK *Tringa erythropus*

Rare migrant in western Alaska. Extremely rare elsewhere in North America, but has shown up at widely scattered places. ▶ Size and shape of a yellowlegs (p. 182), but with very thin, long bill. Has *red legs,* red base of bill. In spring, all *blackish* with small white spots. Winter birds very gray.

TEREK SANDPIPER *Xenus cinereus*

Rare migrant in western Alaska. Found on mudflats with other shorebirds, running about very actively while feeding. ▶ Odd *bill shape:* long, rather thick, slightly *upcurved.* Short *yellow-orange* legs. Plain gray-brown above, usually with dark line above wings.

RARE SANDPIPERS

fall
juvenile

Ruff
10"–12"

female

spring males
(quite variable) in
courtship display

fall
juvenile

Curlew Sandpiper
8½"

spring
adults

Wood
Sandpiper
8"

spring

Gray-tailed
Tattler
10½"

spring

Spotted
Redshank
13"

Common
Sandpiper
8"

Terek
Sandpiper
9"

193

PIGEONS

and doves are in the **family Columbidae**. All have rather small round heads and short straight bills. The term "pigeon" is usually applied to the larger species, "dove" to the smaller ones.

ROCK PIGEON *Columba livia*

The familiar city pigeon, native to wild rocky areas of Europe but domesticated worldwide. Now lives in a semiwild state over much of North America. Mostly nests on buildings and bridges, but a few nest on cliffs in wilder areas. ▶ The ancestral type has pale gray body, darker head, white rump, two black bars on wings. In flight, shows contrasty white underwings. Feral flocks include a wide variety of other color forms, some of which might suggest the wild native species shown below. ♪**Voice:** soft cooing, with hollow gurgling sound.

BAND-TAILED PIGEON *Patagioenas fasciata*

This big wild pigeon of the west may be common all year on the Pacific seaboard, in oak woods, pines, foothills. In the interior, mostly a summer resident and mostly in the mountains. Travels in flocks, feeding on acorns, berries. ▶ Large and colorful. Note narrow *white band across nape* (absent on juvenile), yellow base of bill, wide *gray tail band*. Purplish pink on head and chest, with green iridescence on neck. ♪**Voice:** a deep, double-noted cooing, *huh-whoooo.*

WHITE-CROWNED PIGEON *Patagioenas leucocephala*

South Florida only, mainly in Everglades and on the Keys. Flocks roost in mangroves, fly to inland stands of hardwoods in daytime. This pigeon feeds mostly on berries up in trees, not on the ground. Readily travels among islands, and some fly from Florida to the Caribbean for the winter. ▶ Dark, slaty (often looks black) with striking *white cap*, green iridescence on neck. Female is duller, and juvenile has grayish cap. ♪**Voice:** deep cooing, *woo, coocarooo.*

RED-BILLED PIGEON *Patagioenas flavirostris*

South Texas only. Uncommon in summer, rare in winter, mostly in dry woods along Rio Grande. Most easily seen when it perches in treetops at dawn. Widespread in Mexico and Central America. ▶ Very dark overall: maroon on head and chest, slaty below. Despite the name, bill is mostly *yellowish white* (red only at base). Some Rock Doves are similarly dark-bodied but have different bill pattern. ♪**Voice:** deep cooing with staccato pattern, *woooo, up-chuck-a-pup.*

PIGEONS

Rock Pigeon
13"

color
variants

juvenile

male

**Band-tailed
Pigeon**
14"

female

**Red-billed
Pigeon**
13"

female

**White-crowned
Pigeon**
14"

male

MOURNING DOVE *Zenaida macroura*

Common everywhere except deep woods and far north, often seen perched on roadside wires or walking on ground, alone or in flocks. When it takes flight, its wings make a whistling noise. In warm climates, a pair may raise up to six broods per year. The nest is a flimsy platform of sticks. ▶ *Long, pointed tail* shows *white spots* along edge in flight. Mostly plain, with black spots on wings. Adult male is tinged pinkish on chest, blue-gray on crown; female is duller plain brown. Scaly-looking young bird sometimes mistaken for Inca Dove or Common Ground-Dove (next page). ♪**Voice:** slow, mournful cooing, *cooowaah, cooo, coo, coooo.*

WHITE-WINGED DOVE *Zenaida asiatica*

A big southwestern dove, common in summer in deserts, towns, brushy country. Most go to tropics for winter. Also common all year in parts of Florida. Sometimes wanders far north of mapped range. ▶ Bulkier than Mourning Dove, with shorter tail. Big *white wing patches* and white tips on outer tail feathers, most obvious in flight. ♪**Voice:** rich cooing, *too soon to tell;* also a repeated *koolah kooow, koolah kooow.*

EURASIAN COLLARED-DOVE *Streptopelia decaocto*

Native to Old World. Became established in Florida in 1980s. Now rapidly expanding range to west and north; has reached Arizona, Montana, New York; likely to colonize much of continent. Mostly lives in towns and suburbs, less often in wild areas. ▶ Pale brown with narrow *black neck ring,* big white patches in outer tail feathers. Compare to Ringed-Turtle-Dove. ♪**Voice:** harsh cooing, *cuk-KOOOO-cooo;* hoarse shriek.

RINGED TURTLE-DOVE *Streptopelia risoria*

This domesticated variety sometimes lives in a semiwild state around cities, but does not seem to thrive without regular handouts from humans. ▶ Like Eurasian Collared-Dove but usually paler, especially on *undertail coverts* (white, not gray) and wingtips. Voice differs. ♪**Voice:** cooing with drawn-out rolling sound, *cooo-krrrroooooooo.*

SPOTTED DOVE *Streptopelia chinensis*

Introduced from Asia to southern California, now found locally in parks and suburbs from San Diego to Bakersfield. ▶ Size of Mourning Dove but bulkier, tail more rounded, *lacks* black spots on wings. Best mark is black *collar* with white spots (less obvious on young birds). ♪**Voice:** hoarse cooing, *coo-WOOH-cooh* or *coo-cooo-CWOOH.*

LARGER DOVES

Mourning Dove
12"

juvenile

adults

adults

White-winged Dove
12"

adults

juvenile

Eurasian Collared-Dove
12½"

Ringed Turtle-Dove
12"

Spotted Dove
12"

197

SMALLER DOVES

These are found mostly in warmer climates. Like other doves, they lay their eggs in remarkably flimsy nests made out of twigs.

INCA DOVE   *Columbina inca*

A tame little dove of southwestern lawns. Very common in some towns and cities, less common in wild habitats. Gentle and sociable; several will often roost huddled shoulder to shoulder. ▶ Small and *long-tailed*, with a dark *scaly pattern* all over. When it flies, *rusty red wing feathers* and *white outer tail feathers* are obvious. Common Ground-Dove also shows reddish wing flash in flight, but its tail is short, with tiny pale corners. See juvenile Mourning Dove (previous page), which also looks somewhat scaly. ♪ **Voice:** sad cooing, *hooh hooh* (or "no hope"). Sometimes *hooo kahooo*. Wings make dry rattle on takeoff.

COMMON GROUND-DOVE   *Columbina passerina*

This tiny dove walks about on the ground, often in pairs or small flocks. Not so much of a town bird as the Inca Dove, it favors brushy places, edges of woodlands. Formerly common, it has declined in numbers in many areas, especially in the southeast. ▶ Small and *short-tailed*, with a *scaly pattern* on chest and head. Base of bill pink. In flight, the wings show bright rusty red and the short black tail shows pale corners. See juvenile Mourning Dove (previous page), which has scaly pattern and may be short-tailed at first. ♪ **Voice:** soft rising *hoowup . . . hoowup . . . ,* often repeated on and on. Wings make a soft rattling sound on takeoff.

RUDDY GROUND-DOVE   *Columbina talpacoti*

Rare but regular visitor to southwest, mostly in winter. Often found with flocks of Inca Doves. ▶ Similar to Common Ground-Dove, but redder overall (especially males) and slightly longer-tailed. *Lacks* scaly pattern on chest and pink on bill. Both ground-doves have black spots on wings, but Ruddy also has them up on scapulars, *above* the wings. ♪ **Voice:** rising *huh wup*, repeated monotonously, similar to Common Ground-Dove's.

WHITE-TIPPED DOVE   *Leptotila verreauxi*

South Texas only. Walks about on the ground in dry woods; if alarmed, it walks away into the thickets or flies away swiftly and low. ▶ May suggest a Mourning Dove (previous page), but much rounder-bodied and shorter-tailed, has pale eyes, and lacks black ear spot and black spots on wings. In flight, it shows rich dark *chestnut* under the wings. ♪ **Voice:** low-pitched, ghostly *hu-whhoooooooah*, like the sound of someone blowing over mouth of a bottle.

SMALLER DOVES

Inca Dove
8½"

adults

female

Common Ground-Dove
6½"

male

Ruddy
Ground-Dove
(rare)
6¾"

male

female

White-tipped Dove
(Texas only)
11½"

adults

199

CUCKOOS

(family Cuculidae) include some odd birds, like roadrunners and anis (see below). Typical North American cuckoos are slender, long-tailed birds. Secretive, more often heard than seen, they move about through heavy foliage of trees, feeding on hairy caterpillars and other insects.

YELLOW-BILLED CUCKOO   *Coccyzus americanus*

Fairly common in summer in leafy forest, but easily overlooked, hiding in foliage. In west, found in trees along lowland rivers; has become rare with loss of such habitat in California. ▶ From below, long tail looks *black,* with *big white spots.* Rusty red in wing is obvious in flight. Yellow on lower mandible shows at close range. Juveniles in fall may have paler, duller tail pattern, less yellow on bill. ♪**Voice:** staccato clatter, slowing down: *kakakakakakah-kah-kah-kowp kowp kowp kowp.* Also mellow, cooing *kooowp kooowp kooowp.*

BLACK-BILLED CUCKOO   *Coccyzus erythropthalmus*

Sometimes fairly common in summer in leafy woods east of Rockies, but may be even more secretive and elusive than Yellow-billed Cuckoo. ▶ From below, tail looks *gray,* with *narrow white spots.* Bill is all black; *no* rusty red in wings. Adult has narrow red eye-ring. Juvenile in late summer and fall has buff eye-ring, and its tail may show even less contrast than adult's. ♪**Voice:** fast series of short hollow notes, *cucucu, cucucucu,* etc. May sing at night.

MANGROVE CUCKOO   *Coccyzus minor*

Florida only. Scarce, elusive, slipping furtively through coastal mangrove swamps. Usually hard to see (especially in winter, when mostly silent). Extremely rare visitor elsewhere along Gulf Coast. ▶ Resembles Yellow-billed Cuckoo (big white tail spots, yellow on bill) but washed with *warm buff below,* has more obvious *black mask,* and usually looks grayer on crown. ♪**Voice:** rough, throaty *gah-gah gaww gaww gaww gawww.*

COMMON CUCKOO   *Cuculus canorus*

Rare visitor to western Alaska, mostly in early summer. Widespread in Old World. ▶ Large, long-winged, long-tailed; suggests a hawk in flight. Males and some females are gray, with narrow barring on belly. Some females are rusty brown with heavy black barring. Note: Oriental Cuckoo (*Cuculus saturatus*) also strays to western Alaska very rarely, is almost identical.

OTHER CUCKOOS

Roadrunners and anis belong to the cuckoo family, but look so different from the species above that they are treated in other parts of this guide, with birds that they resemble more closely.

CUCKOOS

Yellow-billed Cuckoo 12"

Mangrove Cuckoo 12¼"

juvenile

adult

Black-billed Cuckoo 11¾"

OTHER CUCKOOS
(not to scale)

Common Cuckoo (rare visitor) 13"

Groove-billed Ani (see p. 336)

Greater Roadrunner (see p. 148)

PARROTS AND PARAKEETS

We have no surviving native members of the parrot family **(Psittacidae)**. The Carolina Parakeet is extinct, and the Thick-billed Parrot (opposite) no longer occurs here naturally. However, parrots from all over the world are kept here as cagebirds. Some escapees are seen free-flying, and in mild climates they may survive for years, even forming well-established feral nesting populations. Here are some of the most frequently seen species.

Monk Parakeet *(Myiopsitta monachus)* 12"

Native to South America. Now well established in Florida and in many eastern towns, north to Chicago and New England. Noisy colonies build stick nests in trees.

Black-hooded Parakeet *(Nandayus nenday)* 14"
Native to South America.

Yellow-chevroned Parakeet *(Brotogeris chiriri)* 9"
Native to South America. Well established in parts of Florida and California.

White-winged Parakeet *(Brotogeris versicolorus)* 9"
Native to South America. Some in Florida and California.

Cockatiel *(Nymphicus hollandicus)* 11"
Native to Australia.

Budgerigar *(Melopsittacus undulatus)* 7"
Native to Australia. Colonies established in Florida. Escapees seen widely.

Peach-faced Lovebird *(Agapornis roseicollis)* 7"
Native to Africa. Feral in Phoenix and elsewhere.

Yellow-headed Parrot
(Amazona oratrix) 14"
Native to Mexico, feral in
California and elsewhere.

Red-crowned Parrot
(Amazona viridigenalis)
13"
Native to Mexico. Feral in
Texas, Florida, California.

**Lilac-crowned
Parrot**
(Amazona finschi)
13"
Native to Mexico.

**Rose-ringed
Parakeet**
*(Psittacula kra-
meri)* 15"
Native to Asia.

**Thick-billed
Parrot**
*(Rhynchopsitta
pachyrhyncha)* 16"
Native to Mexico.
Formerly strayed
into southwest.

**Blue-
crowned
Parakeet**
*(Aratinga
acuticaudata)*
12"
Native to
South America.

**Green
Parakeet**
*(Aratinga
holochlora)* 13"
Native to Mexico.
Many present in
south Texas.

**Red-masked
Parakeet**
*(Aratinga
erythrogenys)*
13"
Native to South
America.

Mitred Parakeet
(Aratinga mitrata) 14"
Native to South America.
Feral in California and
Florida. Often seen with
Red-masked Parakeet.

NIGHTHAWKS

are not related to hawks and are often active in daylight as well as at night, flying high, pursuing insects. Other members of the nightjar family **(Caprimulgidae)** — including the Pauraque, below, and birds on next page — are strictly nocturnal and are heard far more often than they are seen.

COMMON NIGHTHAWK *Chordeiles minor*

On summer evenings, the nighthawk chases insects in the sky, gliding and fluttering about with erratic beats of its long wings. It is often common over farmland, open woods, and even cities, where it may lay its eggs on gravel roofs instead of in its usual nest sites on bare ground. However, numbers are mysteriously declining in many areas. ▶ White bar across outer part of angled, pointed wings. At rest, note heavily barred underparts. In Florida and southwest, see next two species. ♪ **Voice:** calls often in flight, buzzy *pzeeent*. In aerial display, male dives steeply, then pulls up with a rushing or booming sound.

LESSER NIGHTHAWK *Chordeiles acutipennis*

In the southwest, this bird replaces the Common Nighthawk in desert and dry brushland. ▶ Very similar to Common Nighthawk, not always identifiable. Pale bar across wing is closer to wingtip on Lesser, and on female Lesser this bar is *buff*, not white. Lesser often flies closer to the ground, with smoother, less erratic wingbeats, and usually maintains an eerie silence. ♪ **Voice:** nasal whinnying trill, not often heard.

ANTILLEAN NIGHTHAWK *Chordeiles gundlachii*

Florida only. A summer resident of Florida Keys, mostly from Marathon to Key West; rarely south Florida mainland. ▶ Almost identical to Common Nighthawk. A bit smaller, and females have smaller pale wing patches. Identified with certainty only by sound. ♪ **Voice:** some notes suggest Common Nighthawk, but a sharp nasal *pittick* or *pitty-pick-pick is* distinctive.

COMMON PAURAQUE *Nyctidromus albicollis*

On back roads through south Texas brushlands, this tropical nightjar may be seen in the headlight beams at night. By day, it roosts in dense thickets. Name is pronounced "pa-RAW-kee." ▶ Large and long-tailed. In flight, shows *white bar* across *rounded* wingtips, and tail shows broad white stripes (male) or smaller buff spots (female). At rest, chestnut ear patch and big dark spots on scapulars (above wings) are good marks. Note: nighthawks and three other nightjars (next page) also occur in south Texas. Nighthawks have pointed wings, different habits; other nightjars lack white in wings. ♪ **Voice:** husky, throaty *guh guh guh-weeeeerr.*

NIGHTHAWKS, ETC.

males

female

male

Common Nighthawk
9½"

female

male

Lesser Nighthawk
8½"

female

male

female

Antillean Nighthawk
(Florida only)
8½"

females

males

female

Common Pauraque
11½"

males

are much easier to identify by sound than by sight. Active only at night, they roost on the ground by day; if disturbed, they flutter away quietly. They build no nests, simply laying their eggs on flat ground.

WHIP-POOR-WILL   *Caprimulgus vociferus*

In leafy woods of the northeast (and locally in mountains of the southwest), the Whip-poor-will chants its name on summer nights. Discovered by day, may sit quietly and allow close approach. ▶ Camouflaged in mottled brown and gray. In flight, wingtips are broadly rounded (unlike nighthawks, on previous page); corners of tail are white (male) or buff (female). ♪ **Voice:** rolling chant, *whip, prrr-WEEL,* last note highest. Often repeated rapidly for minutes at a time at night. Mexican Whip-poor-wills in southwest mountains have lower, rougher voice, might be a separate species.

CHUCK-WILL'S-WIDOW   *Caprimulgus carolinensis*

A big brown nightjar of southern woods. Lurks in thickets by day; wary, it may fly away if approached. Like other nightjars, shows pink or orange eye-shine in headlight beams at night. ▶ Larger than Whip-poor-will, rich *buffy brown* all over. Chest often looks darker than throat (opposite of Whip-poor-will's pattern). Shows less white in tail in flight. ♪ **Voice:** rolling chant, *chuk weeyo WEEdow.* Often repeated steadily over and over at night.

COMMON POORWILL   *Phalaenoptilus nuttallii*

In the west, this little nightjar haunts dry foothills, desert canyons, rocky outcrops on prairie. Sits on open ground at night, fluttering up to catch passing insects. Some Poorwills remain through winter in the southwest, hibernating in cold weather. ▶ Smaller and *shorter-tailed* than other nightjars. Mottled gray-brown, with white band across lower throat. Shows small white or buff tail corners in flight. ♪ **Voice:** mellow whistle, *poor-WILL,* second note higher. At close range, soft third note is audible: *poor-WILL-ip.*

BUFF-COLLARED NIGHTJAR   *Caprimulgus ridgwayi*

A tropical bird, very rare in summer in a few rugged canyons of southern Arizona and southwestern New Mexico. May not be present every year. ▶ Looks very much like Whip-poor-will (which also can show a buffy collar). Males may show more white in tail than Arizona race of Whip-poor-will. Best identified by sound. ♪ **Voice:** odd staccato clucks rising to a crescendo, *cuk-cuk-cuk-cuk-cuk-cukaCHEEyah.*

NIGHTJARS

male

Whip-poor-will
10"

female

**Whip-poor-will
tail patterns**

male   female

Chuck-will's-widow
12"

adults

tail pattern
of male

**Common
Poorwill**
8"

Poorwill
In flight

**Buff-collared
Nightjar
(rare)**
9"

207

KINGFISHERS AND TROGONS

Kingfishers **(family Alcedinidae)** have big heads, big bills, small feet; they perch (or hover) above water, dive to catch small fish in their bills. For nesting, they dig tunnels in dirt banks. Trogons **(family Trogonidae)** are tropical birds with vertical posture and long tails. They perch motionless, then flutter out to pluck a berry or insect. Trogons nest in holes in trees.

BELTED KINGFISHER   *Ceryle alcyon*

A solitary bird of the waterside almost everywhere, seen perched on branches above streams and lakes or on low coastal rocks. Flies with irregular wingbeats, often drawing attention with its rattling call. ▶ Unmistakable in most areas; near Mexican border, see next two species. (Blue Jay, p. 272, is also blue-gray and crested, but has very different shape and markings.) Female has two chest bands, blue-gray and rusty; the latter is lacking on males. ♪ **Voice:** loud harsh rattle.

RINGED KINGFISHER   *Ceryle torquatus*

Texas only. Mainly in lower Rio Grande Valley below Falcon Dam, a few farther north, sometimes into central Texas. Often seen on high perches above rivers, lakes. ▶ Bigger than Belted Kingfisher, with underparts *all rusty red* (crossed by blue chest band on female). White collar, pale bill base may be conspicuous. ♪ **Voice:** clattering rattle, with wilder sound than Belted. Measured *chack . . . chack* in flight.

GREEN KINGFISHER   *Chloroceryle americana*

Along narrow streams in southern Texas (and very locally in southern Arizona), this little kingfisher perches low and flies low over the water; may be easy to overlook. ▶ Very small with outsized bill (like a sparrow with a heron's beak). Darker above, with less obvious crest than other kingfishers. *White outer tail feathers* are obvious in flight. ♪ **Voice:** hard ticking notes.

ELEGANT TROGON   *Trogon elegans*

A sought-after prize for birders, this trogon summers in southeast Arizona, mostly where tall sycamores grow along streams in wooded canyons. A few may stay through the winter. ▶ Distinctive shape, red belly, white chest band, yellow bill. Tail shows narrow barring below, coppery sheen above. Head and back brownish (female and young) or golden green (male). ♪ **Voice:** hoarse echoing croak, *kowaa kowaa kowaa . . .*

EARED QUETZAL   *Euptilotis neoxenus*

Very rare visitor to mountains of southern Arizona at any season (has nested). ▶ Larger than Elegant Trogon. *Lacks* white chest band, has darker bill. Tail bluish above, solid gray and white below (without barring). ♪ **Voice:** squealing *kwee-ee-chuk*. Also a loud descending cackle.

KINGFISHERS, TROGONS

young
female

**Belted
Kingfisher**
13"

male

female

female

**Green
Kingfisher**
9"

male

male

female

**Ringed
Kingfisher**
16"

male

male

female

**Eared
Quetzal
(rare)**
14"

female

**Elegant
Trogon**
12½"

female

male

209

WOODPECKERS

(family Picidae) cling with strong toes and brace themselves with stiff tail feathers as they hitch their way up trees, seeking insects in and under the bark. They also eat nuts and berries at times. They excavate their own nest holes in trees, usually in dead wood. For other tree-climbing birds, see the nuthatches and creepers (p. 286).

RED-HEADED WOODPECKER   *Melanerpes erythrocephalus*

Most woodpeckers have some red on the head, but not as much as this one. Locally common (but declining) in the east, in open woods, orchards, isolated groves in open country. Winters where acorns or other wild nuts are plentiful. ▶ Adults unmistakable, solid black, white, and red, with big white wing patches. In west, see Red-breasted Sapsucker (p. 216). Young bird has *brown head*, dark bars across white wing patch; brown is replaced by red gradually during first winter. ♪ **Voice:** loud croaking *woaarrghh*, with mournful sound.

ACORN WOODPECKER   *Melanerpes formicivorus*

A clown-faced, noisy bird of western oak woods. Lives in groups all year; colonies harvest acorns in fall, storing them in holes riddled in dead wood, feeding on them during winter and spring. Seldom wanders away from colony sites. ▶ Black above and on chest, red cap, strong *face pattern*, white eyes. In flight, shows white rump, small white wing patch. Female has black bar separating red cap from white forehead. ♪ **Voice:** noisy; hoarse *ratchet, ratchet,* and various other calls.

LEWIS'S WOODPECKER   *Melanerpes lewis*

A bizarre woodpecker, scarce and localized in the west, mostly around groves of tall trees in open country. Does much of its feeding by flying out from a perch to catch insects in midair. Broad wings make it look rather crowlike in flight. ▶ Odd colors: oily-green back, red face, pink belly, silver-gray collar. Young bird mostly dark at first, with only a hint of adult colors. ♪ **Voice:** Usually silent; in nesting season, weak chattering and chirring notes.

WHITE-HEADED WOODPECKER   *Picoides albolarvatus*

Fairly common but localized in mountain pine forest of Pacific states. ▶ Black body and *white head* are diagnostic (but Acorn Woodpecker, seen at a distance, is sometimes mistaken for this species). Male has red patch on back of head. Large white patch on outer part of wing, more obvious in flight. ♪ **Voice:** a sharp *whick* or *whick-ick,* and a shrill rattling.

WOODPECKERS

Acorn
Woodpecker
9"

males

female

Red-headed
Woodpecker
9¼"

adults

juvenile

White-headed
Woodpecker
9"

female

male

Lewis's
Woodpecker
11"

adults

juvenile

"ZEBRA-BACKED" WOODPECKERS

RED-BELLIED WOODPECKER *Melanerpes carolinus*

Numerous, noisy, and noticeable in southeastern woods, the Red-bellied is extending its range northward. Found everywhere from deep forest and swamps to city parks, suburbs. ▶ Narrow black and white bars on back, buffy brown chest and face, bright red stripe over top and back of head (female has less red). Despite name, red on belly is usually hard to see. In flight, shows white patches on wings and rump. ♪ **Voice:** loud repeated *chiff, chiff,* a rolling *churrrr,* other notes.

GOLDEN-FRONTED WOODPECKER *Melanerpes aurifrons*

A Texas specialty (also southwest Oklahoma), replacing Red-bellied in drier woods. ▶ Black and white bars on back. Chest and head buffy brown, with *orange-yellow* nape, yellow over bill; male has red cap. (Red-bellied Woodpecker sometimes has orange replacing red on head.) In flight, white patches flash in wings and on rump. ♪ **Voice:** loud, harsh *check-eck,* rolling *churr.*

GILA WOODPECKER *Melanerpes uropygialis*

A brash, noisy woodpecker of desert regions. Common in riverside trees, stands of giant saguaro cactus, palm groves. Excavates nest holes in cactus as well as in trees. ▶ Black and white bars on back, wings, tail; head and underparts all buffy brown. Male has small red spot on crown. ♪ **Voice:** very noisy. Harsh *yarp yarp yarp,* rolling *churrr,* various other notes.

NUTTALL'S WOODPECKER *Picoides nuttallii*

This and the next species are related to the Downy Woodpecker (next page), not to the three above. West of the mountains in California, Nuttall's Woodpecker is fairly common, from oak groves and canyons in the foothills to larger trees on the coast. ▶ Black back with narrow white barring; thin white stripes on black face. Male has red crown patch. ♪ **Voice:** sharp *ka-teak,* as if announcing itself; also a chattering whinny or rattle.

LADDER-BACKED WOODPECKER *Picoides scalaris*

In dry country of the southwest, the Ladder-backed survives wherever there are even small trees along rivers, desert washes. ▶ Similar to Nuttall's but with more white on face, wider white bars on back (especially noticeable on upper back). Drier habitat and different range are best clues. The two species sometimes interbreed where their ranges meet. ♪ **Voice:** sharp *chik* and a descending, chattering whinny.

"ZEBRA-BACKED" WOODPECKERS

female

Red-bellied Woodpecker
9½"

males

Golden-fronted Woodpecker
9½"

male

female

male

female

Gila Woodpecker
9¼"

female

female

male

male

Nuttall's Woodpecker
7½"

female

Ladder-backed Woodpecker
7¼"

BLACK-AND-WHITE WOODPECKERS

DOWNY WOODPECKER *Picoides pubescens*

Common almost everywhere there are trees (except the dry southwest), even in suburbs and city parks. Will forage on dried weed stalks as well as tree trunks, and comes to feeders for suet. ▶ *White back,* striped face, very *short* bill. Male has red nape spot. In Rockies, less white spotting on wings. ♪**Voice**: chirping *pik* or *chik* and a descending, chattering whinny. Drums with bill on resounding dead branches like other woodpeckers.

HAIRY WOODPECKER *Picoides villosus*

Like a bigger version of the Downy, usually less common, requiring bigger trees. ▶ With practice, can be told from Downy by much *longer bill,* larger size. White outer tail feathers usually *lack* dark bars (but these can be hard to see on Downy also). Birds in some regions have darker chest or less spotting on wings. ♪**Voice**: sharper than Downy's, a high *peek!* and a lower, fast rattle, more or less on one pitch, not descending.

AMERICAN THREE-TOED WOODPECKER *Picoides dorsalis*

Widespread in north and mountains but usually rare or uncommon, quiet, hard to find. May be more numerous where trees have been killed by fire. Flakes off bits of bark to find insects beneath. ▶ Black barring on sides; back varies from mostly white to heavily barred black. Male has *yellow* crown spot. Some young Hairy Woodpeckers also have yellow on crown, bars on sides. ♪**Voice**: sharp *pick,* not often heard.

BLACK-BACKED WOODPECKER *Picoides arcticus*

Like the preceding species, a scarce woodpecker of conifer forest, with only three toes on each foot. Favors burned-over areas, forest edge with standing dead trees. Sometimes strays south of range in east. ▶ Back *solidly black;* bars on sides. Less white on face than Three-toed Woodpecker. Male has yellow on crown. ♪**Voice**: sharp *pick,* not often heard.

RED-COCKADED WOODPECKER *Picoides borealis*

Rare and localized, living in small colonies in mature pine forest of southeast; an endangered species. Nest may be located by rings of oozing white sap on pine trunks. ▶ Back barred with black and white; big *white cheek patch,* black cap. Small red "cockade" behind eye of male is seldom noticeable. See other bar-backed woodpeckers (previous page). ♪**Voice**: harsh, rather weak *sshriff* (suggests call of young starling).

WOODPECKERS

male

female

Downy Woodpecker
6½"

female on weed stalk

female

Hairy Woodpecker
9"

male

female

Black-backed Woodpecker
9"

male

male

American Three-toed Woodpecker
9"

female

Red-cockaded Woodpecker
7½"

male

female at nest hole

SAPSUCKERS AND ARIZONA WOODPECKER

Sapsuckers are odd woodpeckers that drill rows of "sap wells" in bark, then return to drink oozing sap. They tend to be quiet, sluggish, and rather tame. Arizona Woodpecker is part of the Downy group (previous page).

YELLOW-BELLIED SAPSUCKER *Sphyrapicus varius*

Widespread in northern forest in summer, wintering in southeast. ▶ Long *white stripe* on folded wing; mottled back, striped face. Throat is red on male, white on female. Young birds have *brown heads* in fall, gradually molting to resemble adults by late winter. ♪ **Voice**: often silent, but may give catlike *meeyah*. When drumming on dead wood, has staccato beat, several short bursts of rapid-fire taps. All other sapsuckers sound similar.

RED-NAPED SAPSUCKER *Sphyrapicus nuchalis*

Replaces Yellow-bellied Sapsucker in Rocky Mountain region. Common in summer in aspen groves, pine forest. In migration and winter, seen in big trees of lowland valleys. ▶ Similar to Yellow-bellied. Usually some *red* on upper *nape*. Male has more red on throat; female has throat *partly red* (not all white). Young in late fall resemble adults (not brown-headed).

RED-BREASTED SAPSUCKER *Sphyrapicus ruber*

A richly colored bird, most numerous in humid forests of Pacific Northwest. ▶ Body and wings like other sapsuckers, but *head* and chest *all red*. Birds in northern part of range tend to be darker, with brighter yellow below; farther south, head is paler red with hint of white stripes. May interbreed with Yellow-bellied or Red-naped sapsuckers where their ranges meet.

WILLIAMSON'S SAPSUCKER *Sphyrapicus thyroideus*

Widespread in western mountains, but often scarce, quiet, hard to find. Occasionally strays in winter to lowlands, where may occur in planted evergreens. ▶ Male and female *strikingly different*. Male mostly *black,* with white wing patch, white rump, yellow belly, thin face stripes. Female has barred back, brown head; suggests Gila Woodpecker (p. 212), but has black on chest.

ARIZONA WOODPECKER *Picoides arizonae*

Uncommon resident of oak and pine-oak woods in canyons near Mexican border. Quiet, easily overlooked. Formerly called Strickland's Woodpecker. ▶ Solid *brown back* (*no* barring) is diagnostic. Patterned face, brown spots on white underparts. Adult female lacks red nape spot. ♪ **Voice**: sharp *schick*, short whinnying rattle, and a hoarse *wheak-wheak-wheak-wheak* . . .

SAPSUCKERS, ETC.

Red-naped Sapsucker 8½"

male

female

juvenile in late fall

Yellow-bellied Sapsucker 8½"

female

male

northern form (not to scale)

Red-breasted Sapsucker 8½"

southern form

female

Williamson's Sapsucker 9"

male

Arizona Woodpecker 7½"

male

female

FLICKERS AND PILEATED WOODPECKER

Flickers are common throughout North America, often feeding on the ground in open places. The big Pileated prefers deep woods.

NORTHERN FLICKER   *Colaptes auratus*

"Yellow-shafted"

This big brown woodpecker often feeds on the ground, seeking ants. When it flies, it flashes bright colors under the wings and tail, as well as a white rump. Found everywhere from deep woods to city parks. Two distinct forms, eastern/northern **"Yellow-shafted Flicker"** and western **"Red-shafted Flicker,"** named for color of feather shafts in wings. ▶ Brown back with narrow black bars, black chest patch, spots on belly. **"Yellow-shafted"** form has bright *yellow* under wings and tail, *red crescent* on back of head, tan face, gray crown; male has *black* mustache stripe. **"Red-shafted"** has *salmon-pink* under wings and tail, gray face, brown crown; male has *red* mustache stripe. Where the forms meet (southwestern Canada, western Great Plains) they interbreed freely, producing many intermediates. ♪**Voice:** loud, clear *kleeyah!* Also ringing *wik-wik-wik . . .*, long continued, heard especially in spring.

"Red-shafted"

GILDED FLICKER   *Colaptes chrysoides*

Common in the Arizona desert, excavating nest holes in giant saguaro cactus or in riverside trees. ▶ Bright yellow under wings and tail, but no red on back of head; gray face, with red mustache mark on male. Some intergrades between "Red-shafted" and "Yellow-shafted" flickers show similar combination, but true Gilded shows much *more black on underside of tail,* brighter *cinnamon crown.* Note: Gilded and "Red-shafted" flickers interbreed at middle elevations in Arizona (e.g., Sonoita Creek, Verde River), producing birds with intermediate markings. ♪**Voice:** much like Northern Flicker's, slightly higher-pitched.

PILEATED WOODPECKER   *Dryocopus pileatus*

Our biggest woodpecker (except for the Ivory-billed Woodpecker, now extinct in North America). Requires big trees, digging deep into dead wood for carpenter ants and other insects. The Pileated became scarce with the clearing of forest but is now making a comeback, even appearing in city parks. ▶ Very large, mostly black, with *red crest,* white stripe on neck. White under wings flashes in flight. Forehead and mustache red on male, black on female. ♪**Voice:** loud, ringing series of notes, suggesting one call of Northern Flicker, but with a wilder sound.

LARGE WOODPECKERS

male

female

"Yellow-shafted"
form

Northern
Flicker
13"

"Red-shafted"
form

female

male

Pileated
Woodpecker
17"

female

male

male

Gilded
Flicker
11½"

female

219

HUMMINGBIRDS

(family Trochilidae) are flying jewels, with amazing powers of flight and often glittering iridescent colors. They hover at flowers to sip nectar, also come to sugar-water feeders. Most of the 300-plus species live in the American tropics. Males may have bright colors, especially on the throat (often called the gorget), but females can be very hard to identify.

RUBY-THROATED HUMMINGBIRD   *Archilochus colubris*

The only *eastern* hummer seen regularly (others stray in). Common in summer but easily overlooked, in forest edge, parks, gardens. Most winter in tropics; a few remain in southeast (but a wintering hummer on Gulf Coast is more likely a western stray). ▶ Adult male has iridescent ruby throat, looking black in most lights. White chest contrasts with dark throat, green sides; tail all black, forked. Female green above, whitish below, with white tips on outer tail feathers; best identified by range. ♪ **Voice**: soft *tew*, varied chattering notes.

BLACK-CHINNED HUMMINGBIRD   *Archilochus alexandri*

The common summer hummer in lowlands of many parts of west. Very rare in winter in southeast. ▶ *Purple band* below male's black chin is hard to see; more obvious is *white collar* below that. Female almost identical to female Ruby-throated; told from similar hummers in west by long bill, pale underparts, callnotes. Flips and spreads tail actively while hovering. ♪ **Voice**: soft *tew* and chattering, identical to voice of Ruby-throated.

ANNA'S HUMMINGBIRD   *Calypte anna*

The familiar year-round hummer of the west coast, common in gardens, parks, streamsides, open woodland. ▶ Adult male has *rose red* on throat *and crown* (looks black or gold in some lights). Female plain green above, dingy gray below, often with red spots on throat. More stocky than Black-chinned or Costa's; unlike them, tends to hold tail still while hovering. ♪ **Callnote**: hard *tchip*. **Song**: male sings from perch, long scraping sputter interrupted by two harder notes.

COSTA'S HUMMINGBIRD   *Calypte costae*

A desert hummer, most numerous in very dry country, coming into edges of towns in Arizona and California. ▶ Adult male has *purple crown and throat*, with gorget feathers extending back to point. Female smaller and shorter-billed than female Anna's or Black-chinned, with *shorter tail*, paler belly, different voice. ♪ **Callnote**: light *tik*, sometimes run into rattle. **Song**: perched or in display flight, male gives high-pitched long whistle.

HUMMINGBIRDS

females

adult males

Ruby-throated Hummingbird
3³⁄₄"

female on nest

Black-chinned Hummingbird
3³⁄₄"

adult males

Anna's Hummingbird
4"

females

adult male

young male Costa's

female

adult male

Costa's Hummingbird
3¹⁄₂'

"SELASPHORUS" HUMMINGBIRDS

Common in the west. Adult males are mostly distinctive, but females and immatures are all extremely similar.

BROAD-TAILED HUMMINGBIRD   *Selasphorus platycercus*

Around meadows in the mountain west, male Broad-tails are often heard before they are seen: their wings make metallic trilling in flight. Like other mountain hummers, appears regularly in lowlands during migration. ▶ Male has rose throat, green back and sides, some rusty in tail. See Ruby-throated (east) and young male Anna's Hummingbird (west), previous page. Female green above, buff on sides; like female Rufous (below) but has larger tail. ♪**Voice:** musical *chip,* buzzy chattering. Wing-trill of male is sound most often heard.

RUFOUS HUMMINGBIRD   *Selasphorus rufus*

The most widespread western hummer, reaching southeast Alaska in summer, wintering to southern Mexico. Small but feisty, often chasing other hummers. Of all the western hummingbirds, this is the one that strays most often to the east; small numbers live along Gulf Coast every winter. ▶ Adult male bright *coppery rufous* above, with dark throat shining red in good light. Females and young have green back, spotted throat, orange-buff wash on sides and at base of tail. ♪**Voice:** musical *chip,* buzzy chattering. Male's wings make slight trilling sound in flight.

ALLEN'S HUMMINGBIRD   *Selasphorus sasin*

Locally common in chaparral, open woods, suburbs, along Pacific Coast from southwest Oregon to southern California (Rufous Hummingbird migrates through this region). Very early migrant, arriving in late winter. Those on Channel Islands and Palos Verdes Peninsula, California, are present all year. ▶ Adult male like Rufous Hummingbird but with green back. Females and young identical to those of Rufous. Note: some male Rufous Hummingbirds also have green backs, so Allen's not safely identified outside its normal range.

CALLIOPE HUMMINGBIRD   *Stellula calliope*

Our tiniest bird, fairly common in mountain meadows. Often feeds at low flowers, close to ground, although males may perch atop tall trees. ▶ Adult male has smeary magenta stripes on throat, pale green on sides. Female and young smaller than female Rufous, with *shorter bill;* short, rounded tail, with very little rusty at base; often shows a pale buff wash clear across chest. ♪**Voice:** high, thin *tsip.*

WESTERN HUMMINGBIRDS

adult female

male

Broad-tailed Hummingbird 4¼"

male

Allen's Hummingbird 3¾"

males

Rufous Hummingbird 3¾"

males

adult female

immature

adult female

immature

Calliope Hummingbird 3¼"

male

223

These live mainly near the Mexican border, rarely stray north or east.

BROAD-BILLED HUMMINGBIRD   *Cynanthus latirostris*

Mainly southern Arizona. Locally common in summer in streamside woods, foothills, canyons. A few remain through winter. Active, flips tail about while hovering. ▶ Adult male dark blue-green, with *red-based bill.* Tail *blue-black,* slightly forked; undertail coverts white. Female has less red on bill, smooth gray below, white face stripe; note tail action and pattern. See White-eared Hummingbird (rare), next page. ♪**Voice:** dry chatter.

BUFF-BELLIED HUMMINGBIRD   *Amazilia yucatanensis*

Mainly southern Texas, more common in summer, around woodland edges, towns. In winter, may wander up Gulf Coast, a few reaching Louisiana or even farther east. ▶ A stocky hummer, mostly green (brighter on throat), with *chestnut tail, red bill* with black tip, pale *buff belly.* In Arizona see Berylline Hummingbird (next page). ♪**Voice:** hard *chik,* often run into a rapid chatter.

MAGNIFICENT HUMMINGBIRD   *Eugenes fulgens*

A big long-billed hummer of southwestern mountains. Often in dry, open pine forest. Sometimes winters at feeders. ▶ Male's green throat and purple crown flash in good light, but usually bird looks all dark, with white spot behind eye. Female plainer; note size, long bill, white stripe behind eye, mottled gray-green sides, *small* pale tips on outer tail feathers. ♪**Voice:** hard *tchip.*

BLUE-THROATED HUMMINGBIRD   *Lampornis clemenciae*

This flashy big hummer is uncommon, usually near streams in mountain canyons of southwest. A few have wintered at feeders. ▶ Blue on throat is hard to see on male, lacking on female. Best known by size, white stripe behind eye, and especially *big white corners* on big *black tail.* Female Magnificent Hummingbird similar but more mottled below, has smaller pale corners on duller tail. ♪**Voice:** loud, sharp *sseek.* Male may perch in shadows and call repeatedly.

VIOLET-CROWNED HUMMINGBIRD   *Amazilia violiceps*

Uncommon and local near Mexican border. Mostly near streams, around sycamores in canyons at low elevations. A few have wintered at feeders. ▶ Strikingly *white underparts,* red-based bill. Dull gray-green above, with plain tail, violet reflections on crown. Female similar to male or slightly duller. ♪**Voice:** hard *chizk,* sometimes run into a rapid chatter.

HUMMINGBIRDS

young male

Broad-billed Hummingbird
4"

female

adult male

Buff-bellied Hummingbird
4¹/₂"

fcmale

male

Magnificent Hummingbird
5¹/₄"

female

Blue-throated Hummingbird
5"

male

Violet-crowned Hummingbird
4¹/₂"

LUCIFER HUMMINGBIRD   *Calothorax lucifer*

A Mexican desert hummingbird, scarce and local in summer in west Texas, southeast Arizona, extreme southwest New Mexico. Mostly in desert areas with agave and ocotillo plants; wanders up into lower edges of mountain canyons. ▶ Small hummer with *heavy, curved bill.* Male has long black tail (sometimes looks forked), purple throat. Female warm pale buff below and on face, with dusky ear patch. Note that several other southwestern hummers have slightly curved bills. ♪ **Voice:** dry, thin *chip.*

WHITE-EARED HUMMINGBIRD   *Hylocharis leucotis*

This Mexican mountain hummer reaches southeastern Arizona almost every summer. Very rare visitor in west Texas. Favors coniferous forest of mountains, canyons. ▶ *Broad white ear stripe,* blackish cheek patch. Male has shining green and purple on head (but often looks dark), red bill base. Female and young have duller bill, paler underparts with green spotting. Note that some other hummers have white ear stripes. Broad-billed Hummingbird (previous page) can be very similar but has longer bill, more blue-black in tail; usually in drier habitat. ♪ **Voice:** hard metallic *ktink.*

BERYLLINE HUMMINGBIRD   *Amazilia beryllina*

Almost every summer, a few Beryllines reach southeastern Arizona; they have nested there a few times. Likes streamsides with tall trees, at middle elevations in mountain canyons. ▶ Mostly apple green, with *chestnut red* in the tail *and wings.* Some reddish on bill; belly may be buff or gray. Buff-bellied Hummingbird (previous page), found in Texas, lacks chestnut in wings. ♪ **Voice:** buzzy *skizzz;* also soft *too-doo-deet,* last note higher.

GREEN VIOLET-EAR   *Colibri thalassinus*

Widespread in tropics. Strays to Texas almost annually, but has wandered much farther, even reaching Canada. Might appear at a hummingbird feeder almost anywhere. ▶ Rather large, with straight bill. Dark green with *blue-violet ear patch* and *chest.* Tail blue-green, crossed by *blackish band.* ♪ **Voice:** dry rattle or chatter.

PLAIN-CAPPED STARTHROAT   *Heliomaster constantii*

Rare wanderer into southern Arizona, mostly in summer and mostly at low elevations. ▶ Large, long-billed, drab (red on throat seldom obvious). Has broad *white whisker mark,* white tuft near base of wings. *White rump patch* distinctive (but beware partial albinos of other hummer species).

GREEN-BREASTED MANGO   *Anthracothorax prevostii*

Rare wanderer into southern Texas. ▶ Big and dark, with *curved bill* and *reddish purple tail.* Adult male has all-green body; female white below with smeary *dark central stripe,* white spots on tail tip. Immature like female but with some cinnamon color at sides of throat.

RARE HUMMINGBIRDS

male

female

male

Lucifer Hummingbird
3½"

male

males

White-eared Hummingbird
3¾"

female

Green Violet-ear
4¾"

Berylline Hummingbird
4¼"

immature

Green-breasted Mango
4¾"

Plain-capped Starthroat
5"

227

SWIFTS

(family Apodidae) are among the most aerial of all birds, feeding on insects captured in midair during rapid flight. Unlike the swallows (next pages), an unrelated family of songbirds, swifts are never seen perching on wires, because they can't: their tiny feet can only cling to vertical surfaces.

CHIMNEY SWIFT *Chaetura pelagica*

In the skies above eastern towns in summer, pairs and trios of Chimney Swifts zoom about with very rapid stiff wingbeats and glides. Formerly nesting in hollow trees, they now nest mainly inside chimneys, using their sticky saliva to plaster a nest shelf against the vertical wall. They winter in South America. Very rare summer visitor in west. ▶ Gray overall, best known by shape: stubby at both ends, with scimitar-shaped wings (sometimes called "a cigar with wings"). ♪**Voice:** sharp *chip*, often run together into shrill chattering series.

VAUX'S SWIFT *Chaetura vauxi*

Fairly common in summer in northwest, but declining, as it loses its major nesting sites: hollow trees in mature forest. May roost overnight in chimneys, and sometimes nests there. Migrates mostly west of Rockies. Very rare in midwinter on Gulf Coast (but more likely than Chimney Swift at that season). ▶ Very similar to Chimney Swift but a bit smaller. Slightly paler on throat and rump, contrasting more with dark body plumage (hard to see on flying birds). Best known by range. ♪**Voice:** thin chittering, weaker than Chimney Swift's.

WHITE-THROATED SWIFT *Aeronautes saxatalis*

One of our fastest-flying birds, this little torpedo zooms along cliffs and canyons of the west, often in chattering flocks. Nests in crevices in cliffs, sometimes in cracks in buildings. ▶ Our only swift with white and black pattern. Tail longer than in other swifts, and slightly forked. Violet-green Swallow (next page), often seen flying in same areas, is similar but has shorter wings, slower flight, lacks black stripe on side below wing. ♪**Voice:** shrill chattering *je-je-je-je-je-je*.

BLACK SWIFT *Cypseloides niger*

This big swift inhabits wild country of the west, nesting on sea-cliffs and behind waterfalls. Scarce and elusive, never seen in large numbers. ▶ Larger than other swifts, tail moderately long, slightly forked. Mostly uniform blackish gray; at close range, shows frosting of whitish on forehead. High overhead, might suggest Purple Martin (next page) but has much longer, narrower wings. ♪**Voice:** sharp twitter, seldom heard.

SWIFTS

Chimney Swift
5"

Chimney Swift clinging to tree

Vaux's Swift
4½"

White-throated Swift
6½"

on nest

Black Swift
7¼"

229

(family Hirundinidae) are usually seen in graceful flight, often low over streams or ponds; they feed mostly on insects, caught in midair. Flocks of swallows often line up on wires, especially when they gather for fall migration. Swallows resemble swifts (previous page) but are more closely related to typical songbirds (section begins p. 250).

PURPLE MARTIN — *Progne subis*

Widespread and popular in the east, where most colonies nest in multiroomed martin houses. Scarcer in west, where they mostly use natural nest sites: holes in trees or in giant cactus. Winters in South America, but returns to southeastern states very early in spring (January in some places). ► Our biggest swallow. Angular, pointed wings, forked tail. Male glossy blue-black all over, female and young grayer below, with white belly. Starlings (p. 330) are somewhat similar and will nest in martin houses, but have longer bills, browner wings, different behavior. ♪ **Voice:** musical, burry *dzeeb-dzurr,* other notes. Often heard high overhead at dawn.

TREE SWALLOW — *Tachycineta bicolor*

Common and widespread in summer, nesting in holes in trees or in birdhouses (especially bluebird boxes). Unlike most swallows, winters regularly in southern states, feeding on berries when insects are scarce. Forms huge flocks in fall. ► Sharply bicolored, dark above, *clean white below.* Adults are glossy blue or green above, with dark cap down to level of eye. Juveniles dusky brown above, often have gray-brown wash across chest (Bank Swallow, next page, is much more sharply marked on chest). ♪ **Voice:** clear *tdeet,* liquid twittering.

VIOLET-GREEN SWALLOW — *Tachycineta thalassina*

Western only, very common in summer in clearings of evergreen forest, mountains, canyons, riversides. Nests in holes in trees or cliffs. ► A bit smaller than Tree Swallow, with faster wingbeats, less gliding. Dark above (glossed violet and green in good light), with *white rump patches* that almost meet above tail, white circling up *on face.* Female duller, with smudged face. Juvenile gray-brown above, dingy on face, may be hard to tell from young Tree Swallow. ♪ **Voice:** liquid twitters.

BAHAMA SWALLOW — *Tachycineta cyaneoviridis*

Native to pine forest in Bahamas, where it nests in holes in trees. Very rare visitor to Florida. ► Suggests Tree Swallow (clean white below, dark above), but has very long, deeply forked tail, more white on underside of wings. Barn Swallow (next page) is similar in shape, can be very pale below.

SWALLOWS

females

Purple Martin
8"

adult
male

juvenile

**Tree
Swallow**
5¾"

adult
male

male

**Violet-green
Swallow**
5¼"

female

male

**Bahama
Swallow**
(rare visitor)
6"

adults

BARN SWALLOW *Hirundo rustica*

A familiar swallow of open country, nesting in barns or sheds or under bridges, making cup-shaped nest with mud foundation. Graceful in flight, its forked "swallow tail" often folded in a long point. Like some other swallows, gathers in very large flocks for migration. ▶ *Long forked tail* (with white spots, which may be hidden). Steel blue back, chestnut throat. Chest and belly vary from deep buff to white. Young birds have shorter tails. ♪ **Voice**: musical twittering, clear liquid *kweap.*

CLIFF SWALLOW *Petrochelidon pyrrhonota*

Very common in west, less numerous in east, in open country. Colonies often nest under bridges or on sides of buildings, making gourd-shaped mud nest with small opening at one end. ▶ Short square-tipped tail. Seen from above, *buffy rump* contrasts with dark back and tail. Throat deep chestnut, forehead usually pale (some in southwest have dark foreheads). ♪ **Voice**: low *churr*, soft rasping and creaking notes.

CAVE SWALLOW *Petrochelidon fulva*

Formerly nested only in caves, now nests under bridges and culverts, has become locally common in Texas and nearby areas. Also very locally in south Florida. Strays sometimes appear well to the north, especially on Atlantic Coast in late fall. ▶ Like Cliff Swallow (buffy rump, square tail) but has *pale buff throat*, black cap, dark forehead. ♪ **Voice**: clear *weet*, soft rasping notes.

BANK SWALLOW *Riparia riparia*

This small brown swallow nests in holes excavated in vertical dirt banks. Highly social, with many nest holes crowded close together. ▶ Brown above, white below, with *white throat* and sharply defined *dark chest band.* (Compare to juvenile Tree Swallow, previous page.) Smaller than Rough-winged Swallow, with faster wingbeats. ♪ **Voice**: dry buzzy chattering.

NORTHERN ROUGH-WINGED SWALLOW *Stelgidopteryx serripennis*

Not as sociable as most swallows, often seen as isolated pairs, rarely gathering in large flocks. Nests in holes dug in vertical dirt banks, or in holes in cliffs or buildings; does not form colonies like Bank Swallow. ▶ Brown above, *dull dingy gray-brown on throat*, fading to *white* on belly and undertail coverts. ♪ **Voice**: buzzy *fzzzt*, often repeated several times rapidly.

SWALLOWS

Barn Swallow
7"

at nest

Cliff Swallow
5½"

Cliff Swallow nests

Cave Swallow
5½"

at nest

Bank Swallow
4¾"

nests in
dirt bank

**Northern
Rough-winged Swallow**
5½"

233

(family Tyrannidae) are found mostly in the American tropics, where there are more than 350 species. Flycatchers in North America are known (and named) for their habit of perching in one spot, looking about, and then flying out to catch insects in the air. The term "tyrant" flycatcher reflects the bold, aggressive behavior of some species, notably kingbirds (below).

Some groups of flycatchers are quite difficult to identify. Studies have shown that they may recognize their own kind mainly by voice. Birders may have to recognize some of them the same way. Even seasoned experts have to let some flycatchers go as unidentified. Here are some well-defined groups of flycatchers to know:

Kingbirds often perch in the open, may chase birds much larger than themselves.

Crested flycatchers, p. 242, usually have some yellow below, reddish in wings or tail, and bushy crests. Found in woods or desert.

KINGBIRDS
These two white-bellied kingbirds occur in the east.

EASTERN KINGBIRD   *Tyrannus tyrannus*

Common in summer in open country, forest edge, farms, roadsides, perching on fences or treetops. Conspicuous for its bold behavior, attacking and chasing crows, hawks, or other large birds that come too near the kingbird's nest. Migrates in flocks; winters in South America. ▶ Broad *white band* at tip of black tail is diagnostic. Blackish above, white below, with gray wash across chest. A narrow strip of red feathers on the crown is usually hidden. ♪ **Voice:** high-pitched *bzzeent*, often run into a rapid chattering series.

GRAY KINGBIRD   *Tyrannus dominicensis*

Mainly Florida (a few elsewhere along coast in the southeast), also widespread in Caribbean. Conspicuous in summer in mangroves, roadsides, even cities near coast. Perches in the open, gives loud calls. ▶ Whitish below, *gray above,* with darker mask. Tail notched at tip, with *no* white band. Heavy black bill. ♪ **Voice:** loud, trilled *pi-teerr-it* and other metallic, sputtering calls.

Phoebes (left), p. 240, perch in upright posture. Their rather long tails are frequently wagged or dipped in a gentle motion.

Wood-pewees (above), p. 238, have wing-bars but no eye-rings. Perch upright in forest trees.

Empidonax flycatchers (right), p. 244, can be very challenging to identify. All 11 species are small and plain, with wing-bars and (usually) eye-rings. In summer on the nesting grounds, habitat is a good clue and songs are distinctive. Their feeding behavior, flying out from a perch to take insects in the air, helps distinguish the Empids from other small birds with wing-bars and eye-rings, including kinglets, p. 294, and vireos, p. 296.

Eastern Kingbird
8½"

Gray Kingbird
9"

build cup-shaped nest of grass and twigs, usually well up in a tree; may harass and chase much larger birds that venture too close.

WESTERN KINGBIRD   *Tyrannus verticalis*

A bold, spunky flycatcher, common in the west, perching on wires or fences in open country, roadsides, even cities. May nest on utility poles, towers. Strays reach the Atlantic Coast every fall; a few spend winter in Florida. ► Yellow belly, gray chest and head (with darker mask). Notice *black* tail with *narrow white outer edges.* Compare to other yellow-bellied kingbirds (below), crested flycatchers (p. 242). ♪ **Voice:** sharp *kep;* also a staccato sputtering or "bickering," rising and falling in pitch.

CASSIN'S KINGBIRD   *Tyrannus vociferans*

Fairly common in west, in riversides and canyons, favoring more wooded areas than Western Kingbird. Noisy. Often perches among foliage of tall trees. ► Like Western Kingbird, but *darker gray* head and chest contrast more with *white chin.* Tail has pale tip, but only faint white edges. Bill larger, wings have more obvious *scaly pattern.* ♪ **Voice:** loud rough *chibeer,* sometimes run into excited series, *kideer-kideer-kideer.* Also (mainly at dawn) a rising rough series, *berg-berg-berg-BERG.*

COUCH'S KINGBIRD   *Tyrannus couchii*

Texas only, common in lower Rio Grande Valley and southern coast. Favors native woodland, trees near ponds and rivers. Much less numerous in winter. ► Like Western and Cassin's but tail *dusky brown,* with *notch* at tip; yellow extends farther up chest; bill heavier. Tropical Kingbird (next), scarce in south Texas, almost identical but has different voice. ♪ **Voice:** hard *kep,* throaty *berreeer.* Also rolling *puweeer, puweer-puWEEchew!*

TROPICAL KINGBIRD   *Tyrannus melancholicus*

Southern Arizona, scarce and local in summer in big trees by lowland ponds, streams. Recently a few pairs year-round in southern Texas. Rare fall visitor on Pacific Coast, very rare elsewhere. ► Chest yellow (not gray), tail dull brown, notched at tip. Almost identical to Couch's Kingbird; best told by range or (in Texas) by sound. ♪ **Voice:** fast twittering with hard metallic sound.

THICK-BILLED KINGBIRD   *Tyrannus crassirostris*

Southeast Arizona, extreme southwest New Mexico, scarce and local in summer. Perches high in big trees along streams. ► Sooty above with blacker head, *whitish below* with pale yellow wash on belly. Very *heavy* black bill. ♪ **Voice:** loud, arresting *ka-RREEP!,* metallic buzzing *prreeer.*

KINGBIRDS

Western Kingbird 8"

Cassin's Kingbird 8½"

(identify Couch's and Tropical by range and voice)

Couch's and Tropical Kingbirds 9"

Thick-billed Kingbird 9½"

237

PEWEES AND TYRANNULET

The four pewees (including Olive-sided) are drab flycatchers that perch upright, usually rather high in trees.

EASTERN WOOD-PEWEE *Contopus virens*

Common in summer in eastern forests, often perching high among foliage; heard more often than seen. ▶ Very plain, with faint wing-bars, no eye-ring. Note length of wingtips. Empidonax flycatchers (p. 236) have shorter wingtips, most have eye-rings (but see Willow Flycatcher). Western Wood-Pewee almost identical, recognized by range, voice. ♪ **Song**: plaintive whistles, *peee-yerr* and *pee-ya-weeee*. **Callnotes**: rising *prreee*, short *chip*.

WESTERN WOOD-PEWEE *Contopus sordidulus*

Common in summer in woods of canyons and riversides. ▶ Confusingly plain, with faint wing-bars, no eye-ring. Most Empidonax flycatchers have eye-rings, but see Willow Flycatcher (p. 236), which has shorter wingtips. Eastern Wood-Pewee averages *slightly* paler but most safely identified by range, voice. ♪ **Song**: buzzy, descending *bzeeyeer*. May alternate with clear notes: *tew, tee-deet . . . bzeeyeer*. **Callnote**: short *chip*.

OLIVE-SIDED FLYCATCHER *Contopus cooperi*

Uncommon in summer in coniferous forest, usually near water. Typically on bare twig at top of tree, flying out to catch insects, returning to same perch. ▶ *Dark, mottled sides* contrast with *white stripe* down center of chest (like unbuttoned vest). Has big-headed, short-tailed look. Tuft of white may show above wing. ♪ **Song**: whistled *quick-three-beers!* **Callnote**: sharp *pip-pip*.

GREATER PEWEE *Contopus pertinax*

Uncommon in summer in mountain pine forests of southwest. Usually perches high in fairly open spots. A few may stay through winter in lowlands. ▶ Rather uniform plain gray with short crest, noticeable *orange lower mandible*. Looks darker, more crested, brighter-billed, and bigger than Western Wood-Pewee. ♪ **Song**: whistled *ho-say, ma-ree-ah*. **Callnote**: sharp *pip-pip*.

NORTHERN BEARDLESS-TYRANNULET *Camptostoma imberbe*

Uncommon in Arizona, rare in Texas, in streamside woods. An odd little tropical flycatcher, easily overlooked. ▶ Suggests an Empidonax (p. 236) but even smaller, with bushy-headed look, thin stubby bill. Has slight dark line through eye but *no obvious eye-ring*, vague wing-bars. Often bobs tail up and down. ♪ **Voice**: odd squeaky *spee-yuk*; descending whistled *peer, peer, peer, peer*.

FLYCATCHERS

Eastern Wood-Pewee
6½"

Western Wood-Pewee
6½"

(identify the two wood-pewees by range and voice)

juvenile

Olive-sided Flycatcher
7½"

Greater Pewee
8"

Northern Beardless-Tyrannulet
4½"

239

Phoebes are slim flycatchers that perch upright, wagging or dipping their tails downward in a gentle movement.

EASTERN PHOEBE *Sayornis phoebe*

One of the earliest spring migrants to return in the northeast, the phoebe sings its name as it perches low along streams, wagging its tail down-up repeatedly. Its nest (with mud foundation) is plastered against a streambank, or placed under a bridge or the eaves of a building. ▶ Shows strong contrast between whitish throat and *sooty brown head*. Otherwise rather plain, off-white below, gray-brown above, with no obvious marks. In fresh fall plumage, has yellow wash below, faint wing-bars. ♪**Callnote**: sharp *peep*. **Song**: soft *fee-bee*, second note lower, with a rolled or burry quality.

BLACK PHOEBE *Sayornis nigricans*

A typical bird of streamsides in the southwest, rarely found away from the water. Perches on low branches, dipping and fanning its tail, calling frequently. Often nests in culverts or under bridges. ▶ Mostly dark charcoal gray, blacker on head, with white belly. Note slim shape, upright posture. Juveniles in summer have rusty edges on wing and back feathers. ♪**Callnote**: sharp ringing *peep*. **Song**: thin, shrill whistles, *pee-teeer*, repeated.

SAY'S PHOEBE *Sayornis saya*

A dry-country phoebe, often seen perched on fences or hovering over barren fields. May nest around barns or ranch houses. ▶ Soft dusty gray, with pale *orange-buff* belly, *black tail*. Wags tail like other phoebes. (Note: in regions with red soil, Eastern Phoebe can have belly stained orange like Say's, but it shows much more contrast on the face.) ♪**Callnote**: soft, descending *peeer* or *peeyeer*. **Song**: same notes, run together in fast series.

VERMILION FLYCATCHER *Pyrocephalus rubinus*

A brilliant exception to the general drabness of flycatchers, locally common near streams and ponds in the southwest. A few wander east along Gulf Coast in winter. Usually perches fairly low among scattered trees, dipping its tail like a phoebe. Male performs display flight, puffing himself up and fluttering high while singing. ▶ Male's pattern unmistakable (compare to Scarlet Tanager, p. 328). Female and young mostly gray and white with faint *streaks on chest,* wash of pink or yellow on belly; note tail-dipping habit. ♪**Callnote**: very high-pitched *teek*. **Song**: high, thin sputtering series, rising and falling, often given in flight.

PHOEBES AND VERMILION

juvenile

Eastern
Phoebe
7"

Black
Phoebe
7"

adult

Say's
Phoebe
7½"

Vermilion
Flycatcher
6"

young
male

female

adult
male

have bushy heads, yellow on belly, usually reddish brown in tail and/or wings. These all nest in holes in trees or cactus (or in birdhouses). Colors may suggest kingbirds (p. 236), but those are more typically out in the open, perch more horizontally, and lack reddish in tail and wings.

GREAT CRESTED FLYCATCHER *Myiarchus crinitus*

Common in eastern forest in summer but sometimes overlooked, staying high among dense foliage. May be heard more often than seen. Has odd habit of adding a piece of shed snakeskin to its nest lining. ▶ Olive-brown head and back; clear gray throat and chest contrasting with bright yellow belly. Bright *reddish brown* in tail and wings, obvious when the bird flies. Bushy-crested look not always apparent. ♪**Voice:** loud, whistled *wheeeap!* and rough *berrg, berrg.*

ASH-THROATED FLYCATCHER *Myiarchus cinerascens*

A pale flycatcher of dry country in the west, often common in summer. Where it overlaps in range with other crested flycatchers, it favors more arid, open habitats. Rarely strays to east coast in late fall. ▶ Very *pale* gray throat grades into whitish chest, then pale yellow belly. From below, notice pattern of reddish and dark brown in tail (with dark brown along outer edge spreading out more at tip of tail). ♪**Voice:** rough or rolled notes, *brrk* or *kabrick* or louder *prrt-wheeer;* many variations.

BROWN-CRESTED FLYCATCHER *Myiarchus tyrannulus*

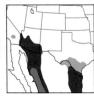

The big crested flycatcher of the southwest and south Texas, fairly common in summer around riverside trees, saguaro cactus desert, foothills canyons. ▶ Like Ash-throated Flycatcher but has *bigger bill,* more *contrasting* yellow belly, bushier crest. Tail pattern differs (hard to see). Great Crested Flycatcher (migrant through south Texas) is much darker gray on chest, olive-brown on back, with orange at base of lower mandible. ♪**Voice:** loud *whit!* and rough *brrrk, brrrk,* repeated. At dawn, a rolling *three-for-two.*

DUSKY-CAPPED FLYCATCHER *Myiarchus tuberculifer*

A sad-voiced flycatcher of oak woods, summering in canyons and streamsides near the Mexican border. Almost never ventures into desert. ▶ Small with relatively large bill; gray throat and chest *contrast* with yellow belly. Smaller than Brown-crested Flycatcher, more contrasty than Ash-throated, and shows less reddish in tail than either. ♪**Voice:** clear, mournful *wheeeaahh,* rising slightly and then falling. Also rolling *prrree, pyerrr.* Sometimes a soft *whit.*

Ash-throat in faded summer plumage

Great Crested Flycatcher
8½"

at nest hole

Ash-throated Flycatcher
8"

Brown-crested Flycatcher
9"

Dusky-capped Flycatcher
7"

EMPIDONAX FLYCATCHERS

Eleven confusing little birds, with wing-bars and (usually) eye-rings, all looking very much alike. They favor different habitats and have different songs, but it is often safest just to call them all "Empids."

LEAST FLYCATCHER   *Empidonax minimus*

Common in east, scarce in west, around forest edge, clearings. Stays fairly low in partly open areas. Like other Empids, often jerks its tail up slightly and flicks its wings while perched. ▶ Gray or brown-gray above, white on throat, with contrasting wing-bars and eye-ring. Smaller than most eastern Empids. ♪ **Song:** snappy, hard *che-beck!* **Callnote:** dry *whit.*

YELLOW-BELLIED FLYCATCHER   *Empidonax flaviventris*

Fairly common in summer in wet conifer forest, bogs. May stay fairly low in dense cover. In spring, migrates north later than most flycatchers. ▶ All Empids show some yellow on belly; this one also has yellow wash on *throat.* Back tinged green; wing-bars contrasty. In west, see Western Flycatcher (next page). ♪ **Song:** *chebunk,* much softer than Least's. **Callnote:** soft *perwee* or *pyew.*

ACADIAN FLYCATCHER   *Empidonax virescens*

Mainly southeastern states, in swamps, streamside woods. Stays at midlevels inside forest; loud calls often heard before bird is seen. ▶ Has contrasting wing-bars and eye-ring like other Empids, but tends to look quite pale below, green above. Fall birds may be very yellow below; bigger bill, longer wingtips than Yellow-bellied. ♪ **Song:** explosive *PEET-ssah.* **Callnote:** loud, flat *peek!*

ALDER FLYCATCHER   *Empidonax alnorum*

Nests farther north than most Empids, favoring thickets of alder and birch around ponds, swamps, streams. Migrates through the eastern states. Formerly lumped with the next species, under name of Traill's Flycatcher. ▶ Large Empid with greenish gray back, large bill, white throat. Eye-ring sometimes not well defined. ♪ **Song:** buzzy *freeBEEEyeer,* accent on *second* syllable. **Callnote:** flat *peep* or *kep,* more tone quality than Willow's.

WILLOW FLYCATCHER   *Empidonax traillii*

Favors thickets of willow and other low trees along streams, ponds. The race nesting along southwestern rivers is now endangered. ▶ Almost identical to Alder Flycatcher (and formerly considered same species). Tends to be browner and show less obvious eye-ring, but safely identified only by voice. ♪ **Song:** *FITZ-bew,* buzzy, accent on *first* syllable. **Callnote:** dry *whit.*

EMPIDONAX FLYCATCHERS
(BEST IDENTIFIED BY VOICE)

Least
Flycatcher
5¼"

Yellow-bellied
Flycatcher
5½"

Acadian
Flycatcher
5¾"

Willow Flycatcher
and
Alder Flycatcher
5¾"

EMPIDONAX FLYCATCHERS OF THE WEST

"WESTERN FLYCATCHER"

Pacific-slope

Cordilleran

The two species under this heading (**Pacific-slope Flycatcher**, *Empidonax difficilis*, and **Cordilleran Flycatcher**, *E. occidentalis*) are *very* close relatives, identical in looks, differing only in range and in details of voice. Usually it is better just to call them "Western Flycatchers." Common in summer in wet coniferous forest, along streams, shaded canyons. Nests on streambanks, sometimes on cabin porches. ▶ Tinged greenish above, with distinct *yellow wash on throat*. Eyering extends behind eye in *teardrop shape*. From below, bill looks wide, with orange lower mandible. ♪**Voice:** up-slurred *suweeat* (Pacific-slope) or broken *pit-peet* (Cordilleran); also high thin *peet* (both species).

HAMMOND'S FLYCATCHER   *Empidonax hammondii*

A compact dark Empid of cold western forests. Usually nests higher in mountains than Dusky Flycatcher, in forest of spruce, Douglas-fir, aspen. ▶ Short-billed and short-tailed, and often shows contrast between gray head and olive back, but can look exactly like Dusky. ♪**Song:** series of rough notes, *chpit . . . brrrrk . . . grrip!* Lower than Dusky's. **Callnotes:** distinctive sharp *peek*.

DUSKY FLYCATCHER   *Empidonax oberholseri*

Drab and confusing, between Hammond's and Gray in many ways. Summers at midelevations in mountains, where tall conifers meet leafy thickets, or in aspen groves. ▶ Has eye-ring and wing-bars, but otherwise lacks obvious marks. Bill and tail slightly longer than Hammond's, shorter than Gray. ♪**Song:** *chrip . . . grreep . . . pweet!*, higher than Hammond's. **Callnote:** dry *whit*.

GRAY FLYCATCHER   *Empidonax wrightii*

Favors dry country: sagebrush and juniper flats in summer, mesquite desert in winter. Often perches low, flies to ground to pick up insects. ▶ Best mark is behavior: instead of flipping tail up like other Empids, it *dips* its tail *downward* gently, like a phoebe. Paler than other Empids, relatively long tail and bill. ♪**Song:** short notes, *chuwip . . . teeah . . . chuwip . . .* etc. **Callnote:** dry *whit*.

BUFF-BREASTED FLYCATCHER   *Empidonax fulvifrons*

Scarce and local in summer in southeast Arizona (mostly Huachuca Mountains), in open pine forest. ▶ Smaller, paler, and browner than most Empids. Unique pale *buff wash* on chest (may be hard to see on faded midsummer birds). ♪**Song:** squeaky *cheebit* or *chebeet!* **Callnote:** dry *pit*.

WESTERN EMPIDONAX
(BEST IDENTIFIED BY VOICE)

"Western
Flycatcher"
5½"

Hammond's
Flycatcher
5½"

Gray
Flycatcher
6"

Dusky
Flycatcher
5¾"

Buff-breasted
Flycatcher
5"

DISTINCTIVE FLYCATCHERS

SCISSOR-TAILED FLYCATCHER   *Tyrannus forficatus*

An elegant summer bird of the southern plains. Perches on fences and wires; flutters over open fields, spreading its tail wide, as it chases flying insects. Sometimes wanders far from mapped range. Small numbers winter in Florida. ▶ Pale overall with dusky wings, black and white tail (slightly shorter on female), *orange-pink* on sides and under wings. Young bird has shorter tail; resembles Western Kingbird (p. 228) but paler. ♪ **Voice:** snappy sputtering, much like Western Kingbird's.

FORK-TAILED FLYCATCHER   *Tyrannus savana*

Rare visitor from the tropics. May show up almost anywhere, but most records are on Atlantic Coast in fall. ▶ Adult has *long,* flexible black tail streamers. Gray back contrasts with *black head,* dark wings. (Scissor-tailed Flycatcher has pale head, white in tail.) Young Fork-tails (and molting adults) have shorter tails, but show same pattern of head and back.

GREAT KISKADEE   *Pitangus sulphuratus*

A south Texas specialty, common in riverside woods, trees near ponds. (Also common in Bermuda, where it was introduced.) Brash, noisy, may perch in the open. Feeds on insects and berries, sometimes plunges into water to catch minnows. ▶ Bright *rusty wings and tail,* yellow belly, black-and-white-striped head. Unmistakable in our area (but some other tropical flycatchers are similar). ♪ **Voice:** loud *gweeap!* and slow *kiss-kah-deee!*

SULPHUR-BELLIED FLYCATCHER   *Myiodynastes luteiventris*

Uncommon in summer in Arizona, in big sycamores along streams. Has loud voice but often sits silently among foliage, easily overlooked. Nests in holes in trees. Very rare visitor to Texas and along Gulf Coast; winters in South America. ▶ Bright *rusty tail,* long heavy bill, dark face patch, *heavily streaked* above and below. Unlike any other flycatcher in our area (but some in tropics are very similar). ♪ **Voice:** *ka-reek-ah, ka-REEK-ah,* other notes, with shrill squeaky quality.

ROSE-THROATED BECARD   *Pachyramphus aglaiae*

Rare in summer in southeast Arizona, very rare in all seasons in south Texas. Easily overlooked among dense foliage of tall trees. Builds messy football-shaped nest suspended from a twig, with entrance low on one side. ▶ Looks big-headed. Adult male gray, with blacker cap, small rose spot on throat. Female and young have brown back, dark cap, pale buff to dingy white below. ♪ **Voice:** thin, whiny *tseeeyo;* also rapid whining chatter.

FLASHY FLYCATCHERS

Scissor-tailed
Flycatcher
13"

Fork-tailed
Flycatcher
(rare visitor)
14"

Great
Kiskadee
10"

Sulphur-
bellied
Flycatcher
8¹/₂"

males

Rose-throated
Becard
7"

female

Almost half the birds in this guide—from swallows (p. 230) through the end of the book—are classified in the **order Passeriformes,** or perching birds. Most of these (but not the flycatchers, considered a more primitive group) are often collectively known as songbirds. Not all of them are good songsters by any means, but they are often familiar and common birds, living in our neighborhoods and parks. The major families of songbirds are introduced below.

Thrashers and mockingbirds, p. 260. Slim and long-tailed. Impressive singers.

Thrushes, p. 252. A varied group. Many are good singers. Often feed on ground.

Shrikes, p. 264. Predatory; impale prey on thorns.

Waxwings, p. 266. Sociable, with soft voices. Feed on berries.

Silky-flycatchers, p. 266. Southwestern. Crave mistletoe berries.

Dippers, p. 268. Aquatic songbirds of western streams.

Pipits and wagtails, p. 268. Walk on the ground in open country, often wagging their tails.

Jays and crows, p. 272. Large omnivores
with strong bills, harsh voices.

Larks, p. 270.
Walk and run
on barren open
ground.

Chickadees and titmice, p. 280.
Small treetop acrobats, in
cheery flocks in cold weather.

Nuthatches, p. 286.
Clamber down tree
trunks headfirst.

Creepers,
p. 286. Like bits
of bark, creep-
ing up trees.

Wrens, p. 288.
Active little
brown birds,
fussy and
curious.

Gnatcatchers, p. 292. Tiny,
active, long-tailed birds. See
also bushtits and verdins, p. 294.

Kinglets, p. 294. Tiny,
short-tailed, hyperactive.

Vireos, p. 296.
Persistent singers
of treetops and
thickets, seeking
insects among
dense foliage.

See also these other groups of songbirds, which are major enough to merit
their own sections of the book: Warblers (p. 302), Blackbirds and Tanagers
(p. 328), Sparrows (p. 344), and Finches and Buntings (p. 364).

ROBINS AND VARIED THRUSH

The first birds of the thrush family **(Turdidae)** are shown here. We have only one widespread robin, but a couple of others wander in from Mexico; related species (next page) stray in from Europe or Asia. The Varied Thrush has similar colors but different shape and behavior.

AMERICAN ROBIN   *Turdus migratorius*

Common and familiar almost everywhere, from wilderness to city parks. Often seen running and hopping on lawns, hunting earthworms. Nest (built with mud and grass) is sometimes placed on windowsills. In winter, gathers in large flocks to feed on berries, wild fruits. Winter range varies from year to year, with large flocks sometimes invading southern areas. ▶ Brick-red chest, gray back, streaks on white chin. Small white spots around eyes and (usually) on tail corners. Male usually has blacker head, slightly richer colors than female. Juvenile can be confusing at first: heavily spotted below, mottled on back, pale marks on face. Look for reddish tinge on chest. ♪**Song**: rich caroling, *cheerup cheerio cheerup,* often beginning well before dawn. **Callnotes:** thin *seleeet;* chuckling *tuh-tuh-tuh-tuh.*

VARIED THRUSH   *Ixoreus naevius*

Shaped somewhat like a very chunky robin, but usually acts shier. Common but elusive in wet forest of the northwest. Usually in trees or undergrowth, but sometimes comes out on lawns, roadsides. May wander widely in winter, even reaching east coast. ▶ Orange throat and eyebrow, *dark chest band, orange wing markings.* Female duller than male. Juvenile mottled on chest, but has same *wing pattern* as adults. ♪**Song**: long breathy whistle in minor key, with sound like humming and whistling at same time. **Callnote:** soft *tuck.*

CLAY-COLORED ROBIN   *Turdus grayi*

Very scarce resident in extreme southern Texas in woodland, native brush, suburbs. Has nested there several times and may be increasing. Usually fairly shy. ▶ Has shape and actions of American Robin, but entirely *dull brown,* paler below. Dull yellow or yellow-green bill. ♪**Song**: rich whistles like those of American Robin. **Callnotes:** mellow two-part whistle, *tooweee hoowaah,* second part lower; also low chuckling notes.

RUFOUS-BACKED ROBIN   *Turdus rufopalliatus*

Rare visitor from western Mexico. Most records are in Arizona in winter, but sometimes reaches Texas, New Mexico, California. Shy, often hides in wooded areas, dense brush. Attracted to berries and wild fruits, like other robins. ▶ Very similar to American Robin but has *no white around eye;* usually stronger throat pattern and brighter yellow bill; *rufous* wash across *back and wings.* ♪**Callnotes:** thin *seeet,* soft low *chgk.*

ROBINS AND VARIED THRUSH

males

female

American Robin
10"

juvenile
robins
have
spots

female

Varied Thrush
9¹/₂"

male

Clay-colored
Robin
10"

Rufous-backed
Robin
9¹/₂"

253

NORTHERN WHEATEAR   *Oenanthe oenanthe*

Uncommon in summer in Alaska and in northwestern and northeastern Canada. Lives on ground on rocky tundra. Very active, bobbing its tail, flitting among boulders. Though scarce on this continent, it is common across Eurasia; almost all our wheatears go back to Old World for winter, but a few show up in northeast every fall. ▶ Striking *tail pattern* (like inverted black T on white) and *white rump*. Dark mask and wings in summer (female duller). Fall immatures mostly warm buff; note tail pattern, perky behavior. ♪**Song**: fast series of varied notes. **Callnotes**: *weet* and *chack*.

BLUETHROAT   *Luscinia svecica*

Uncommon in summer in western and northern Alaska. Mainly in scrub willow thickets close to water, hard to see when not singing. Nests all across northern Europe and Asia; Alaskan birds go to southern Asia for winter. ▶ Mostly pale and drab except for male's bright *blue throat* (with red central spot). Female and young have white throat with dark border; on all, note *rusty patches* at base of tail. ♪**Song**: long, varied, ringing notes and imitations of other birds. **Callnote**: *chack*.

FIELDFARE   *Turdus pilaris*

Very rare visitor to eastern Canada and northeast U.S., mostly in winter. A few Alaskan records. (Common in Europe, also found in Greenland.) May associate with American Robins in woods, swamps. ▶ Like a bulky robin with pale gray rump and neck contrasting with black tail, chestnut brown back and wings. *Peachy tinge* on chest may be partly obscured by heavy blackish spots. ♪**Callnote**: harsh *chak-chak-chak*.

EYEBROWED THRUSH   *Turdus obscurus*

Rare visitor to islands of western Alaska, mostly during spring migration. ▶ Like a washed-out American Robin but with gray chest, white eyebrow, no white tail corners. Similar birds seen south of Alaska are almost certain to be pale variants of American Robin, *not* stray Eyebrowed Thrushes.

DUSKY THRUSH   *Turdus naumanni*

Very rare visitor to western Alaska, mostly in spring migration. ▶ Robin-shaped but with bright *rusty wings*, blackish mottling on head and chest.

AZTEC THRUSH   *Ridgwayia pinicola*

Rare visitor from Mexico to mountain forest of Arizona and west Texas, mostly in late summer. Shy, quiet, easily overlooked. ▶ Male blackish with white belly, strong *white pattern* in wings, black tail with broad white tip. Female similar pattern but browner. Juvenile has similar wing and tail pattern but body is brown with buff spots and streaks. ♪**Callnote**: soft *zhheer*.

SMALL NORTHERN THRUSHES

summer male

Northern Wheatear
6"

fall immatures

summer female

Bluethroat
5½"

female

male

RARE VISITORS

Fieldfare
10"

Dusky Thrush
10"

female

Aztec Thrush
9"

Eyebrowed Thrush
8½"

male

Bluebirds are small thrushes with beautiful colors and gentle voices. Living in open country, they nest in holes in trees or in birdhouses. In winter, flocks wander in seach of berries and wild fruits. Solitaires are slim, long-tailed thrushes that hide their nests on the ground.

EASTERN BLUEBIRD   *Sialia sialis*

Fairly common in farmland, parks, forest edge. Perches in the open, flutters to ground for insects, perches in trees to eat berries. Once suffering from lack of natural nest sites, bluebirds are making good comeback, partly thanks to nest boxes put out for them. ▶ Bright blue above, reddish brown on throat and chest, belly white. Female paler, duller than male. Juvenile heavily spotted, has telltale traces of blue above. ♪ **Song**: soft warbling notes in short series. **Callnote**: rich musical *true-lee*.

WESTERN BLUEBIRD   *Sialia mexicana*

Widespread in west, sometimes common in open country. Large flocks may gather in juniper woods in winter. ▶ Male deep purplish blue on upperparts and throat, reddish brown on chest and sometimes center of back; belly gray. *Blue throat* and gray belly are distinctions from Eastern Bluebird. Female much duller and grayer than male, with solid gray throat. Juvenile is spotted. Lazuli Bunting (p. 374) has white wing-bars, thicker bill. ♪ **Song**: short mellow warble. **Callnotes**: include soft *tung* or *tew,* often given in flight.

MOUNTAIN BLUEBIRD   *Sialia currucoides*

This ethereal bird haunts wide-open spaces: mountain meadows, high prairies, rangeland. In winter, also in juniper woods, desert, plowed fields. Hovers in midair before dropping to pick up insects from ground. Rarely strays east in winter. ▶ Sky-blue male almost unmistakable; see blue buntings on p. 374. Female gray with blue tinges; *gray flanks* contrast with white belly; longer wings and tail than other bluebirds. ♪ **Song**: a soft musical warble. **Callnote**: low *zhirr* or *zheew*.

TOWNSEND'S SOLITAIRE   *Myadestes townsendi*

Fairly common in west, in forest edge in mountains, juniper woods. Winters where it finds a good supply of berries, including juniper groves on plains. As name implies, never in flocks. ▶ Slim, long-tailed, perches upright. Smooth gray with *white eye-ring,* white outer tail feathers. *Buff wing patch* shows in flight. Mockingbird (p. 264) perches more horizontally, lacks eye-ring. Juvenile quite different, heavily spotted. ♪ **Song**: a long rich warble. **Callnote**: soft but far-carrying bell-like note.

BLUEBIRDS AND SOLITAIRE

female Eastern Bluebird, southwest race

Eastern Bluebird 7"

female

male

juvenile bluebirds have spots

female

Western Bluebird 7"

males

Townsend's Solitaire 8½"

adults

Mountain Bluebird 7¼"

female

male

BROWN THRUSHES

These shy forest birds are among our finest singers. They forage mostly on the ground. Also see Wood Thrush (next page).

HERMIT THRUSH　　*Catharus guttatus*

The only brown thrush likely in cold weather; migrates earlier in spring, later in fall than other thrushes. When alarmed, flicks wings, raises and lowers tail. ▶ *Red-brown tail* contrasts with duller back (can be hard to see). Overall color varies. Usually shows strong *eye-ring*. See Fox Sparrow (p. 346), also reddish tailed. ♪ **Song**: slow clear note followed by fast soft warble; repeated on different pitch. **Callnotes**: *chuck;* nasal *vreee?*

VEERY　　*Catharus fuscescens*

A common summer thrush of leafy woods of the northeast; scarce and local in west. Winters in South America. ▶ *Warm tawny-brown* above, with very little spotting on chest; *face* looks pale and *plain*. Western Veeries duller, with slightly more spots on chest. ♪ **Song**: breezy, spiraling whistles, gradually dropping, *veeyurr, veeyur, veeer, veer.* **Callnote**: soft descending *veeyew.*

SWAINSON'S THRUSH　　*Catharus ustulatus*

Common in summer in moist, cool forest of north and west. Elsewhere, often a numerous migrant in late spring and early fall. ▶ Usually shows bold buff eye-ring, buff at sides of chest. Back usually olive-brown (a bit redder along Pacific Coast). Winters in tropics; similar birds seen in winter are likely Hermit Thrushes. ♪ **Song**: starts with short clear note, then short phrases ending on higher pitch. **Callnote**: soft, liquid *hwoit.*

GRAY-CHEEKED THRUSH　　*Catharus minimus*

This shy thrush summers in far northern forest, winters in South America, migrates through east. In migration, usually seems outnumbered by Swainson's. ▶ Dull brown back, spotted chest. Paler around eye, but no sharp eye-ring. Face and neck *grayish,* lack strong buff tones. ♪ **Song**: breathy, rather nasal whistles, descending, *veeyer, vede veer, du veer.* **Callnote**: thin *veeyr.*

BICKNELL'S THRUSH　　*Catharus bicknelli*

Extremely similar to Gray-cheeked Thrush, safely identified only by range. Nests on a few mountaintops in New England and New York, also Quebec and Maritime Provinces, in forest of short trees. ▶ Like Gray-cheeked but tends to have more yellow on lower mandible, more chestnut tinge on tail. ♪ **Song**: like that of Gray-cheeked but sounds thinner, may rise at end.

BROWN THRUSHES

western

eastern

Hermit Thrush
7"

Veery
7"

Pacific Coast form

Swainson's Thrush
7"

Bicknell's Thrush
6³/₄"

Gray-cheeked Thrush
7¹/₄"

WOOD THRUSH, THRASHERS, AND CATBIRD

Wood Thrush is related to the birds on the previous page. Thrashers, catbirds, and mockingbirds **(family Mimidae)** are slim, long-tailed birds. They build open cup-shaped nests, well hidden in shrubs or cactus.

WOOD THRUSH *Hylocichla mustelina*

Biggest and spottiest brown thrush. Summers in eastern forest, sometimes in shady suburbs, foraging mostly on the ground. Declining numbers in recent years. ▶ Round *black spots* on white chest. Brown above, shading to reddish brown on head; bold eye-ring. Stronger markings than other brown thrushes. Brown Thrasher striped (not spotted) below, has yellow eyes, longer tail. ♪**Song:** slow, rich, fluty whistle, *eeyoh-lay*. **Callnotes:** include snappy *pep-pep-pep-pep*.

BROWN THRASHER *Toxostoma rufum*

A foxy-brown bird that lurks in eastern thickets. Usually feeds on ground or in bushes, but may sing from treetops. A few spend winter north and west of mapped range. Declining numbers in many areas. ▶ Rufous-brown above, striped below, with *long tail, yellow eyes*. In south Texas, see Long-billed Thrasher. ♪**Song:** long series of short, richly whistled phrases, each phrase usually given twice. **Callnotes:** hard *smack;* nasal *chaahh*.

LONG-BILLED THRASHER *Toxostoma longirostre*

South Texas only; very rarely farther north. Mostly in dense native brush, thickets. ▶ Like Brown Thrasher but has more *gray* on face, brighter orange eye, slightly longer curved bill. ♪**Song:** series of short whistled phrases; may double the phrases like Brown Thrasher. **Callnote:** whistled *cheeowp*.

SAGE THRASHER *Oreoscoptes montanus*

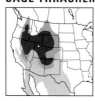

A drab thrasher of western sagebrush flats. Moves into other habitats in winter, including juniper woods, feeding on berries. Rarely strays far east. ▶ Shorter bill and tail than most thrashers. Dusty gray above, striped below, with white tail corners. Faded summer birds are less streaky; see Bendire's Thrasher (next page). ♪**Song:** repetition of clear warbled phrases. **Callnote:** *chuk*.

GRAY CATBIRD *Dumetella carolinensis*

Sometimes the catbird lurks in dense shrubbery, making odd noises; sometimes it forages boldly in the open, seeking insects on ground or eating berries in trees. Very common in east, uncommon and local west of the plains. A few linger through winter north of mapped range. ▶ Slim and long-tailed. Smooth gray with *black cap, chestnut undertail coverts*. ♪**Song:** disjointed series of clear notes, squeaks, whines. **Callnote:** catlike *meyew*.

Wood Thrush
7³/₄"

Brown Thrasher
11¹/₂"

Long-billed Thrasher
11¹/₂"

Sage Thrasher
8¹/₂"

Gray Catbird
8¹/₂"

Most of these use their bills to "thrash" the soil or leaf-litter in search of insects; they also eat many berries.

CURVE-BILLED THRASHER   *Toxostoma curvirostre*

Common in desert and arid brush, perching boldly in the open and calling loudly. Can thrive even in towns if it finds cholla cactus, its favored nest site. ▶ Moderately curved black bill; yellow-orange eyes. In east part of range (Texas), tends to have more obvious chest spots. Juvenile has shorter bill, sharper spots on upper chest. ♪ **Song:** long series of abrupt phrases with rich tone. **Callnote:** sharp *whit-wheet!* as if whistling for attention.

BENDIRE'S THRASHER   *Toxostoma bendirei*

Uncommon in southwest deserts. Usually outnumbered by Curve-billed Thrasher, but Bendire's is more numerous in some areas, such as desert grassland, farm edges. ▶ Short, *straight* bill slightly *paler at base;* yellow eyes, narrow sharp spots on upper chest. Juvenile Curve-billed can look almost identical. ♪ **Song:** long, sweet, continuous warble, unlike the choppy songs of most thrashers. No loud callnotes like Curve-billed.

CALIFORNIA THRASHER   *Toxostoma redivivum*

In chaparral and brushy hills near the Pacific Coast, this big thrasher is fairly common but hard to see except when it perches atop a tall bush to sing. Forages on ground under dense thickets. ▶ *Strongly curved* bill, plain dark brown overall, with pale eyebrow, dark eyes, buff wash on belly. ♪ **Song:** long series of choppy phrases, some whistled, some guttural. **Callnote:** low *chuck.*

CRISSAL THRASHER   *Toxostoma crissale*

The largest thrasher of the dry southwest, and the most elusive in dense cover. Fairly common along desert washes, locally in oaks of foothills. ▶ *Strongly curved* bill, *chestnut* undertail coverts. Dark whisker mark, *plain* breast, eyes dull gold to brown. ♪ **Song:** abrupt musical phrases, sometimes repeated, like other thrashers. **Callnote:** rolling *chorrychorry,* audible at some distance.

LE CONTE'S THRASHER   *Toxostoma lecontei*

A pale wraith of barren deserts, uncommon and local on arid saltbush flats. Shy, hard to approach; runs away on open ground with tail held high. ▶ Overall *pale sandy look* with contrasting darker tail, pale buff undertail coverts. Bill deeply curved but not as heavy as those of Crissal or California thrashers. ♪ **Song:** abrupt musical phrases, sometimes repeated, like other thrashers. **Callnote:** rising *too-reep.*

WESTERN THRASHERS

Curve-billed
on cactus

Curve-billed
Thrasher
11"

Bendire's
Thrasher
10"

California
Thrasher
12"

Crissal
Thrasher
11½"

Le Conte's
running

Le Conte's
Thrasher
11"

MOCKINGBIRDS AND SHRIKES

Mockingbirds are related to the thrashers and catbirds (previous pages). Shrikes (**family Laniidae**) are songbirds that live more like birds of prey, watching from high perches and then flying out to capture large insects, rodents, lizards, even small birds. They may impale dead prey on thorns or barbed wire, earning the nickname "butcher-bird." Their nests are well hidden in dense or thorny trees.

NORTHERN MOCKINGBIRD   *Mimus polyglottos*

Familiar in warmer climates, in cities, farms, woodland edges, desert. Often seen running on lawns, stopping to spread its wings abruptly. Eats mostly insects in summer, also many berries in winter. May sing all night on moonlit nights. Most common in south, it is called "Northern" because other mockingbirds live in the tropics. ▶ Slim, long-tailed. Pale gray with white wing patches (mainly visible in flight), white outer tail feathers. Juvenile has dark streaks on chest, darker eyes than adult. ♪**Song:** repeats a short phrase over and over, then switches to a different phrase, on and on, often including imitations of birds or other sounds. Sometimes leaps into the air and flutters back down while singing. **Callnotes:** loud *tchack* and nasal *sseee*.

BAHAMA MOCKINGBIRD   *Mimus gundlachii*

Very rare visitor to southeastern Florida. ▶ Bigger and dingier than Northern Mockingbird. Lacks white wing patch and white outer tail feathers (has small white tips on tail). Has heavy *dark streaks along flanks* (but note that juvenile Northern Mockingbird is also streaked below).

LOGGERHEAD SHRIKE   *Lanius ludovicianus*

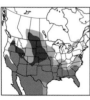

An open-country bird, perching on wires or bush tops. Still fairly common in south and west, but declining; mostly gone from northeast. ▶ Slim, perches horizontally. *Black mask,* black wings and tail with white markings visible mostly in flight. Juvenile has very narrow gray barring. In cold climates, see Northern Shrike. ♪**Song:** simple short phrase, clear or burry, repeated at intervals. **Callnotes:** include rasping *schaak, schaak.*

NORTHERN SHRIKE   *Lanius excubitor*

Summers in the far north, in spruces or thickets at edge of tundra. In winter, appears in farmland, open country farther south. ▶ Adult like Loggerhead Shrike but larger, with *mask distinctly reduced in front of eye;* faint gray *barring* on underparts; base of lower mandible often paler. Immature in first winter distinctly tinged *brown,* with narrow dusky mask and barring on chest. ♪**Song:** surprisingly musical, includes imitations of other birds. **Callnotes:** include harsh rasping notes.

MOCKINGBIRDS, SHRIKES

juvenile

Northern Mockingbird 10½"

adults

Bahama Mockingbird (rare) 11"

Loggerhead Shrike 9"

adult

juvenile

Northern Shrike 10"

immature

adult

fall juvenile (not to scale)

Waxwings **(family Bombycillidae)**, named for the waxy red tips on certain wing feathers, have soft voices and soft colors. Highly sociable, they are usually seen in flocks, eating berries or catching small flying insects. The Phainopepla belongs to the silky-flycatcher family **(Ptilogonatidae)**, mostly Central American birds that feed on mistletoe and other berries. Bulbuls **(family Pycnonotidae)** live mainly in Africa and southern Asia.

CEDAR WAXWING   *Bombycilla cedrorum*

These elegant little nomads may be present by the hundreds one month, absent the next, as their flocks rove about in search of wild berries. Their flocks break up into pairs for nesting in midsummer, but otherwise they are almost always in groups — it is rare to see just one waxwing. ▶ *Yellow band on tail tip,* narrow dark mask and throat, yellow belly, short crest. In far north or in winter, compare to Bohemian Waxwing. Juvenile has blurry streaks on plumage but shows diagnostic yellow tail band. ♪**Voice:** thin, high-pitched *sseee.*

BOHEMIAN WAXWING   *Bombycilla garrulus*

The Bohemian has its stronghold in the far northwest, summering in spruce forest and bogs. Winter flocks visit the prairie provinces and northern Rockies, and sometimes wander much farther afield, appearing unpredictably. Lone Bohemians may associate with Cedar Waxwing flocks. ▶ Like Cedar Waxwing (with crest and yellow tail tip) but larger and grayer, with *chestnut* undertail coverts, yellow and white pattern in wings. Streaky juvenile differs from young Cedar by color of undertail coverts. ♪**Voice:** rougher than that of Cedar Waxwing, a burry trilling sound.

PHAINOPEPLA   *Phainopepla nitens*

In southwestern desert, this slim bird perches bolt upright atop a shrub, guarding a clump of fruiting mistletoe. Sometimes gathers in flocks when other berries are abundant. Nomadic, may be locally numerous in some seasons, scarce in others. ▶ Slim and long-tailed, with spiky crest, red eyes. Male glossy black; *white wing patches* show mainly in flight. Female gray with paler wing edgings. ♪**Song:** soft musical gurgling. **Callnote:** soft *wurp?* with rising tone.

RED-WHISKERED BULBUL   *Pycnonotus jocosus*

Florida only (native to southern Asia). Escaped cagebirds established a wild population in the Miami suburb of Kendall in 1960, but have not spread far from there. ▶ Unlike any native bird, with black crest, white and red "whisker," red undertail coverts.

CRESTED BIRDS

Cedar Waxwing
7"

juvenile

female

male

Bohemian Waxwing
8"

males

Phainopepla
8"

adult

female

Red-whiskered Bulbul
7"

adult

DIPPER AND WAGTAILS

Dippers **(family Cinclidae)** are odd aquatic songbirds. Wagtails are found mostly in the Old World, reaching our area mainly in Alaska. Along with pipits (next page), they make up the **family Motacillidae**.

AMERICAN DIPPER *Cinclus mexicanus*

Along rushing mountain streams of the west, this stubby gray bird flies low over the water, pauses to bob up and down on a rock, then jumps into the water, swimming and diving, then walking on the stream bottom. The Dipper builds its nest of moss and twigs on a streambank, under a bridge, etc., often very close to water. Solitary at most seasons, it is never seen in flocks and almost never seen away from the water. ▶ Chunky, short-tailed, and gray all over, although white eyelids sometimes flash noticeably. Juvenile has pale bill, pale edgings on wings. ♪**Song**: loud, varied warbles, trills, metallic notes. **Callnote**: metallic *kz-z-z-zeet* with arresting sound, audible over noise of rushing water.

EASTERN YELLOW WAGTAIL *Motacilla tschutschensis*

On tundra in western and northern Alaska in summer, this slim bird perches atop low willows or walks on the ground, wagging its long tail up and down. Wagtails are mainly Old World birds, and the Eastern Yellow Wagtails that nest in Alaska (and in northeastern Asia) go to southern Asia or beyond for the winter. ▶ Dull olive above, yellow below. Rather long tail, black with white edges. Females somewhat duller than males. Yellow Wagtails reported in summer in the Rockies are probably American Pipits (next page), which can be bright buff below and unstreaked in breeding plumage. ♪**Call-note**: loud, slightly buzzy *tzeeeap*.

WHITE WAGTAIL *Motacilla alba*

Scarce and local in western Alaska in summer. Favors gravel bars, rocky streambeds; may nest under debris, in abandoned buildings, etc. Extremely rare visitor farther south on west coast in fall and winter. ▶ Strong black and white face pattern, black bib, pale gray back, big white wing patches. *Long tail* is especially obvious in flight. Immatures and winter adults have throat mostly white. ♪**Callnote**: loud *shizzik*.

BLACK-BACKED WAGTAIL *Motacilla lugens*

A bird of coastal Asia, rare in spring in far western Alaska. Has been found a few times farther south on west coast in fall and winter. ▶ Very similar to (and closely related to) White Wagtail, but adult in summer has *blacker back,* usually more white on chin. Larger white wing patch is evident only in flight. Immatures almost identical to young White Wagtails.

DIPPER AND WAGTAILS

American Dipper
7¹/₂"

juvenile

Eastern Yellow Wagtail
6¹/₂"

female

male

Black-backed Wagtail
7"

male

adults

White Wagtail
7"

walk and run on the ground in open places. Most larks **(family Alaudidae)** are found in the Old World. Pipits are related to wagtails (previous page). Males of all these birds may sing while fluttering high above the ground.

HORNED LARK *Eremophila alpestris*

Horned Larks love barren ground. They live in flocks in most seasons, on plowed fields, overgrazed pasture, tundra, shores. Nesting season begins early: males can be heard singing overhead in late winter. ▶ Black chest and ear marks (less obvious on females); tiny black "horns" hard to see. Face varies from white to yellow. In flight, looks pale with black on tail. Juveniles are duller, with streaks, spots. ♪**Song**: weak tinkling or twittering, from ground or in flight. **Callnotes**: thin *ssee-tilee.*

SKY LARK *Alauda arvensis*

Europe's most famous songbird, introduced many years ago to Vancouver Island, British Columbia, still found in small numbers around Victoria. Rarely strays from Siberia to islands of western Alaska. ▶ Rather thin bill, heavy streaks on back and chest, short crest, white outer tail feathers. ♪**Song**: torrent of musical trills and warbles, given while circling high in the air.

AMERICAN PIPIT *Anthus rubescens*

During the cooler months, flocks of these slim birds walk in open fields and mudflats, wagging their tails up and down. If flushed, the flock makes off with undulating flight and sharp calls. For summer, they go to tundra of far north and high mountains. ▶ Gray-brown above, whitish to buff below, with streaked chest. In summer, richer pinkish buff below with fainter streaks. Narrow white outer edge on tail; legs usually *blackish*. ♪**Song**: in high flight, continuous *chwee chwee chwee . . .* **Callnote**: sharp *djeet* or *jeejeet*, often while flying.

SPRAGUE'S PIPIT *Anthus spragueii*

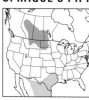

This prairie pipit never joins flocks; lone birds walk on ground among tall grass. ▶ Shorter-tailed than American Pipit, with *pale legs, scaly or striped* back pattern, black streaks on crown. Pale face makes dark eye conspicuous. White outer tail feathers obvious on takeoff. ♪**Song**: series of thin descending notes, repeated over and over in flight. **Callnote**: harsh *chaip* when flushed.

RED-THROATED PIPIT *Anthus cervinus*

A scarce summer bird in western Alaska, on hilly tundra. Very rare in fall farther south along Pacific Coast, with flocks of American Pipits. ▶ Spring male has pink chest, throat, and face. Females and fall birds duller, and fall immatures lack pink. All have strong stripes on back, pale legs, sharp face pattern. **Callnote**: sharp whiny *tsseeo.*

BIRDS OF OPEN GROUND

juvenile

female

Horned Lark
7½"

males

Sky Lark
7¼"

winter

American
Pipit
6½"

summer

Red-throated
Pipit
6"

fall
immature

spring
male

Sprague's Pipit
6½"

271

JAYS

The jays, crows, ravens, and magpies **(family Corvidae)**, often called "corvids" as a group, are thought to be among the most intelligent of birds. Most have strong, heavy bills, and most feed on a wide variety of items. Jays tend to be more colorful than other members of the family.

BLUE JAY *Cyanocitta cristata*

Brash, flashy Blue Jays are common in woods, parks, and yards throughout the east. Often noisy, can also slip quietly through the treetops. Most are permanent residents, but some move south in fall, and big flocks may pass some points on coast or lakeshores. ▶ Note crest, black necklace, white wing-bars and tail corners. Other blue-colored jays lack white pattern in wings and tail. Bluebirds (p. 256) and buntings (p. 374) are *much* smaller. ♪**Voice**: screaming *jayyy! jayyy!* is well known. Also musical *beadle-beadle,* many other notes, including good imitation of Red-shouldered Hawk.

STELLER'S JAY *Cyanocitta stelleri*

In shady forests of western mountains and coast, this dark jay is common, often lurking at picnic grounds or visiting bird feeders. It rarely wanders to plains or deserts in winter. ▶ The only all-dark jay with a crest. Small spots on forehead and near eye may be white (especially inland) or blue (near the coast). In the eastern Rockies, sometimes interbreeds with Blue Jay, producing intermediates. ♪**Voice**: harsh, scraping *kesssh, kessssh,* and fast *shek-shek-shek.* Also soft whistles, hawklike screams, many other notes.

GREEN JAY *Cyanocorax yncas*

Texas only. This gaudy tropical jay is common in riverside woods, parks, suburbs, oak groves, and dry brushland of southern Texas, often traveling in small flocks. ▶ Unmistakable. Mostly green, paler and yellower below, with purple and black head, bright *yellow outer tail feathers.* ♪**Voice**: wide variety of notes, including harsh *ch-ch-ch-ching,* fast *beetle-beetle,* and odd low snore.

BROWN JAY *Cyanocorax morio*

Texas only. A huge jay of the tropics, barely crossing the Rio Grande in the Falcon Dam area, where it lives in dense riverside woods. In small flocks, usually somewhat wary and elusive. ▶ *Large* and long-tailed. Dark sooty brown, paling to whitish on belly. Juveniles have yellow bills. Compare to Plain Chachalaca (p. 148). ♪**Voice**: shrill, explosive *pow!* or *keyoww!,* often heard when flock is on the move.

JAYS

Blue
Jay
11"

coastal
form

Steller's Jay
11½"

inland
form

Green Jay
10½"

juvenile

adult

Brown Jay
(rare, Texas only)
16"

273

BLUISH JAYS WITHOUT CRESTS

Several of these jay species have odd and complicated social lives, which have been the subjects of major ongoing field studies.

WESTERN SCRUB-JAY   *Aphelocoma californica*

The common "blue jay" of parks, yards, and woodlands of coastal California. Also widespread inland in the west, in scrub oaks or pinyon-juniper woods. Often seen in small groups. Omnivorous, but especially favors acorns. ▶ White throat bordered by streaked necklace; gray back contrasts with blue head, wings, and tail. Birds of the interior are distinctly paler, duller, and grayer than those along the coast. ♪ **Voice**: varied harsh calls, including *sshrreeap* and fast *shek-shek-shek*.

FLORIDA SCRUB-JAY   *Aphelocoma coerulescens*

Only in Florida, where it is restricted to native scrub oak habitats. These habitats are threatened, and so is the bird; both are unique and deserve protection. This jay lives in social groups at all seasons, even nesting as a group activity. ▶ Like Western Scrub-Jay, but with paler forehead. No other Florida bird is similar. Blue Jay (previous page) has crest, white spots in wings and tail. ♪ **Voice**: hoarse, rasping *shrreck* and various other notes.

ISLAND SCRUB-JAY   *Aphelocoma insularis*

Lives only on Santa Cruz Island, one of the Channel Islands off the coast of southern California. ▶ Like Western Scrub-Jay but *larger, more richly colored*, with heavier bill. The only jay on the Channel Islands.

MEXICAN JAY   *Aphelocoma ultramarina*

In mountain canyons and oak woods near the Mexican border, this jay is locally common. Found in flocks in all seasons, and even nests as a group activity. Formerly called Gray-breasted Jay. ▶ Plain dull blue above, *smooth gray* below. Juveniles in Arizona/New Mexico have pale bills at first, gradually becoming blackish. More heavily built than Western Scrub-Jay, and *lacks* contrasting white throat and dark necklace. ♪ **Voice**: nasal *zheek?* or *wink?*, softer than calls of most jays.

PINYON JAY   *Gymnorhinus cyanocephalus*

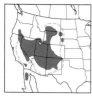

In arid pinyon pine and yellow pine woods of the west, this odd short-tailed jay (more like a small blue crow) wanders in large flocks. Highly sociable, almost never seen singly. Well named, it feeds very heavily on seeds of pinyon pine. ▶ Stocky, short-tailed, spike-billed, and *dull blue all over*. Juvenile is grayer. Other blue-colored jays have different shape, are paler below. ♪ **Voice**: nasal *eye-eye-eye*, laughing *yah-ah-ah-ah*, many other notes.

JAYS WITHOUT CRESTS

inland form

Western Scrub-Jay
11½"

coastal form

Florida Scrub-Jay
11½"

Island Scrub-Jay
(Santa Cruz Island only)
13"

juvenile

Mexican Jay
12"

adult

subadult

juvenile

adult

Pinyon Jay
10½"

BLACK-BILLED MAGPIE   *Pica hudsonia*

This flashy, long-tailed bird is very common over much of the west, in open country, ranchland, forest edge, streamside trees, towns. Often seen in pairs or small flocks, walking on the ground in open fields. Builds bulky, domed stick nests in trees. Rarely wanders a little east of range in winter; those seen farther afield may be escaped cagebirds. Formerly called Black-billed Magpie. ▶ Unmistakable in most areas. Green and blue gloss on wings and long tail. Big white wing patches flash out in flight. In California, see Yellow-billed Magpie. ♪**Voice**: harsh chattering *che-che-che-che-chek;* rising whine, *neeeyick;* varied other notes.

YELLOW-BILLED MAGPIE   *Pica nuttalli*

California only. Fairly common in some central valley regions (but may be declining), in areas with open pastures or farmland next to groves of oak or cottonwood. Magpies are omnivores, but insects make up a major part of their diet; also eat many acorns in winter, and will feed on carrion. ▶ Unmistakable in its range. Like American Magpie but a bit smaller, with *yellow bill,* variable yellow skin near eyes. ♪**Voice**: similar to that of American Magpie.

GRAY JAY   *Perisoreus canadensis*

In the north woods and in high mountain forests, this jay is often oddly tame, following hikers or entering campsites and picnic grounds to beg for scraps. Often in small family groups, but not in large flocks. Very seldom moves away from dense evergreen forest. ▶ Fluffy and gray, paler below. Head pattern varies by region: blackish patch on nape may be very limited or may extend to top of head. Juvenile is mostly dark charcoal gray at first, with *paler whisker mark.* ♪**Voice**: soft whistled *weeoo,* low *tuck,* and a variety of other notes.

CLARK'S NUTCRACKER   *Nucifraga columbiana*

A spike-billed bird of mountains, often at high elevations, near treeline. Fearless around campgrounds and scenic overlooks, seeking handouts. Gathers and buries large numbers of pine seeds in fall, finds them to eat during winter. In drought winters, a few nutcrackers may wander down out of the mountains. ▶ Unmistakable. Big white patches in wings and tail very noticeable in flight. Gray Jay lacks white in wings and tail, has *much* smaller bill. ♪**Voice**: variable, including a hoarse, scraping *kkhhhaaaaaaa,* audible at some distance.

MAGPIES, ETC.

Black-billed Magpie 19"

Yellow-billed Magpie 17"

adults

juvenile

Gray Jay 11½"

Clark's Nutcracker 12"

juvenile

adult

277

AMERICAN CROW *Corvus brachyrhynchos*

Widespread and familiar, mostly in open country, but increasingly numerous in cities also. Often in flocks; may gather in huge roosting concentrations in winter. ▶ All black with strong bill, rather short square-tipped tail. Compare to other crows and ravens, below. Members of the blackbird family (see p. 332) are all smaller, with different voices and shapes. ♪ **Voice:** harsh *caw! caw!* familiar in many regions. Also other hoarse notes.

FISH CROW *Corvus ossifragus*

Common in parts of southeast, extending range north on coast and inland along rivers. Typically near water, foraging on beaches, in swamps. ▶ Slightly smaller than American Crow, but recognized with certainty only by sound. ♪ **Voice:** high-pitched, nasal *kah-hah*, second note lower. Also other nasal caws (but young American Crows also have high-pitched, nasal voices at first).

NORTHWESTERN CROW *Corvus caurinus*

Northwest coast only, immediate coast and islands from southern Alaska to Washington State. Often forages on beaches, in tidal pools. ▶ Very similar to American Crow (may be only a local subspecies); slightly smaller, with somewhat hoarser voice. Best recognized by range and habitat.

TAMAULIPAS CROW *Corvus imparatus*

South Texas only, scarce visitor to Brownsville area (especially around landfills). ▶ *Small* for a crow, glossy blue-black. Chihuahuan Raven (common in south Texas) much larger, with wedge-shaped tail. Great-tailed Grackle (p. 336) has pale eyes, usually longer tail. ♪ **Voice:** very low croak.

COMMON RAVEN *Corvus corax*

A "songbird" the size of a hawk. Mostly scarce (but increasing) in the east, common in the north and west, in forests, mountains, deserts. Also moving into cities in some regions. A resourceful predator and scavenger. Pairs often seen soaring high in the sky. ▶ Much larger than crows but best known by wedge-shaped tail, very thick bill, shaggy throat feathers. ♪ **Voice:** deep echoing croak; other notes including screams, whistles, gurgles.

CHIHUAHUAN RAVEN *Corvus cryptoleucus*

Common in wide-open grassland of the Chihuahuan desert. Unlike Common Ravens in the southwest, often gathers in very large flocks. ▶ Shape of Common Raven but slightly smaller, with smaller bill, different voice. Usually in open grassland (in southwest, Common Raven is mostly in mountains or in drier cactus desert). ♪ **Voice:** flat, dry *kraaaak*, without deep resonant tone.

CROWS AND RAVENS

American Crow 19"
Northwestern Crow 16"
Fish Crow 17"
(identify by voice, range)

Tamaulipas Crow 15"

Chihuahuan Raven 20"

ravens in flight

Common Raven 25"

CHICKADEES

Chickadees and titmice **(family Paridae)** are little acrobats of the treetops, flitting about and clambering on branches and twigs, seeking insects. All nest in holes in trees, and all are essentially non-migratory.

BLACK-CAPPED CHICKADEE   *Poecile atricapillus*

Little roving flocks of Black-capped Chickadees are often the brightest spark of life in bleak winter woods. They are also popular visitors to bird feeders, dropping in for sunflower seeds or suet. In the northeast, quite a few sometimes move south in fall, but flight only reaches the southern edge of usual range. ▶ Small and lively, with black cap and bib, gray back, buff wash on sides. Almost identical to Carolina Chickadee; see below (and other chickadees on next page). Male House Sparrow (p. 344) is sometimes misidentified as a chickadee. ♪ **Song:** clear whistled *fee bee* or *fee bee-ee*, first note higher. Easily imitated. **Callnotes:** quite varied, including a chattering *chick-a-dee-dee-dee*.

CAROLINA CHICKADEE   *Poecile carolinensis*

Very common in woods of the southeast, replacing Black-capped Chickadee abruptly along a boundary that spans half the continent. Like other chickadees, it regularly comes to feeders for seeds or suet. ▶ Extremely similar to Black-capped Chickadee. Averages slightly smaller (difference not apparent in the wild). In fresh plumage (late fall and winter), Black-capped shows more obvious white edgings on feathers of forward part of wing, while Carolina is plain gray there, but both can look plain gray-winged in worn summer plumage. Black bib may have neater lower edge on Carolina, more ragged edge on Black-capped. Range is best clue (see detail map). ♪ **Song:** usually fast four-noted whistle, *see-bee-see-bay,* first and third notes very high-pitched. Where Carolina and Black-capped Chickadees meet, each may learn to sing the song of the other. **Callnotes:** varied, including fast *chick-a-dee-dee-dee*.

MOUNTAIN CHICKADEE   *Poecile gambeli*

This chickadee replaces its relatives in higher mountains of the west, and is often very common in tall pines and other evergreens. Except when nesting, it travels with mixed flocks of other small birds. A few sometimes wander into the lowlands in winter. ▶ Typical chickadee pattern, but black cap is broken by distinct *white eyebrow.* Eyebrow may be broad or narrow; may be hard to see on summer birds in worn plumage. ♪ **Song:** whistled *see dee dee,* first note higher. **Callnotes:** varied, including a fast, husky *tsick-a-dee-dee*.

280 TYPICAL SONGBIRDS

CHICKADEES

fledgling

Black-capped Chickadee
5¼"

adults

Mountain Chickadee
5¼"

Carolina Chickadee
4¾"

For identifying chickadees in the eastern U.S., check the map: Carolina Chickadee to the south of the line, Black-capped to the north of it (plus a few at high elevations in southern Appalachians, shown in paler color).

CHESTNUT-BACKED CHICKADEE   *Poecile rufescens*

A dark, colorful chickadee of the northwest. Usually in dense, wet evergreen forest; in California, also ranges into pine-oak woods, streamside willows. ▶ Rich *chestnut back and sides* contrasting with gray wings; sooty brown cap (may look black). (In the form found along the central California coast, the sides are gray, not chestnut.) Where it overlaps with Boreal Chickadee locally in northwest, Chestnut-backed is always much more richly colored. ♪ **Voice**: husky, burry *schick-a-zhee-zhee;* varied other notes.

BOREAL CHICKADEE   *Poecile hudsonica*

A dusty brown chickadee of northern forest. Fairly common but easy to overlook as it forages in dense spruces. South of the mapped range it is only a rare stray, but it may move some distance south, usually in the same winters that have big southward flights of Black-capped Chickadees. ▶ Dingy look with *brown cap, brown sides.* Wings always plain, without obvious pale edgings on feathers. Overall color varies from warmer to grayer brown, but always has *dusky wash on cheeks,* showing less white there than other chickadees. ♪ **Voice**: varied; includes a hoarse *schick-ah-zzay-zzay.*

GRAY-HEADED CHICKADEE   *Poecile cincta*

Rare and seldom seen, a resident of willow scrub in northern Alaska and northwest Canada, mostly in areas that are far from any roads. ▶ Usually paler and grayer than Boreal Chickadee, with slightly longer tail, paler edgings on wing feathers. Best distinction is Gray-headed's very large clear *white cheek patch.* Many reports of this species are based on grayish juvenile Boreal Chickadees in summer. ♪ **Voice**: varied; includes a thin, whining *deee deeer.*

MEXICAN CHICKADEE   *Poecile sclateri*

Common in the mountain forests of Mexico, this chickadee reaches our area only in Chiricahua Mountains (Arizona) and locally in Animas Mountains (New Mexico). There it lives mainly in dense coniferous forest at upper elevations. ▶ Most easily known by range, as it is the only chickadee in these mountains. (Elsewhere in the southwest, it is replaced by Mountain Chickadee; see p. 272.) Note the *large* black bib, extensive *gray wash on sides.* ♪ **Voice**: wheezy *schick-ah-dzzee,* variety of other notes.

CHICKADEES

central California
coast

**Chestnut-backed
Chickadee**
5"

widespread
form

**Boreal
Chickadee**
5¼"

**Gray-headed
Chickadee**
5½"

**Mexican
Chickadee**
5"

TITMICE

are in the same family as chickadees but have crested heads.

TUFTED TITMOUSE *Baeolophus bicolor*

Active and conspicuous in the treetops of eastern forests, also city parks and suburbs, often visiting feeders for sunflower seeds. In pairs or small flocks, will join flocks with other birds in winter. Has expanded its range northward in recent decades. ▶ Mostly gray and white with perky crest, pale face, black forehead, *rusty* sides. ♪ **Song:** whistled *peeto-peeto-peeto.* **Callnotes:** varied; include whining scolds, *see-nyahh* or *sesee-jjeeer.*

BLACK-CRESTED TITMOUSE *Baeolophus atricristatus*

Replacing the Tufted Titmouse in parts of Texas and southwest Oklahoma, formerly treated as part of the same species. ▶ Mostly gray and white with white forehead, *black crest.* Where range meets that of Tufted Titmouse, they interbreed, and some birds have intermediate markings. ♪ **Voice:** like that of Tufted Titmouse; whistled *peeto-peeto-peeto,* whining scolds.

OAK TITMOUSE *Baeolophus inornatus*

Drab but perky, in pairs in all seasons. Common in oak woods of California, also well-wooded suburbs. Oak and Juniper Titmice were formerly considered one species, Plain Titmouse. ▶ Gray or brownish gray with very plain face, slightly paler underparts. Short crest may be raised or almost flattened against head. Compare to other small gray birds such as Bushtit (p. 294), also next species. ♪ **Song:** fast whistled *peta-peta-peta-peta . . .* **Callnotes:** include a harsh *tsick-a-dee-dee.*

JUNIPER TITMOUSE *Baeolophus ridgwayi*

Widespread and sometimes common in dry woods of juniper and pinyon pine in the inland west. ▶ Very similar to Oak Titmouse, usually a bit grayer (less brownish). Best identified by range, entirely separate except very locally in northeast California. ♪ **Song:** fast whistled *di-di-di-di-di,* usually less two-syllabled than in Oak Titmouse. **Callnotes:** varied; include a fast *tsikadeedee.*

BRIDLED TITMOUSE *Baeolophus wollweberi*

Common in its limited U.S. range, mainly in oak woods of foothills and canyons near Mexican border. Also found in big cottonwoods along lowland streams, especially in winter. ▶ Black and white "bridle" pattern on face, gray and black crest. Sometimes confused with Mountain Chickadee (p. 280). ♪ **Song:** fast series of short whistles. **Callnotes:** varied; include a fast *tsikadeedee.*

TITMICE

Black-crested
Titmouse
6½"

Tufted
Titmouse
6½"

Oak
Titmouse
5¾"

Juniper
Titmouse
5¾"

Bridled
Titmouse
5½"

285

NUTHATCHES AND CREEPER

Nuthatches **(family Sittidae)** are short-tailed birds that walk up, down, and around tree trunks and limbs. They nest in holes in trees. Creepers **(family Certhiidae)** tuck their nests under loose bark.

WHITE-BREASTED NUTHATCH   *Sitta carolinensis*

Common in leafy forest, also thrives in parks and suburbs with big trees. Visits bird feeders for sunflower seeds or suet. In winter, often travels in flocks with chickadees and other birds. ▶ *All-white face* and chest, set off by narrow *black* (or dark gray) crown stripe. Can show much orange-brown on lower belly. ♪ **Voice:** nasal notes, slow *yaank, yaank,* and fast *wahwahwahwahwah.*

RED-BREASTED NUTHATCH   *Sitta canadensis*

Favors dense conifers of the north and the high mountains in summer, but may be in other trees, especially in fall migration. Often rather quiet and tame. In some years, large numbers move south and into lowlands in fall. ▶ Typical head-down nuthatch behavior, *black* eye stripe, *white* eyebrow. Buffy orange below, blue-gray back. ♪ **Voice:** nasal *hennk, hennk,* rather high and soft.

PYGMY NUTHATCH   *Sitta pygmaea*

Common in pine forest of western mountains, also locally along coast. Usually in small flocks, clambering on high twigs and pine cones, making little piping notes. Rarely wanders to lowlands in winter. ▶ Gray-brown cap down to eye, pale below, gray back, white spot on nape. In southeast, replaced by next species. ♪ **Voice:** high thin *peep,* repeated, and squeaky *weevee.*

BROWN-HEADED NUTHATCH   *Sitta pusilla*

In pine woods of the southeast, this nuthatch may be heard before it is seen. Travels in pairs or small groups, often staying in treetops, feeding on insects and pine seeds. ▶ Brown cap down to eye, pale below, gray back, white nape spot. Almost identical to Pygmy Nuthatch, best identified by range. ♪ **Voice:** squeaky *ki-dee,* sometimes running into excited chatter; also fast *dip dip.*

BROWN CREEPER   *Certhia americana*

Like a piece of bark come to life, the creeper creeps up tree trunks and major limbs, bracing itself with its stiff tail feathers. Reaching the top of one tree, it flies down to base of next. Often common but easily overlooked, may join flocks of chickadees and nuthatches in winter. ▶ Streaked back, pale eyebrow, rusty base of tail. Behavior unmistakable. ♪ **Callnote:** high, reedy *tseeeee.* **Song:** thin high series, *tee see, teesyew, seee.* Pattern varies.

SMALL TREE-CLIMBERS

White-breasted Nuthatch 5½"

Red-breasted Nuthatch 4½"

Brown-headed Nuthatch 4¼"

Pygmy Nuthatch 4¼"

Brown Creeper 5"

287

WRENS

Wrens (**family Troglodytidae**) are very active little birds, mostly with plain colors but impressive voices. The four below all nest in holes in trees or in birdhouses or other cavities.

HOUSE WREN — *Troglodytes aedon*

Fussing in brushpiles, singing its bubbling song from trees, the House Wren is familiar from deep woods to back yards. Shy but curious; popping up in the open, it may hold its tail straight up. ▶ Small, hyperactive, with thin bill. Plainer than most wrens; shows faint eyebrow, thin *eye-ring,* bars on wings and tail. Some in Arizona mountains (intergrades with "Brown-throated" race of western Mexico) are warmer buff on throat. ♪ **Song:** very fast, musical, jumbled or bubbling series. **Callnotes:** rough, nasal *dzzhheer,* other harsh, scolding notes.

WINTER WREN — *Troglodytes troglodytes*

A stub-tailed gnome that haunts northern evergreen forest in summer, moving south in winter. Often very hard to see, creeping like a rodent under fallen logs, through dense thickets, along streambanks. ▶ Small and dark. Suggests House Wren but has *shorter tail,* stronger dark barring on flanks, different callnote. ♪ **Song:** very high-pitched, tinkling, trilling series, running on and on. **Callnotes:** squeaky *kimp-kimp,* unlike harsh scold of House Wren; sometimes a dry chatter.

BEWICK'S WREN — *Thryomanes bewickii*

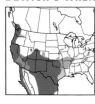

Common in parts of west, in dry woods, thickets, riversides. Has mysteriously vanished from most of eastern range. Pairs move actively in undergrowth and low trees. ▶ *White eyebrow;* longish tail, often flipped about. Eastern birds more richly colored, can suggest Carolina Wren, but note *white corners of tail,* paler underparts. ♪ **Song:** variable. In west, usually two trills, buzzy or musical. In east, more complex, suggesting Song Sparrow. **Callnotes:** varied. Harsh *dzheerr* and *djjk,* low *burdick.*

CAROLINA WREN — *Thryothorus ludovicianus*

In undergrowth of southeastern woods, these chunky wrens live in pairs in all seasons. Scarcer toward the north, but some reach Canada, though numbers drop after harsh winters. ▶ Richly colored: chestnut above, butterscotch below, with bold white eyebrow. Lacks white tail corners of Bewick's. ♪ **Song:** rollicking, full-toned chant, *liberty-liberty-liberty-whew.* Many variations. Members of a pair may sing duets. **Callnotes:** ringing, descending *cheeyr-r-r-r-r-r.* Also metallic *dink dink* and wide variety of other notes.

WRENS

House Wren
4³/₄"

House Wren
at birdhouse

Winter Wren
4"

western
form

eastern
form

Bewick's Wren
5¹/₄"

Carolina
Wren
5³/₄"

MARSH WREN   *Cistothorus palustris*

Heard more often than seen, this wren flits furtively through the cattails and bulrushes of dense marshes. Sometimes sings in the open or pops up to investigate odd noises. Nest is a globe-shaped mass attached to stems above water. ▶ Bold white eyebrow, solid brown crown, *white stripes* on black triangle in center of back. ♪ **Song:** variable rush of sputtering, scraping, squeaking, and bubbling notes. **Callnote:** dry *chuk-chuk.*

SEDGE WREN   *Cistothorus platensis*

Sometimes found with Marsh Wren but more often in short-grass marshes, damp sedge meadows. Uncommon, may be declining. Usually very secretive. ▶ Buffy overall with *narrow streaks* on crown and back. Has shorter bill, much less obvious eyebrow, more pattern on wings than Marsh Wren. Compare to marsh sparrows (p. 348). ♪ **Song:** dry staccato chatter speeding into a dry trill. **Callnotes:** rich *chyip,* dry *dzzt.*

ROCK WREN   *Salpinctes obsoletus*

A pallid wren of rocky desert, badlands, rockslides. Usually on ground or bobbing up and down atop a boulder. Nests inside rock crevices; makes odd "sidewalk" of pebbles in front of nest. ▶ Overall pale look; fine streaks on chest not always apparent. As it flies away, short tail shows rusty at base, *buff* outer corners. ♪ **Song:** short phrases, each repeated several times, like a weak mockingbird. **Callnote:** loud ringing *tk-keeer.*

CANYON WREN   *Catherpes mexicanus*

The clear, ringing song of this wren seems well suited to wild rocky canyons. Often hard to see as it scoots about in boulder piles and cracks in canyon walls, seeking insects in crevices with its very long bill. ▶ Mostly dark chestnut with clear *white throat and chest.* Black bars on short *reddish* tail. ♪ **Song:** rippling cascade of clear notes, *tetetetetete tew tew teew twee tewee tuweee,* becoming slower and lower toward end. **Callnote:** short *bzzzt.*

CACTUS WREN   *Campylorhynchus brunneicapillus*

Brash, noisy, often in family groups, Cactus Wrens are conspicuous in the desert. Also in dry brushland, suburbs. Football-shaped nest built in cactus, spiny shrub. ▶ More boldly barred, striped, and spotted than other desert birds, with sharp white eyebrow. See Sage Thrasher (p. 260). Juvenile has less spotting on chest. ♪ **Voice:** harsh *chug-chug-chug,* loud scraping notes.

WET AND DRY WRENS

Sedge
Wren
4 1/2"

Marsh Wren
5"

Rock
Wren
6"

Canyon
Wren
6"

singing
adult

Cactus
Wren
8 1/2"

juvenile
Cactus
Wren

GNATCATCHERS AND WRENTIT

Gnatcatchers **(family Sylviidae)** are tiny birds with long tails that they flip about as they hop actively through foliage. The underside of the tail provides an important field mark but is often hard to see.

BLUE-GRAY GNATCATCHER   *Polioptila caerulea*

Common in eastern forest, but may be hard to see in summer as it flits about high in leafy trees. More easily observed in the west, where it inhabits lower oaks and junipers. ▶ Blue-gray above, whitish below, with white eye-ring. *White outer tail feathers* (tail looks *all white* from below). In spring and summer, male has thin black eyebrow. ♪**Callnote:** thin, whining *shpeew*. **Song:** thin, squeaky warble, with whining notes tossed in.

BLACK-TAILED GNATCATCHER   *Polioptila melanura*

A desert bird, thriving in dense mesquite brush or on sparse open flats. In pairs in all seasons. ▶ Outermost tail feathers (seen from below) have white edges and tips, most of tail *black*. In spring and summer, male has *black cap*. Blue-gray Gnatcatcher (wetter habitats in summer) reaches desert in winter. ♪**Voice:** varied, including scraping *ch-ch-ch-cheh;* hard *chip-chip-chip* like call of Verdin (next page); light lisping; harsh *djjeer.*

CALIFORNIA GNATCATCHER   *Polioptila californica*

Rare and local on coastal slope of southern California; an endangered species. Restricted to areas with dense low cover of native plants (especially coastal sage scrub). ▶ Tail mostly black, with narrow white edges showing from below; male has black cap in summer. Like Black-tailed Gnatcatcher (in deserts east of the mountains in California) but *darker gray* below. ♪**Voice:** varied; includes kittenlike *meeyew,* rising and falling.

BLACK-CAPPED GNATCATCHER   *Polioptila nigriceps*

(Not illustrated.) Very rare in southern Arizona, in desert canyons, dense brush of mesquite, hackberry. ▶ Underside of tail *mostly white* (as on Blue-gray Gnatcatcher), but male has *black cap* in spring and summer (like male Black-tailed). Female like Blue-gray, *slightly* longer-billed. ♪**Voice:** includes thin *speeyeew,* more drawn-out than note of Blue-gray.

WRENTIT   *Chamaea fasciata*

An odd little bird that skulks in dense low thickets and chaparral near Pacific Coast. Usually hard to see, but its loud voice is heard often. Perhaps related to babblers **(family Timaliidae)** of Old World. ▶ Long tail, stubby bill. Overall gray-brown to reddish brown, with staring *pale eye,* blurry stripes on chest. ♪**Voice:** loud ringing note repeated over and over, usually running into a rapid trill. At close range, a low *trr, trrr.*

GNATCATCHERS AND WRENTIT

female

Blue-gray Gnatcatcher
4½"

male

juvenile

female

Black-tailed Gnatcatcher
4½"

summer male

California Gnatcatcher
4½"

summer male

Wrentit
6¼"

Kinglets (**family Regulidae**), Verdin (**family Remizidae**), and Bushtit (**family Aegithalidae**) are among the smallest songbirds.

RUBY-CROWNED KINGLET *Regulus calendula*

A hyperactive midget, common in winter in woods and thickets of south. Harder to see in summer, when often high in tall conifers. Flicks wings open and shut, especially when excited. ▶ Tiny, short-tailed, with wing-flicking action, bold *white eye-ring*. Wings usually show one strong white wing-bar, with a *black bar* just behind it. Male's ruby crown patch raised only in excitement. *Empidonax* flycatchers (p. 244) more upright, longer-tailed. See Hutton's Vireo (next page). ♪**Callnote**: dry *chi-dit*. **Song**: starts with thin notes, turns surprisingly loud: *see see see syoo syoo syoo chifferty chifferty chifferty.*

GOLDEN-CROWNED KINGLET *Regulus satrapa*

Unlike the Ruby-crown, this kinglet prefers evergreens in all seasons and is often hard to see in dense cover of tall conifers. Flicks its wings open and shut as it forages. Migrates late in fall, sometimes seen in flocks in November. ▶ Tiny, short-tailed, with wing-flicking action, *stripes on face,* no eye-ring. Center of crown orange on male, yellow on female. Wing pattern like Ruby-crown's. ♪**Callnote**: very high, thin *see-see-see*. **Song**: thin *see* notes, like call, speeding up to a very high trill.

BUSHTIT *Psaltriparus minimus*

Long-tailed western birdlets, common in oak woods, junipers, scrub. In flocks for most of year; flock may go unnoticed in a dense tree until thirty or more fly out, in single file. Nest is a hanging pouch, tightly woven of plant material. ▶ Tiny, plain, with small bill, longish tail. Females have pale eyes, males dark eyes. Head browner on coastal birds. Young males in west Texas may have black ear patches. ♪**Voice**: light ticking and lisping, given constantly by flocks on the move.

VERDIN *Auriparus flaviceps*

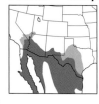

This little bird thrives in desert, arid brushland, open suburbs. Feeds on insects, perches on flowers to take nectar, visits hummingbird feeders. In pairs or solitary in all seasons. Nest is a bulky, twiggy globe with entrance on side. ▶ Very small, mostly gray, long-tailed. Adults have some yellow on head, red on shoulder (often hidden). Juvenile plain gray; suggests Bushtit, but has pale bill base, different habitat and voice, and is never in flocks. ♪**Voice**: varied; includes clear *cheeyilp*, hard rapid chipping, whistled *tee tyew tep tep.*

VARIOUS MICRO-BIRDS

Ruby-crowned Kinglet 4"

Golden-crowned Kinglet 3³/₄"

male

female

western interior

female

Pacific Coast

Bushtit 4¹/₂"

"Black-eared" form

male

Verdin 4¹/₂"

adults

juvenile

295

Vireos **(family Vireonidae)** seek insects among foliage of trees and thickets and sometimes eat berries as well. Most are persistent singers (and have harsh, scolding callnotes as well). Compared to warblers (next section), vireos are mostly larger, thicker-billed, and less active.

YELLOW-THROATED VIREO   *Vireo flavifrons*

Fairly common in eastern woods, especially in oaks, but often stays unseen among the foliage. Rather slow and deliberate in foraging, usually remaining in higher levels of trees. ▶ *Yellow "spectacles" and throat,* white wing-bars, gray rump. See Pine Warbler (p. 314) and other warblers. ♪ **Song**: short whistled phrases separated by pauses, given with a hoarse, burry quality: *zeyoo . . . breeyoowit . . . wheeyay . . .* etc.

WHITE-EYED VIREO   *Vireo griseus*

Their snappy little song is often heard in thickets in the southeast, but White-eyeds can be hard to see as they forage in dense undergrowth. ▶ *Yellow "spectacles"* around white eyes. Olive-gray above, whitish below, with two white wing-bars and with yellow tinge on sides. Immatures in first fall and winter have darker gray-brown eyes. ♪ **Song**: short and emphatic jumble, variable but usually beginning and ending with sharp notes: *pick-up-a-reeeal-chick!*

HUTTON'S VIREO   *Vireo huttoni*

A busy little vireo of western oak woods, common but easily overlooked. Surprisingly similar to the Ruby-crowned Kinglet, and even flicks its wings in kinglet style. ▶ Compact and chunky, with eye-ring and wing-bars. Has thicker bill than Ruby-crowned Kinglet, and different wing pattern, *lacking* the black bar behind the second white wing-bar. Also see Cassin's Vireo (next page). ♪ **Song**: simple note, repeated monotonously: *su-wee . . . suwee . . . suwee . . .* or *syoo . . . syoo . . .* etc.

BLACK-CAPPED VIREO   *Vireo atricapilla*

Rare and local in central Texas and Oklahoma in summer, in patches of scrubby oak in rocky hill country; an endangered species. Smaller and more active than most vireos, often hard to see in dense thickets. ▶ Male's *black hood* contrasts with *white spectacles* and throat, red eyes. Greenish back, yellow wash on sides, with two wing-bars. Female has slaty, not black, head; suggests Blue-headed Vireo (next page) but smaller, with much darker head. ♪ **Song**: squeaky phrases broken by pauses: *chiddle-deet . . . veechew . . . chiudeedeet . . .* etc.

VIREOS

Yellow-throated Vireo 5½"

White-eyed Vireo 5"

Ruby-crowned Kinglet for comparison

Hutton's Vireo 4¾"

female

Black-capped Vireo 4½"

male

297

BLUE-HEADED VIREO *Vireo solitarius*

Common in summer in mixed forest of northeast and Appalachians; some winter in southeast. Forages from mid- to upper levels of trees. This and the next two were formerly considered one species, "Solitary Vireo." ▶ White *"spectacles,"* wing-bars. *Blue-gray head* contrasts with white throat, green back, yellow sides. ♪ **Song:** clear whistled phrases with pauses: *suweet . . . seeoo . . . seeoowip . . .* Like Red-eyed Vireo's but higher-pitched.

CASSIN'S VIREO *Vireo cassinii*

Pacific Coast and northwest in summer, mostly in oak and conifer woods. A few winter along rivers in southwest. ▶ Like a duller version of Blue-headed Vireo; best separated by range. Where they overlap, some may not be identifiable. Plumbeous Vireo is more purely gray, slightly larger, less active. Cassin's often flicks its wings nervously, like Hutton's Vireo (previous page). ♪ **Song:** like Blue-headed Vireo's but with burry sound.

PLUMBEOUS VIREO *Vireo plumbeus*

In the inland west, this lead-colored bird summers in pines and oaks of mountain canyons. A few winter along rivers in southwest. ▶ Gray and white, with only a tinge of color in fresh plumage (fall). Contrasting white throat and "spectacles," two wing-bars. In faded plumage of late summer, wing-bars less obvious, resembles Gray Vireo. ♪ **Song:** short whistled phrases with burry quality, much like Cassin's Vireo.

GRAY VIREO *Vireo vicinior*

Fairly common, but may be missed by birders because it inhabits arid, scrubby juniper woods of Great Basin region. Winters mostly in northwest Mexico. ▶ Gray above, whitish below, with *narrow* white eye-ring, usually *one faint wing-bar.* Looks slightly long-tailed, often flips tail up and down. ♪ **Song:** short whistled phrases with burry sound, similar to Plumbeous Vireo's song.

BELL'S VIREO *Vireo bellii*

Usually heard before seen, a shy but noisy vireo of thickets, streamsides. Locally common in southwest and southern plains, endangered in California. ▶ Confusingly plain, with dull wing-bars, *indistinct* eye-ring. Note bill shape, rather long-tailed look. Gray Vireo, even more colorless, has stronger eye-ring. ♪ **Song:** fast jumbled series, *cheedledoo-cheedledeedle-dee? . . . cheedledoo-cheedledeedle-doo!,* with clinking sound, as if the bird has a mouthful of marbles.

VIREOS

Cassin's Vireo 5"

Blue-headed Vireo 5"

Plumbeous Vireo 5¼"

Gray Vireo 5½"

Bell's Vireo 4¾"

299

These five all have plain wings and contrasting pale eyebrow stripes, and all spend the winter deep in the tropics.

WARBLING VIREO *Vireo gilvus*

Plain but musical, this vireo is common in leafy woods in summer, mostly rather high in trees. ▶ Gray and white, sometimes with yellow and olive tinges. No wing-bars. *White eyebrow* is obvious, but darker line through eye is faint, so dark eye is conspicuous on pale face. Listen for the *song* as one of the best clues. See Tennessee Warbler (p. 310). ♪ **Song**: fast musical warble, usually with higher note in middle and again at end.

PHILADELPHIA VIREO *Vireo philadelphicus*

Generally uncommon, and stays out of sight in tall trees. Summers in open deciduous woods in northeast. ▶ Smaller than Warbling Vireo, with variable *yellow* below, distinct *dark lores* (between eye and bill), different song. Yellow brightest on central upper chest (Warbling Vireo may show yellow mainly on sides). See Tennessee Warbler (p. 310). ♪ **Song**: short whistled phrases broken by pauses (suggests Red-eyed Vireo, not Warbling).

RED-EYED VIREO *Vireo olivaceus*

Very common in summer in eastern woods, but much more often heard than seen, singing as it forages slowly high in trees. ▶ Strong head pattern, with *black stripes* setting off white eyebrow, gray crown. White below, often with yellow wash on sides. Larger, longer-billed than Warbling Vireo. Red eye (brown on young birds) hard to see. ♪ **Song**: short whistled phrases separated by pauses, robinlike but choppier. May sing for hours even on hot summer days.

BLACK-WHISKERED VIREO *Vireo altiloquus*

A south Florida specialty, summering in mangroves and other woods near the coast. Rare visitor farther west along Gulf Coast. ▶ Very similar to Red-eyed Vireo but has dark *whisker mark*, sometimes faint; also has longer, heavier bill, often duller head and back. ♪ **Song**: short accented phrases, such as *Whip Tom Kelly*, more emphatic than Red-eye's song.

YELLOW-GREEN VIREO *Vireo flavoviridis*

Rare summer resident in extreme southern Texas. Also very rare visitor to Arizona (mostly summer) and California (mostly fall). ▶ Like Red-eyed but brighter yellow-green on back, bright yellow on sides and undertail coverts; bill larger, head pattern less contrasty. ♪ **Song**: short phrases, with more clipped or chirping tone than Red-eye's song.

VIREOS

Philadelphia Vireo 4¾"

Warbling Vireo 5"

fall immature

Red-eyed Vireo 6"

adults

Yellow-green Vireo 6"

Black-whiskered Vireo 6"

Small, active birds that often hide among foliage, warblers **(family Parulidae)** may go unnoticed by many people. But most experienced birders love the warblers, and look forward to their spring arrival as one of the highlights of the year.

Warblers offer wonderful diversity (with more than 50 species in North America), bright colors, and beautiful patterns. They also offer interesting challenges. Spring males of most species are easy to recognize, but females are usually duller, and young birds in fall can be quite confusing. In some species, adults have completely different patterns in spring and fall. Learning how to identify all the fall warblers can be an absorbing challenge.

fall

spring

male Bay-breasted Warbler

Although most warblers are brightly patterned and flit about in trees, some (like those on p. 324) have more solid colors and skulk in dense cover close to the ground. There are also some brownish warblers that walk on the ground, like waterthrushes and the Ovenbird (p. 322).

Louisiana Waterthrush

Mourning Warbler

The songs of warblers are mostly high-pitched, with thin clear notes, buzzes, and trills. (Few of them could be said to "warble," actually.) Male warblers sing most on their summer territories, but they also sing during spring migration, especially as they get close to the nesting grounds. Warblers also have callnotes, often referred to as "chip notes." Most of these could be written "chip" or "tsick." It takes a sharp ear to tell species apart by these notes; but by listening for chip notes, you may be able to find warblers hiding in the foliage.

Common Yellowthroat

Warblers feed mainly on small insects, so they are mostly warm-weather birds. The main exception is the Yellow-rumped Warbler (p. 308), which also eats many berries; it lingers later in fall and arrives earlier in spring in the north, and winters throughout the warmer parts of North America.

Yellow-rumped Warbler

winter plumage

Most warblers go to the tropics in winter: some to Mexico and Central America, others to the Caribbean, others even going to South America. Some of those that nest the farthest north are among those that winter the farthest to the south, migrating thousands of miles. Some Blackpoll Warblers, for example, may fly from Alaska to Brazil and back every year.

Blackpoll Warbler (spring male)

Eastern North America has more kinds of warblers than the west. During the peak of spring migration in the east, a birder may be able to find more than 20 species of colorful, beautiful warblers in a single day. In the west, fewer warbler species occur regularly. However, almost all the "eastern" warblers show up in the west occasionally, straying off-course during migration (especially in fall), and causing excitement for western birders.

Chestnut-sided Warbler

SOME OTHER SMALL ACTIVE BIRDS

Here are some other small birds that might suggest warblers:

flycatcher

Vireos (p. 296), right, are usually slightly bigger and not quite so active as warblers. Their bills are thicker and they often have loud, repetitive songs.

vireos

Small flycatchers (p. 244), above, usually sit more upright, may fly back to same perch repeatedly.

goldfinch

kinglet

Kinglets (p. 294), right, are tiny and absurdly active, often nervously twitching their wings.

Goldfinches (p. 370), above, have shorter and thicker bills than warblers. Usually seen feeding on seeds, not insects.

Many warblers have bright yellow in their plumage. These four are among the most striking examples.

YELLOW WARBLER *Dendroica petechia*

Very common in summer in open woods, streamsides, orchards, willow thickets. Flits about at midlevels in trees, seeking insects. Its cup-shaped nest is placed in upright fork of shrub or tree. Winters mostly in tropics; rare in winter in the southwest. ▶ Plain yellow face makes dark eye conspicuous; yellow edgings on dark wing feathers. *Yellow spots* in tail (most warblers have white spots). Adult male has *reddish streaks* on chest. Some young females in fall very dull. Compare to other warblers, other small yellow birds, such as goldfinches (p. 370). ♪ **Song:** bright, fast *sweet sweet sweet weetaweet;* exact pattern varies. **Callnote:** loud musical *schip.*

PROTHONOTARY WARBLER *Protonotaria citrea*

A golden sprite of swampy woods, most common in the south. Often sings from high in trees. Unlike most warblers, places nest in a tree hole, sometimes in a birdhouse. ▶ Golden yellow head and chest, white under tail, *blue-gray* wings and tail with white tail spots. Rather short tail and large bill for a warbler. Female duller than male. Compare to other warblers and to female orioles (p. 340). ♪ **Song:** clear, emphatic *weat weat weat weat weat,* all on one pitch. **Callnote:** loud *tchip.*

WILSON'S WARBLER *Wilsonia pusilla*

Common in west, uncommon in east. A small, rather long-tailed warbler that flits about actively in willow groves, thickets, woodland edges. ▶ All yellow or yellow-green, with *no white* in tail or wings. Round *black cap* of males (and some females) is diagnostic. Overall color varies from bright golden on Pacific Coast to dull greenish yellow in east. ♪ **Song:** rather weak *che-che-che-che-cheh,* rising toward end. **Callnote:** squeaky *tchep.*

HOODED WARBLER *Wilsonia citrina*

In leafy forests of the southeast, this warbler lives in shady undergrowth. Males may sing from midlevels in trees, but mostly forage lower, and the nest is placed close to ground in dense shrubs. ▶ *Black hood* surrounding *yellow face* of male diagnostic. Many females show shadow of this hood, but others are plainer. Note their *white outer tail feathers,* often flashed conspicuously. ♪ **Song:** emphatic clear notes, accent toward end, *tawee tawee taweeTEEoh.* **Callnote:** hard, metallic *tchip.*

WARBLERS

females

males

Yellow Warbler
5″

Prothonotary Warbler
5½″

female

male

west coast male

young female

male

Wilson's Warbler
4¾″

female

Hooded Warbler
5¼″

male

Males of these five species all have bluish backs, and the first four have buzzy songs, but their habits vary widely.

NORTHERN PARULA   *Parula americana*

This very small warbler often keeps to the treetops. Its distinctive song may be heard more often than the bird is seen. Hides its nest among Spanish moss, usnea lichen, or similar hanging matter. Winters in tropics; migrants may stray to west coast. ▶ Blue-gray above, white wing-bars, limited yellow on throat, pale eye crescents. Adult male has black and rusty chest bands. ♪ **Song:** thin sputtering buzz that rises and then snaps down at end, *zz-zz-zzz-zzzeeee-wup*. **Callnote:** hard *tsip*.

TROPICAL PARULA   *Parula pitiayumi*

South Texas only: uncommon in summer, rare in winter, in oak groves south of Kingsville and woods along Rio Grande. Widespread in the tropics. ▶ Like Northern Parula, but *lacks* pale eye crescents; yellow from throat extends up side of face, farther down chest. ♪ **Voice:** like Northern Parula's.

BLACK-THROATED BLUE WARBLER   *Dendroica caerulescens*

This dark warbler likes the understory of leafy woods. Often less active than other warblers. Winters mainly in Caribbean; rare stray west of Mississippi River. ▶ Male may look mostly black in the shadows, but has white belly, white wing spot. Female plain dark above, buff below, with white wing spot (faint on some young females), dark cheek patch. ♪ **Song:** hoarse, lazy *zhurr zhurr zhurr zhreee*, last note higher. **Callnote:** soft *tip*.

CERULEAN WARBLER   *Dendroica cerulea*

A treetop bird, often hard to see among leaves of tall sycamores and other riverside trees. Uncommon and declining. Winters in South America; migrants seldom stray to western states. ▶ Adult male is only tiny bird with *blue* back, white throat, black necklace. Female and young duller; have sharp white wing-bars, pale eyebrow, hint of blue on back. ♪ **Song:** fast buzzy series that rises at end, *zhr zhr zhr zezeze zzeeee*. **Callnote:** *chyip*.

CANADA WARBLER   *Wilsonia canadensis*

Undergrowth and midlevels of leafy woods host this warbler. Despite the name, it nests as far south as Georgia and winters in South America. ▶ *Necklace* of sharp black streaks on *yellow* breast, most obvious on adult males, faint on some young females. Bold eye-ring. Blue-gray above, no wing-bars or tail spots. ♪ **Song:** fast musical jumble of notes, often starting with low *chup* and ending with emphatic *pickety-wip*. **Callnote:** *chup*.

WARBLERS

male

Northern Parula
4½"

male

Tropical Parula
4½"

female

young
female

dull
female

female

**Black-throated
Blue Warbler**
5¼"

male

female

**Cerulean
Warbler**
4¾"

male

female

**Canada
Warbler**
5¼"

male

These all have some yellow above the base of the tail: obvious on the Yellow-rumped Warbler, sometimes faint on the other two.

YELLOW-RUMPED WARBLER   *Dendroica coronata*

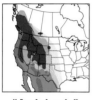

"Myrtle"

"Audubon's"

One of the easiest warblers to learn. Migrates earlier in spring and later in fall than the others, and stays through winter in milder climates, surviving cold snaps (when insects are scarce) by eating berries. Summers in coniferous forest of north and mountains, winters in woodland, parks, riversides, bayberry thickets. Can be very numerous in late fall, especially along coasts. The two distinct types were once considered separate species. ▶ Both types have bright yellow rump patch (obvious as bird flies away), white spots in tail, small yellow patch at side of chest. Eastern **"Myrtle Warbler"** has white throat (may be dull buff in some young birds) wrapping up behind well-defined dark cheek patch. Western **"Audubon's Warbler"** has *yellow* throat, *plainer* face. In both forms, pattern is brightest on spring males, dullest on young females in fall and winter. ♪ Song: simple thin warbling series of notes, without strong pattern. Callnote: loud *tcheck,* that of "Myrtle" sharper and louder than that of "Audubon's."

CAPE MAY WARBLER   *Dendroica tigrina*

A small warbler that summers in northern spruce forest, winters mostly on Caribbean islands. ▶ Adult male striking with sharp black stripes on yellow breast, rich *chestnut ear patch,* yellow spot on side of neck. Yellow-green patch on rump sometimes visible. Female similar but duller, without chestnut ear patch. Fall immatures variable; dullest ones lack yellow, can be perplexing. May suggest "Myrtle," but show more *fine dark streaks* on underparts, shorter tail, hint of pale neck spot. ♪ Song: very high, thin *see see see see see.* Callnote: thin *ssip.*

MAGNOLIA WARBLER   *Dendroica magnolia*

An active warbler that often stays low in trees, flitting about, showing off its distinctive tail pattern. Favors open conifer forest in summer, other trees in migration (has no special connection to magnolias). ▶ Square-edged *white band* across outer tail feathers (from below, tail looks half white, half black). Yellow below, with *streaks on sides;* gray head, small yellow rump patch. Spring male has black mask, black back, much white in wing. ♪ Song: a short sweet warble, *wayta wayta way-teeh;* variable. Callnote: nasal *shleff.*

WARBLERS

winter "Myrtles"

winter male "Myrtle"

spring male

"Myrtle Warbler"

Yellow-rumped Warbler (two forms) 5½"

"Audubon's Warbler"

winter "Audubon's"

spring female "Audubon's"

spring male

fall immature female

Cape May Warbler 5"

female

spring male

immature

Magnolia Warbler 5"

female

spring male

TENNESSEE WARBLER *Vermivora peregrina*

Plain, with a loud staccato song. Summers in bogs and clearings in northern forest, winters mostly in Central America (visiting Tennessee during migration season only). ▶ Spring male white below, *green* on back, with gray cap, white eyebrow. (Warbling Vireo, p. 300, has thicker bill, grayer back.) Female duller. Fall birds mostly yellow below; unlike Orange-crowned Warbler, they have *white* undertail coverts, plain yellow chest. ♪ **Song**: fast dry series that "shifts gears," *chpit chpit chpit chpit tuctuctuctuctuc titititititititititick.* **Callnote**: *tsit.*

ORANGE-CROWNED WARBLER *Vermivora celata*

A plain bird, its orange crown rarely showing, except on frazzled summer adults. Common in west, less so in east. Often stays fairly low in leafy thickets but will also forage in treetops. Unlike most warblers, regularly stays through winter in southern states. ▶ Very plain; more grayish in east, more yellow-green in west. No wing-bars. Dark line through eye, faint broken eye-ring. *Blurry streaks* on chest. Undertail coverts *yellow.* ♪ **Song**: thin trill, usually trailing off at end. **Callnote**: thin *tsit.*

BLUE-WINGED WARBLER *Vermivora pinus*

Not a forest bird like many warblers, the Blue-winged favors thickets, second growth, woodland edges. It winters mostly in Central America. ▶ Bright yellow head and underparts, with sharp *black line* through eye. *Blue-gray* wings with two white wing-bars. Tail short, with white spots in outer feathers. Female duller than male. ♪ **Song**: dry buzzy *beezzzzz-buzzzzzz,* second note lower. **Callnote**: sharp *tsick.*

GOLDEN-WINGED WARBLER *Vermivora chrysoptera*

Uncommon in summer in second-growth woods and swamps in northeast. Declining in numbers as its close relative, Blue-winged Warbler, expands north into its range. ▶ Gray above, white below, with broad *yellow wing-bars, yellow forehead.* Throat patch and narrow mask are black on males, gray on females. ♪ **Song**: *beezz, bz-bz-bzz,* first note higher. **Callnote**: sharp *tsick.*

HYBRID WARBLERS

Unlike most wild birds, Blue-winged and Golden-winged Warblers often interbreed. Their hybrid offspring have informal names, **"Brewster's"** and the rarer **"Lawrence's" Warblers.** They are quite variable; examples are shown here. They may appear wherever the two parent species are found.

WARBLERS

immature

fall adult

spring male

Tennessee Warbler
4³/₄"

spring female

western mountains

eastern

Orange-crowned Warbler
5"

west coast

Blue-winged Warbler
4³/₄"

male

female

Golden-winged Warbler
4³/₄"

male

female

"Brewster's Warbler"

Hybrids

"Lawrence's Warbler"

These five all have plain wings and lack obvious tail spots.

NASHVILLE WARBLER   *Vermivora ruficapilla*

Common and widespread, often in second growth or low trees. May bob its tail up and down. Named as a fluke, since it appears near Nashville during migration only. ► Gray head contrasts with *yellow throat,* olive back, *white eye-ring.* Warblers on p. 324 also have eye-rings and gray heads, but usually lack yellow on throat, and they are large sluggish warblers of dense thickets. ♪**Song**: sweet double notes followed by faster trill, *seeba seeba seeba tetetetetetetetetetetelh.* **Callnote:** sharp *tsick.*

VIRGINIA'S WARBLER   *Vermivora virginiae*

In dry foothills of the west, this plain warbler is fairly common in summer (sometimes hard to see) in scrubby oaks and chaparral. Its nest is hidden on the ground. Often bobs its tail up and down. ► Gray, paler below, with white eye-ring and *yellow* undertail coverts. Yellow wash on chest obvious on adult males, may be faint on young females. ♪**Song**: simple series of notes, on one pitch or rising toward end. **Callnote:** hard *tsick.*

COLIMA WARBLER   *Vermivora crissalis*

West Texas only: Chisos Mountains, Big Bend National Park, in oak-pine woods above 6,000 feet. Arrives mid-April, leaves in August. ► Gray, with white eye-ring and yellow undertail coverts. Virginia's Warbler (migrant through Big Bend) is smaller, *lacks* strong *brown wash* on sides. ♪**Song**: simple musical trill on one pitch, often dropping at end. **Callnote:** hard *tsick.*

LUCY'S WARBLER   *Vermivora luciae*

A pale dry-country bird, the only warbler adapted to the desert. Nests in holes in dead mesquite branches or under loose bark strips. Arrives in early spring, mostly departs in late summer. Often bobs its tail up and down. ► Pale gray above, creamy below, with very pale face. *Chestnut rump patch* sometimes hidden (duller in young birds). Male has chestnut on crown. Fall birds washed buff below. ♪**Song**: fast sweet series of notes, usually changing tempo in middle. **Callnote:** sharp *tsick.*

ARCTIC WARBLER   *Phylloscopus borealis*

Alaska only. Not related to American warblers; belongs to an Old World family and returns "home" every fall, to spend the winter in southern Asia. In Alaska, lives in dense willows along rivers. ► Plain above and below, with obvious whitish eyebrow. See Tennessee Warbler (p. 302), rare in Alaska. ♪**Song**: slow trill on one pitch, with insistent quality. **Callnote:** loud, arresting *tzzzck.*

WARBLERS

Nashville Warbler
4³⁄₄"

female

Virginia's Warbler
4³⁄₄"

male

Colima Warbler
5³⁄₄"

fall

Lucy's Warbler
4¹⁄₄"

spring male

Arctic Warbler
5"

313

BLACKPOLL WARBLER *Dendroica striata*

Common in summer in northern spruce forest. Long-distance migrants, some Blackpolls travel from Alaska to Brazil every year. A few reach west coast every fall. Spring and fall plumages strikingly different. ► Spring male has black cap, white cheeks, striped sides. See Black-throated Gray Warbler (next page), chickadees (p. 280). Spring female duller; note yellow legs. Fall birds olive above with streaks on back, dull yellow below, with blurry streaks on chest, *sharp white wing-bars.* Compare to next two species. ♪ **Song:** very high thin *zi-zi-zi-zi-zi-zi-zi,* fast or slow. **Callnote:** musical *chip.*

BAY-BREASTED WARBLER *Dendroica castanea*

Another warbler that nests in northern conifer forest, winters in the tropics, and changes color with the season. ► Spring male has head/chest pattern of chestnut, black, and buff. Spring female paler, usually has hint of same pattern. Fall birds very much like fall Blackpoll but undertail coverts usually *buff* (not white), chest lacks blurry streaking, sides of neck brighter greenish, legs always dark (some fall Blackpolls have yellow legs). See Pine Warbler, below. ♪ **Song:** very high, thin *weesa weesa weesa weesa.* **Callnote:** musical *chip.*

PINE WARBLER *Dendroica pinus*

A stocky, sluggish warbler that loves pines. Not a long-distance migrant like most warblers; winters mostly in southeast. ► Adults olive above, yellow on chest, with two wing-bars; males have blurry streaks on chest, females plainer. See Yellow-throated Vireo (p. 296). Fall immatures vary, yellowish to gray. Some resemble fall Blackpoll or Bay-breasted, but have duller wing-bars, *no streaks* on back, cheek patch shows more contrast. ♪ **Song:** rich musical trill on one pitch. **Callnote:** *chip.*

BLACK-AND-WHITE WARBLER *Mniotilta varia*

In the forest, this stripy warbler creeps about major limbs and trunks of trees, often acting like a nuthatch. Mostly eastern, but strays turn up in the west. ► Bold stripes, including *white* central crown stripe, black streaks on back and sides. Adult male has black throat and cheeks; female and young paler or whitish there. Compare to Black-throated Gray (next page) and Blackpoll Warblers. Tree-creeping behavior is best mark. ♪ **Song:** insistent *weesee weesee weesee weesee,* all on one pitch. **Callnote:** hard *tchip.*

WARBLERS

dull
fall Blackpoll

bright
fall Blackpoll

Blackpoll Warbler
5"

spring
male

spring
female

Bay-breasted Warbler
5¼"

fall
Bay-breasts

spring
male

spring
female

young female
in fall

Pine Warbler
5½"

male

female

female

fall
male

Black-and-white Warbler
5¼"

spring
male

These five close relatives have different ranges or habitats in summer.

BLACK-THROATED GRAY WARBLER *Dendroica nigrescens*

Dry foothills with oak and juniper host this warbler in summer. A few winter in southwest. Rarely wanders east. ▶ Strong *face pattern* with black cheeks, *solid* black crown. See previous page: Blackpoll has white cheeks, Black-and-white has striped crown. Female grayer, may have throat mostly white. ♪**Song:** hoarse, buzzy series, often rising toward accented end. **Callnote:** hard *tchek.*

BLACK-THROATED GREEN WARBLER *Dendroica virens*

This warbler favors coniferous or mixed forest of the northeast in summer; a few also nest in cypress swamps along the Atlantic Coast. Likes tall trees, often stays high. ▶ *Yellow face* contrasts with black throat, bright moss green back and crown. Obvious white wing-bars. Female and young have black on throat partly replaced by white. ♪**Song:** buzzy *zoo, zee, zoo zoo zee,* with the *zee* notes higher, or *zee zee zee zoo zee.* **Callnote:** flat *teck.*

TOWNSEND'S WARBLER *Dendroica townsendi*

In wet evergreen forest of the northwest, Townsend's is common in summer, usually staying high in trees. Seen throughout the west in migration, rarely wanders east. ▶ Strong *face pattern,* with bright yellow surrounding dark cheek. Green back, yellow chest, white wing-bars, streaked sides. Throat black on adult male, mostly yellow on female and young. ♪**Song:** high-pitched, wheezy or buzzy series, with variable pattern. **Callnote:** *tep.*

HERMIT WARBLER *Dendroica occidentalis*

Fairly common in limited summer range in Pacific Northwest. Most winter in Mexico, a few in California. Townsend's and Hermit may interbreed where their ranges meet, producing hybrid young. ▶ Plain *yellow face,* gray back, white underparts. Throat patch black on adult males, veiled on others, may be missing on young females in fall. ♪**Song:** high-pitched, wheezy series, often ending in accented notes. **Callnote:** flat *teck.*

GOLDEN-CHEEKED WARBLER *Dendroica chrysoparia*

Texas only; an endangered species. A scarce summer bird of juniper-covered hills in central Texas. Winters in southern Mexico, Guatemala. ▶ Male's bright gold cheeks contrast with black crown and back, black eyeline. Female much like female Black-throated Green, may show darker eyeline, whiter belly. ♪**Song:** variable, about five notes with lazy, buzzy sound. **Callnote:** *teck.*

WARBLERS

female

Black-throated Gray Warbler 5"

male

young female in fall

Black-throated Green Warbler 5"

female

male

young male

Townsend's Warbler 5"

male

female

Golden-cheeked Warbler 5¼"

males

Hermit Warbler 5¼"

adult male

young female

CHESTNUT-SIDED WARBLER *Dendroica pensylvanica*

An active little warbler of leafy second-growth woods, forest edges. Hops about in foliage, often rather low, holding its tail up at a perky angle. ▶ Yellow cap, black face stripe around white cheeks, ragged chestnut stripe on sides. In fall, very different: lime green above, white below, with white eye-ring on pale gray face, two yellow wing-bars; may or may not show some chestnut on sides. ♪ **Song**: lively *sweet sweet sweet seesaWEETchew*. Much like song of Yellow Warbler (p. 304) but usually ends more emphatically. **Callnote**: rather low *chup*.

BLACKBURNIAN WARBLER *Dendroica fusca*

A glowing flame of the treetops, fairly common in summer in northeastern spruce woods. Winters mostly in Andes of South America. Migrates through eastern states, very rare in west. ▶ Adult male shows brilliant *orange throat*, black triangle on face, white wing patch, black back with white stripes. Female has same pattern with paler orange-yellow throat, two white wing-bars on black wings. Some young birds in fall very dull, with shadow of adults' pattern; notice *pale stripes* on back. ♪ **Song**: thin and wiry, usually ending in a very high note with strained sound. **Callnote**: strong *tsip*.

YELLOW-THROATED WARBLER *Dendroica dominica*

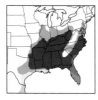

A classic southeastern warbler, arriving on its nesting grounds very early in spring. During summer, likes open pine forest, tall sycamores along rivers; in winter in far southern areas, often in palms. Forages rather slowly and deliberately in high branches. ▶ Brilliant yellow throat contrasts with *white* neck spot, *black face*, black stripes on sides. Gray back, white wing-bars. Grace's Warbler (western) lacks white neck spot. ♪ **Song**: clear descending whistles, last one rising, *teeew teeew teeew teew tuwee*. **Callnote**: loud *tchip*.

GRACE'S WARBLER *Dendroica graciae*

In open pine forests of southwestern mountains, this warbler is common in summer. It usually stays high in trees. ▶ Gray above, white below, with yellow throat and *short yellow eyebrow*. Thin dark streaks on sides. Female and young like adult male but duller. Compare to "Audubon's" Yellow-rumped Warbler (p. 308). ♪ **Song**: thin musical chatter, *ch-ch-ch-ch-chi-chih*, rising in pitch toward end. **Callnote**: *tchip*.

WARBLERS

spring female

Chestnut-sided Warbler
5"

fall immature female

spring male

fall immature female

Blackburnian Warbler
5"

spring male

spring female

Yellow-throated Warbler
5 1/2"

adults

female

Grace's Warbler
5"

male

WARBLERS

These four are usually in thickets or saplings, or close to the ground.

PALM WARBLER *Dendroica palmarum*

Summers in northern bogs, but more birders see this warbler in winter quarters in the southeast, where it usually feeds on the ground in open areas. Can be very drab, but its constant *tail-bobbing habit* identifies it. Migrates earlier in spring and later in fall than most warblers; a few winter on Pacific Coast. ▶ Two types: **"Yellow Palm Warbler"** is less common, nests farther east, has more extensive yellow below. In all Palm Warblers, note *yellow undertail coverts,* tail-bobbing action, well-defined pale eyebrow. ♪**Song**: rough, simple trill with stuttering sound. **Callnote**: sharp *tsipp.*

PRAIRIE WARBLER *Dendroica discolor*

Not well named—favors dense second growth and thickets, not open prairies. In Florida, also common in mangrove swamps. ▶ Olive above, bright yellow below, with two very dull wing-bars. Best mark is face pattern, sharp in adult male, fainter in female and young. Bobs its tail up and down almost constantly. ♪**Song**: very thin, wiry *zee zee zee zee zee zee zee zee . . .* , each note slightly higher. **Callnote**: hard *chip.*

KIRTLAND'S WARBLER *Dendroica kirtlandii*

Very rare, an endangered species. Nests almost exclusively in a few counties in Michigan's lower peninsula, in stands of young jack pines. Winters in Bahamas. Very seldom seen while migrating. Large for a warbler, stays low and moves deliberately, often bobbing its tail up and down. ▶ Blue-gray above, yellow below, with black streaks along sides, narrow white crescents above and below eye. This rare bird should be identified with caution; compare to Palm and Prairie Warblers, also Magnolia (p. 308), Pine (p. 314), and Canada Warblers (p. 306). ♪**Song**: choppy quick jumble of notes, usually rising; low-pitched for a warbler. **Callnote**: low *chup.*

YELLOW-BREASTED CHAT *Icteria virens*

This big warbler acts like a thrasher or catbird, hiding in bushes and making weird noises. Male sometimes sings while fluttering above thickets with legs dangling. ▶ Much larger than most warblers, with thick bill and long tail. Bright yellow throat and breast (may even look orange) contrasting with white belly, olive back. Sharp *white "spectacles"* on dark face. Common Yellowthroat (p. 324) much smaller, with different face pattern. ♪**Song**: remarkable ongoing sequence of hoots, whistles, clucks, gurgles, and short rough chatters, the notes often separated by several seconds.

WARBLERS THAT STAY LOW

fall or winter

spring

Palm Warbler
5"

"Yellow Palm"
spring

"Yellow Palm"
fall

Prairie Warbler
5"

female

male

Kirtland's Warbler
6"

male

female

Yellow-breasted Chat
7"

adults

fall immature

BROWN GROUND WARBLERS

These dull-colored species all live close to the ground, on the ground, or close to water, in deep shade inside the forest.

OVENBIRD   *Seiurus aurocapilla*

Common in summer in eastern woods but easily over-looked as it walks on the ground in slow dainty style, tail cocked up. Domed nest, built on ground, suggests an old-fashioned oven. ▶ Bold white *eye-ring,* striped chest, olive-brown back. Dull *orange* crown stripe bordered by blackish stripes. Brown thrushes (p. 258) lack crown stripes. ♪**Song:** emphatic chant, louder at end, *chertea chertea cherTEA CHERTEA.* **Callnote:** *tchep.*

NORTHERN WATERTHRUSH   *Seiurus noveboracensis*

Waterthrushes wag their tails up and down as they walk the shores of streams, ponds. When disturbed, they fly away into woods, with sharp callnote. ▶ Dark brown back, bright eyebrow, streaked below. Underparts and eyebrow usually tinged *yellow,* sometimes more white; see next species, also pipits (p. 270). ♪**Song:** loud, fast series, ending in lower emphatic notes, *weat weat weat chechechecheche-chewchewchew.* **Callnote:** loud *chink.*

LOUISIANA WATERTHRUSH   *Seiurus motacilla*

A shy warbler that haunts shorelines of southeastern streams, teetering its tail up and down. Arrives very early in spring. ▶ Like Northern Waterthrush but eyebrow always bright white; below white, with *pink-buff tinge* on flanks; bill usually larger, throat usually plain. ♪**Song:** 3–4 clear whistles, *teer teer teer,* running into a short quick jumble of notes. **Callnote:** loud *chink.*

WORM-EATING WARBLER   *Helmitheros vermivorum*

Fairly common but easily overlooked, staying inside forest, low among dense thickets. Despite the name, does not feed on earthworms. ▶ Strong black stripes on warm *buff* head; plain olive-brown on back, wings. Bill heavy for a warbler, sharply pointed. ♪**Song:** flat, dry, thin trill on one pitch; much like song of Chipping Sparrow (p. 350). **Callnote:** hard *djip.*

SWAINSON'S WARBLER   *Limnothlypis swainsonii*

Uncommon and elusive in southeastern woods. Likes tangles and deep undergrowth in swampy places; also drier thickets in Appalachians. ▶ Heavy-billed and plain for a warbler. Olive-brown back, *warmer brown* crown, pale eyebrow. Below tinged gray or yellow. Compare to wrens (p. 288). ♪**Song:** clear, ringing *teer, teer, teer, whiti-perwill.* **Callnote:** loud *tchep.*

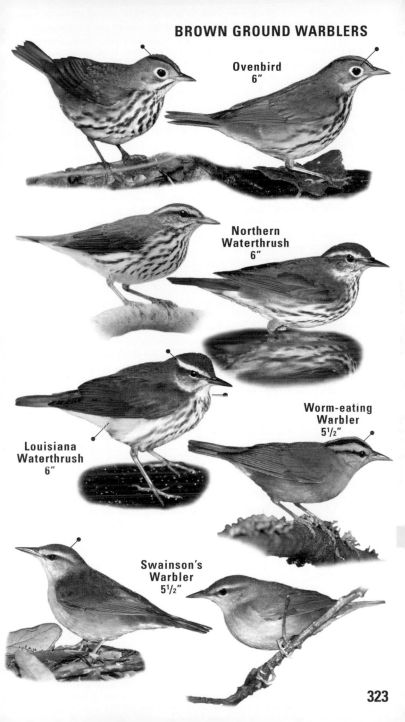

BROWN GROUND WARBLERS

Ovenbird
6"

Northern
Waterthrush
6"

Louisiana
Waterthrush
6"

Worm-eating
Warbler
5¹/₂"

Swainson's
Warbler
5¹/₂"

These five all live close to the ground in dense cover.

COMMON YELLOWTHROAT *Geothlypis trichas*

The only warbler nesting in open marshes. Active, flitting among the reeds, often staying out of sight. Also ranges into thickets and damp woods, especially while migrating. ▶ Male's *bandit mask* contrasts with *yellow throat* and is set off above by paler stripe. Female plainer, can be confusing, but shows contrast between yellow throat and darker face; olive above with plain wings. Notice habitat, calls. ♪**Song**: bright, fast *wichity-wichity-wichity*, variable. **Callnote**: low, guttural *tchuck*.

KENTUCKY WARBLER *Oporornis formosus*

In leafy woods of the southeast, this shy warbler hops and runs on the ground under dense thickets. ▶ Bright *yellow spectacles* set off black crown and black whisker mark. Plain olive above, bright yellow below. Young male Common Yellowthroat similar but lacks obvious spectacles. Also see Canada Warbler (p. 300). ♪**Song**: rich *turree-turree-turrree-turree*. **Callnote**: loud *chep*.

MACGILLIVRAY'S WARBLER *Oporornis tolmiei*

A stocky, sluggish warbler of dense thickets in the west. ▶ Olive above, yellow below, with full gray hood. Sharp *white crescents* above and below eye, best distinction from next two species. Lower throat blackish on adult males, gray on females; chin and throat whitish gray on young birds. ♪**Song**: variable, usually two-parted rolling *jirry jirry jirry, jorry jorry*. **Callnote**: hard *djk*.

MOURNING WARBLER *Oporornis philadelphia*

A skulker in dense low thickets of woodland edge and brushy clearings in the east. Migrates relatively late in spring. ▶ Olive above, yellow below, with gray hood. Adult male has veiled black on throat; female paler, may show narrow eye-ring. Some fall immatures suggest female Common Yellowthroat, but show hint of hood, more evenly yellow belly. ♪**Song**: rolling, two-parted *jirry jirry jirry, jorry jorry*. **Callnote**: flat *jip*.

CONNECTICUT WARBLER *Oporornis agilis*

A rare, elusive warbler of the forest floor. Nests in northern bogs, winters in South America; only a scarce migrant in Connecticut. ▶ On ground, *walks* deliberately (Mourning and MacGillivray's hop). Large, dull, with complete white eye-ring on gray head. Nashville Warbler (p. 312), active up in trees, has yellow throat. ♪**Song**: snappy *took-a-ticket*, repeated. **Callnote**: nasal *jip*.

young male

female

WARBLERS THAT STAY LOW

Common Yellowthroat
5"

males

male

Kentucky Warbler
5¼"

male

female

MacGillivray's Warbler
5¼"

female

fall immature

female

Mourning Warbler
5¼"

male

adult male

Connecticut Warbler
5¾"

fall immature

325

AMERICAN REDSTART   *Setophaga ruticilla*

Active and attractive, the redstart flits about, half-spreading wings and tail to show off patches of color. Common in summer in eastern forest edge, second growth; less common in west. ▶ Adult male mostly black with red-orange patches on wings, tail, sides. Female gray above, white below, seems confusingly plain until her *yellow wing and tail patches* are seen. Young male like female but with black mottling. ♪ **Song**: quite variable, phrases like *weesa weesa weesa* or *ssee ssee ssee suweeo;* songs often alternated. **Callnote**: thin *schip.*

RED-FACED WARBLER   *Cardellina rubrifrons*

In mountain forest near the Mexican border, this beautiful warbler is fairly common in summer. Forages high in trees, but hides its nest on the ground on a hillside or steep bank. ▶ Red and black face pattern diagnostic; otherwise white below and on rump, gray on back. Female slightly duller than male. ♪ **Song**: variable bright phrases, often ends in *suweetchew.* **Callnote**: sharp *tchip.*

PAINTED REDSTART   *Myioborus pictus*

Flashy, showy warbler of mountain canyons of southwest, fairly common in pine-oak woods. Poses with spread tail and wings as it hops on tree limbs, trunks. Nests on ground. ▶ White outer tail feathers and wing patch, red chest, otherwise mostly black. Juveniles may lack red at first. ♪ **Song**: rich warbled whistles, *wheaty wheaty wheaty tew tew tew.* **Callnote**: full-toned *cheeilp.*

OLIVE WARBLER   *Peucedramus taeniatus*

Uncommon; high in pines in southwestern mountains. A few remain through winter. Now classified in a separate family from other warblers. ▶ Adult male has *copper-brown head* with black ear patch; gray back, white wing-bars. On young male, copper replaced by yellow. Female has pale yellow face, dull ear patch; compare to female Hermit Warbler (p. 316). ♪ **Song**: variable phrases, *veeza veeza veeza,* etc. **Callnote**: soft *feeyw.*

RUFOUS-CAPPED WARBLER   *Basileuterus rufifrons*

Rare visitor to Texas and Arizona (has nested), found in dense low thickets. ▶ Reddish cap, white eyebrow, bright yellow throat. Rather long tail often raised above level of back. ♪ **Song**: dry staccato chattering series.

BANANAQUIT   *Coereba flaveola*

Rare visitor to Florida from Bahamas. Often clambers about masses of flowers, feeding on nectar and insects. ▶ White eyebrow, yellow rump, yellow chest. Pink at base of *thin, curved bill.* Young birds are duller.

WARBLERS

female

immature
male

**American
Redstart**
5¼"

adult
male

**Red-faced
Warbler**
5½"

**Painted
Redstart**
5¾"

female

Olive Warbler
5¼"

adult
male

RARE VISITORS

**Rufous-capped
Warbler**
5½"

Bananaquit
4½"

327

TANAGERS

(family Thraupidae) are mainly tropical. A few species reach North America in summer, typically staying in treetops inside the forest.

WESTERN TANAGER   *Piranga ludoviciana*

In early summer, this tanager likes cool conifer forests of northwest and high mountains. During spring and fall migration, may appear in cities, farmland, even desert. ▶ Adult male yellow and black with red face. Female and young dull yellow with gray back and wings, *two wing-bars.* Suggest female orioles (p. 340) but have thicker bill. ♪**Song:** rising and falling whistles, robinlike but hoarser. **Callnote:** dry, rising *pri-di-dit?*

SCARLET TANAGER   *Piranga olivacea*

A stunning summer resident of leafy forests of northeast. Usually stays high; may forage low during migration. ▶ Spring/summer male is our only brilliant red bird with *black wings and tail* (see crossbills, p. 368). In late summer he molts into winter plumage, greenish with black wings. Female dull yellow-green, wings *darker;* note sluggish behavior, thick bill. ♪**Song:** rising and falling phrases, hoarse, like robin with sore throat. **Callnote:** distinctive *chip-brrr,* or just *chip.*

SUMMER TANAGER   *Piranga rubra*

A summer bird of the treetops. Mainly in oak and pine forest in southeast, tall cottonwoods along rivers in southwest. ▶ Adult male bright rosy red all year. Young males may be patchy yellow and red. Female rich yellow, less greenish than female Scarlet; note *large pale bill,* plain wings. ♪**Song:** robinlike whistled phrases, less burry than Scarlet Tanager. **Callnote:** crackling *pikituck.*

HEPATIC TANAGER   *Piranga flava*

In mountains of the southwest, this tanager is an uncommon summer resident of pine-oak forest. Rarely stays into winter in Arizona. ▶ Resembles Summer Tanager, but has contrasting *gray cheeks* and usually a darker bill. Male is more brick red or orange-red. ♪**Song:** robinlike whistled phrases, rising and falling, clearer tone than other tanagers. **Callnote:** dry *chuck.*

FLAME-COLORED TANAGER   *Piranga bidentata*

Rare summer visitor to pine forest of Arizona mountains. ▶ Male orange with bold pattern on black wings, *black stripes on back.* Female resembles female Western Tanager, but may show stripes on back, dark ear patch.

WESTERN SPINDALIS   *Spindalis zena* **("Stripe-headed Tanager")**

Very rare visitor to Florida from Bahamas. ▶ Male unmistakable. Female olive-gray, with pale eyebrow and whisker mark, wing pattern like male's.

TANAGERS

Western Tanager 7¼"
- male
- female

Scarlet Tanager 7"
- summer male
- female

Hepatic Tanager 8"
- males
- female

Summer Tanager 7¾"
- male
- female

RARE TANAGERS
(not to scale)

Flame-colored Tanager 7¾"
- males

Western Spindalis 6¾"
- male

329

STARLINGS AND MYNAS

(family Sturnidae) are native to the Old World. Many starlings in Asia and Africa are very colorful; the one introduced into North America is not. However, it is tough and adaptable, remarkable for its ability to thrive on this continent. Several species of mynas, as escaped cagebirds, have survived in the wild here, but so far none is widespread.

EUROPEAN STARLING   *Sturnus vulgaris*

A chunky, short-tailed bird that waddles about on lawns. Brought to North America in 1890, the starling is now one of the most abundant birds on this continent. Usually in flocks when not nesting; may gather in big roosts that number in the tens of thousands. Not related to American blackbirds but often associates with them, may form mixed flocks. Starlings nest in holes in trees, birdhouses, crevices in buildings, etc.; very aggressive, they may compete with native birds for nest sites, even evicting woodpeckers from their own holes. ▶ Short tail, thin straight bill. Plumage black, with purple and green gloss in spring and summer. In fresh fall plumage, heavily marked with white spots, which gradually wear off during winter. Bill bright yellow in breeding season, with base of lower mandible *blue* in males, *pink* in females. Bill duller at other seasons. Juveniles (seen in flocks in summer) very different, all dusty gray, with dark bills. ♪**Song**: remarkably varied stream of sound, with whistles, gurgles, imitations of other birds. **Call-notes**: include rough chatter, soft whistles. Juveniles in flocks make rough trill, *dzzhhrrrr.*

COMMON MYNA   *Acridotheres tristis*

Escaped cagebirds have established a wild population in Florida and are now spreading and increasing in the southeastern part of the state, from the Keys to Fort Pierce, mostly nesting in urban areas. Native to southern Asia. ▶ Chunky and short-tailed. Dark brown, with *black hood,* yellow bill, bare yellow facial skin. White under wing and white tail tip are obvious in flight. ♪**Voice**: varied, includes whistles, chatters.

CRESTED MYNA   *Acridotheres cristatellus*

Introduced at Vancouver, British Columbia, in the 1890s, and thrived there for years before fading out, finally disappearing in 2003. Escaped cagebirds are sometimes seen elsewhere. Native to Asia. ▶ Chunky and black, with *short bristly crest* on forehead, white wing patch. Yellow bill and legs, pale eyes. ♪**Voice**: melodious whistles, chatters, imitations of other birds.

HILL MYNA   *Gracula religiosa*

Escaped cagebirds have survived for years in southern Florida (mostly in Miami area) and have nested there, but are still uncommon. ▶ Large, glossy black, with orange bill and bright *yellow face wattles.* White wing patch obvious in flight. ♪**Voice**: varied whistles, croaks. A skilled mimic.

STARLINGS AND MYNAS

juvenile

early
spring

European
Starling
8½"

spring
male

juveniles
changing to
first-winter
plumage

winter
adult

Crested
Myna
10"

Common
Myna
10"

Hill Myna
11"

MARSH BLACKBIRDS

The blackbird family (**Icteridae**) includes orioles, meadowlarks, cowbirds, and others, a diverse group found only in the Americas. Many (like the ones on this page) are primarily black. Compare to other black birds such as starlings (previous page) and crows (p. 278).

RED-WINGED BLACKBIRD *Agelaius phoeniceus*

Abundant and familiar, Red-wings nest in practically every marsh and weedy ditch in the temperate parts of North America. Outside the nesting season, they wander in flocks through farmland, marshes, forest edge, walking on ground in open fields. ▶ Male's shoulder patches can be obvious (especially in song display) or mostly hidden by body feathers. Patches usually bordered yellow, but in central California (**"Bicolored Red-wing"**), these can be all red. Females and young very different, streaky brown with buff eyebrow. Resemble sparrows (next section) but have different behavior, spikier bill, darker lower belly. See Bobolink (next page). ♪**Song**: nasal gurgling ending in rough trill, *aawnk-ah-rrreeeeeeee.* **Callnote**: dry *chack.*

TRICOLORED BLACKBIRD *Agelaius tricolor*

Mostly a California specialty. Even there, usually harder to find than its cousin the Red-wing, but when found, it is often in large numbers. Tricoloreds are localized but very social, nesting in dense colonies and traveling in tight flocks. ▶ Very similar to Red-winged Blackbird. Male's shoulder patch deeper red, with *white* (not yellow) border (border can look whitish on faded male Red-wings in late summer). Female and young almost identical to some female Red-wings but darker than most, with streaking mostly obscure, and never have buff or rusty edgings on back. ♪**Song**: nasal *awnk-krr-awnngk,* harsher than Red-wing's.

YELLOW-HEADED BLACKBIRD *Xanthocephalus xanthocephalus*

In western marshes in summer, this blackbird draws attention with striking colors and with the males' awful attempts to sing. Outside the nesting season, flocks wander through open habitats (including farm fields, prairies, feedlots), often mixing with other blackbirds. ▶ Name describes male; also note his white wing patches, obvious in flight. Female a bit smaller, sooty brown, with yellow on face and chest, white streaks on belly, no white wing patches. Immatures have some yellow on head, wing patches small or absent. ♪**Song**: male strains to rasp out a few gurgles followed by long, strangled buzzing noise. **Callnote**: low *tluc.*

MARSH BLACKBIRDS

male "Bicolored"

displaying male

Red-winged Blackbird 9"

females

Red-wing flock in flight

winter male

female

Tricolored Blackbird 9"

maloc

juvenile

females

males

Yellow-headed Blackbird 10"

BIRDS OF OPEN FIELDS

Meadowlarks and Bobolink belong to blackbird family; Dickcissel and Lark Bunting are related to sparrows (section beginning on p. 344).

WESTERN MEADOWLARK *Sturnella neglecta*

Common in grassland, singing from fences, walking on open ground. A chunky, short-tailed bird that flies with quick flaps and stiff glide. Gathers in small flocks in winter. ▶ *Black* V on yellow breast (partly veiled in fall). *White outer tail feathers,* most obvious on takeoff and landing. Told from Eastern Meadowlark by voice, range. ♪**Song:** short rich whistles speeding up to rapid bubbling jumble. **Callnotes:** low *chook;* dry rattle.

EASTERN MEADOWLARK *Sturnella magna*

Widespread in east and southwest, declining in some areas. ▶ Looks like Western Meadowlark; can be slightly darker, more richly colored, but with less yellow on face. Southwestern race paler like Western, but shows more white in tail. Best known by voice, range. ♪**Song:** clear whistles, *te-seeyeer seeeyaayy,* without Western's fast bubbling. **Callnotes:** buzzy *djjerrrt;* dry rattle.

BOBOLINK *Dolichonyx oryzivorus*

Fairly common in summer (but declining) in damp meadows, hayfields. Male flutters over the grass while singing. Winters in South America. ▶ Spring/summer male unmistakable. In late summer he molts to pattern like female and young's: buffy, streaky, with black stripes on crown. See sparrows (next section). ♪**Song:** rich, rapid bubbling, often while flying. **Callnote:** chiming *engk.*

DICKCISSEL *Spiza americana*

Can be abundant in summer on midwestern prairie, but numbers vary. Migrates in dense flocks; most go to South America, a few linger at feeders. ▶ Male has *black* bib on *yellow chest,* rusty shoulder. Female like House Sparrow (p. 344) but with hint of yellow on chest, reddish on shoulder. ♪**Song:** suggests name, rough *djjk, djjk, sizzs-sizzs-sizzs.* **Callnote:** sharp *bzznt* given in flight.

LARK BUNTING *Calamospiza melanocorys*

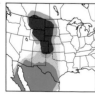

Numerous in summer on prairies just east of Rockies. Winters in tight flocks in brushy grassland of southwest. ▶ Summer male black with white wing patches. Females and all winter birds like very chunky, short-tailed, big-billed sparrows, with pale wing patches. In winter flocks, note contrasty pattern, dark underwings in flight. ♪**Song:** varied rich whistles, trills, buzzes, each repeated several times. **Callnote:** soft, rising *fweee.*

BIRDS OF OPEN FIELDS

**Western Meadowlark
and Eastern Meadowlark**
9½"

fall

summer
female

spring
male

Bobolink
7"

summer
male

immature

Dickcissel
6¼"

female

male

winter
males

Lark Bunting
7"

female

summer
male

GRACKLES AND ANIS

Grackles are long-tailed blackbirds with interesting voices. Anis are similar but unrelated, belonging to the cuckoo family (see p. 200).

COMMON GRACKLE *Quiscalus quiscula*

Very common almost everywhere east of Rockies (and locally farther west) in towns, farms, swamps, woods. Often seen walking on lawns. Nests in colonies; in fall and winter, may travel in huge noisy flocks, sometimes with other blackbirds. ▶ *Long tail* with "crease" down middle, *whitish-yellow eyes,* strong bill. Two forms: on widespread **"Bronzed Grackle,"** bronzy body contrasts with blue-black head; **"Purple Grackle"** of southeast has purple and green gloss, less contrast. Juveniles have dark eyes. Molting birds in late summer have short or ragged tails. ♪**Voice:** includes gurgling and creaking *kssh-ka-leeeea.* Also hard *chack* and *bzzt,* rough *zchaa.*

GREAT-TAILED GRACKLE *Quiscalus mexicanus*

Abundant in southwest, expanding range toward north and west, in towns, farms, riversides, freshwater marsh. Nests in colonies, travels in flocks. ▶ Very long tail, yellow eyes. Male glossy black, more evenly colored than Common Grackle and much larger. Female buff below and on eyebrow, smaller than male. ♪**Voice:** wildly varied, includes whistles, creaks, "flushing" sounds.

BOAT-TAILED GRACKLE *Quiscalus major*

A big grackle of the southeast coast, usually near salt water, though it goes inland in Florida. ▶ Like Great-tailed Grackle but a bit shorter-tailed, rounder-headed. Where they overlap (Texas-Louisiana coast), Boat-tail has *dark eyes* (but young Great-tail does also). From northeast Florida north, Boat-tail has yellow eyes; see Common Grackle. ♪**Voice:** varied squeaks, buzzes, whistles; male in display often gives rough *jeeb jeeb jeeb.*

GROOVE-BILLED ANI *Crotophaga sulcirostris*

A bizarre tropical cuckoo that reaches south Texas, a few wandering east along Gulf Coast and rarely elsewhere. Small groups hop clumsily on ground (often feeding near cattle), perch in the open, fly with several quick flaps and then a glide. ▶ Long tail (often held at odd angles), high narrow bill. Grooves on bill hard to see. ♪**Voice:** squeaky whining whistles.

SMOOTH-BILLED ANI *Crotophaga ani*

Scarce and declining in southern Florida, in brushy country, marsh edges. ▶ Like Groove-billed Ani but with *higher peaked ridge* on bill (and lacks grooves there). ♪**Voice:** thin rising whines, squeaky whistles.

LONG-TAILED BLACK BIRDS

juvenile

Common Grackle
12½"

"Bronzed" form

"Purple" form

Great-tailed Grackle
15"–18"

female

male

Boat-tailed Grackle
14"–16½"

female

males

Smooth-billed Ani
14"

Groove-billed Ani
13"

COWBIRDS AND MID-SIZED BLACKBIRDS

Cowbirds are brood parasites, laying their eggs in the nests of other birds so that their young will be raised by these "foster parents." The other two blackbirds here have more normal nesting habits.

BROWN-HEADED COWBIRD   *Molothrus ater*

This open-country bird has prospered with the clearing of forests. Very common today, its nest parasitism threatens populations of some smaller birds. Named for habit of feeding near cattle and other grazers, cowbirds walk on ground with tails held up. Often flocks with other blackbirds in winter. ▶ Male glossy black, with contrasting *brown head*. Female confusing, plain dusty brown with dark, sparrowlike bill. Juvenile streaked at first. ♪ **Song**: low gurgles and high thin notes. **Callnote**: long, liquid rattle; thin *seee-leeet* in flight.

BRONZED COWBIRD   *Molothrus aeneus*

A chunky southwestern cowbird. Scatters through all habitats in summer, but localized in winter around farms, feedlots. Strays east along Gulf Coast. ▶ Heavier than Brown-headed Cowbird, with longer bill, shorter tail, *red eyes* (hard to see). Neck ruff gives look of hunched shoulders. Females dull black (Texas) or gray-brown (Arizona). ♪ **Voice**: thin scraping whistles, clucks.

SHINY COWBIRD   *Molothrus bonariensis*

Rare visitor from Caribbean, mostly to Florida, but seen elsewhere in southeast. ▶ Size and shape much like Brown-headed Cowbird (females not safely identified), but male is *black all over*, with shiny purple gloss. Most other all-black birds are either much larger or have pale eyes.

BREWER'S BLACKBIRD   *Euphagus cyanocephalus*

A typical bird of the west, often very common in open country. Near Pacific Coast, also in cities, walking about on busy sidewalks. Gather in large flocks in winter. ▶ Shorter-tailed than grackles (previous page), a bit larger than cowbirds. Male all glossy black with whitish eyes. Female dull gray-brown, with *dark eyes*. ♪ **Song**: scraping, creaky *krk-queeee*. **Callnote**: *chuck*.

RUSTY BLACKBIRD   *Euphagus carolinus*

Mostly uncommon and declining, but sometimes seen in large flocks. Nests around bogs in far north, winters in southeastern swamps. Almost always near water, not joining other blackbirds in fields. ▶ In most seasons, dull black (male) or slaty (female), with yellow eyes. Like male Brewer's but less glossy, with thinner bill. In fall, distinctive with *rusty feather edges, buff eyebrow*. ♪ **Song**: high, creaking *kssh-dlleee*. **Callnote**: *chuck*.

BLACKBIRDS

females

Brown-headed
Cowbird
7½"

juvenile

males

Bronzed Cowbird
8½"

females

male

Shiny
Cowbird
(rare)
7½"

male

female

Brewer's
Blackbird
9"

female

male

Rusty
Blackbird
9"

fall
plumage

male

339

ORIOLES

forage for insects in trees, sometimes sip nectar from flowers (and may visit hummingbird feeders). Usually solitary or in pairs, sometimes in small flocks when migrating. Their nests are woven pouches or hanging bags of plant fibers, suspended from twigs.

BALTIMORE ORIOLE *Icterus galbula*

Rich color and whistled song make this oriole a summer favorite in the east, though it often stays hidden among foliage of elms or other shade trees. Winters mostly in tropics, a few in southeast. ► No other eastern bird resembles adult male. Female brown above, tinged orange below, with white wing-bars, variable black on head. On Great Plains, often interbreeds with Bullock's Oriole, producing hybrids with intermediate pattern. ♪ **Song**: series of rich whistles, fast or slow, sometimes with harsh notes included. **Callnote**: dry chatter.

BULLOCK'S ORIOLE *Icterus bullockii*

From the western Great Plains to the Pacific Coast, this oriole is fairly common in summer in treetops along rivers, lowland woods. ► Male resembles male Baltimore Oriole but has *orange face*, more white in wing, different tail pattern. Female usually not as orange as female Baltimore, with grayer back, *whiter belly*, darker eyeline, but some not safely identified. ♪ **Song**: series of short whistles, chatters, creaks. Often less musical than Baltimore Oriole. **Callnote**: harsh, dry chatter.

HOODED ORIOLE *Icterus cucullatus*

Common in summer in southwest, in riverside woods, parks, suburbs. It especially likes palms, often suspending its nest under a frond. A few stay for winter, may visit feeders. ► Adult male has *orange hood*, black throat and back, *white shoulder*. In winter, back looks barred with buff. On Mexican border and in south Florida, see orioles on next page. Female known by overall yellow-green look and thin, slightly curved bill. ♪ **Song**: variable choppy warble. **Callnotes**: nasal *weenk?*; thin chatter.

ORCHARD ORIOLE *Icterus spurius*

A small oriole, common in parts of southeast and midwest, scarcer northward. Favors edge of low woods, suburbs, stands of trees in open country. Migrates south early, on the move in July. ► Adult male unmistakable. Female is *small*, all yellow-green. Lacks orange tone of female Baltimore and Bullock's; *shorter bill* than Hooded. One-year-old male like female but with black throat. ♪ **Song**: fast jumble of whistles and buzzes. **Callnotes**: low *chuck*; thin whistle; dry chatter.

ORIOLES

young male

young female

Baltimore Oriole 8"

adult male

adult female

immature

female

Bullock's Oriole 8"

adult male

young male

Hooded Oriole 7³⁄₄"

winter male

summer male

female

young male

Orchard Oriole 7"

female

adult male

341

SCOTT'S ORIOLE   *Icterus parisorum*

In foothills of the southwest, this striking oriole is widespread but uncommon in summer, in junipers, oak woods, grassland with scattered yuccas. ▶ Brilliant black-and-yellow male unmistakable in range; note black upper back, yellow on rump and in base of tail. Female dusky yellow-green, darker and larger than female Hooded or Orchard Orioles (previous page). Older females and young males may have much black on head. ♪ **Song**: fast, rich, whistled phrases. Suggests Western Meadowlark. **Callnote**: harsh *schuck*.

ALTAMIRA ORIOLE   *Icterus gularis*

South Texas only. Fairly common in native woodland, riverside trees. Builds conspicuous nest, a hanging bag more than a foot long, suspended from a twig. ▶ Like Hooded Oriole (previous page) but has *orange patch* (not white) on shoulder. Larger, with thicker, straighter bill. Immatures duller. ♪ **Song**: fast choppy series of short whistles, rough notes. **Callnote**: rasping *enk enk enk*.

AUDUBON'S ORIOLE   *Icterus graduacauda*

South Texas only. Uncommon in woods along the Rio Grande, ranging into mesquite brushland and oak groves slightly farther north. Quiet, rather shy, easily overlooked. ▶ Adults known by *yellow-green back* contrasting with solid black hood, black tail, mostly black wings. Female slightly duller than male, young birds much duller, lacking black at first. ♪ **Song**: slow, hesitant, like human learning to whistle. **Callnote**: nasal *engk*.

SPOT-BREASTED ORIOLE   *Icterus pectoralis*

Florida only. Native to Mexico and Central America, accidentally introduced into Miami area, where it is uncommon and localized in suburbs. ▶ Only Florida oriole with bright *orange head* and black throat. Spots on sides of chest; much white in black wings. Immature duller, may lack spots. Juvenile all dull yellow at first. ♪ **Song**: rich slurred whistles. **Callnote**: nasal *nyeng*.

STREAK-BACKED ORIOLE   *Icterus pustulatus*

Rare visitor to southern Arizona and California, mostly in winter, but has nested in Arizona. Favors tall trees near water. ▶ Adult male rich orange with narrow black throat, much white in wings, *narrow black streaks on back*. Hooded Oriole (previous page) has scaly pattern on back in winter. Female duller; some young females not safely separated from some female Bullock's Orioles (which can have streaked back). ♪ **Song**: rich warbling whistle. **Callnotes**: dry rattle, soft *weeep*, harsh nasal *nyehhr*.

ORIOLES

Scott's
Oriole
9"

males

females

Altamira Oriole
10"
(Texas only)

adult

adult

Spot-breasted
Oriole
9¹/₂"

(Florida
only)

adult

Audubon's
Oriole
9¹/₂"

(Texas
only)

adult
male

Streak-backed
Oriole
(rare visitor)
8¹/₂"

immature

OLD WORLD SPARROWS

(family Passeridae) are widespread in Europe, Asia, and Africa. Two very adaptable species have been introduced into North America.

HOUSE SPARROW   *Passer domesticus*

This resourceful, spunky bird, adapted to living around humans, thrives even in our biggest cities. Unpopular with some people (partly because it may compete with native birds), this sparrow is undeniably interesting to watch, and it adds a spark of life to urban settings that would be almost birdless without it. ▶ Male has black bib, white cheeks, gray crown, chestnut nape. Female also attractive with a close look, with pale buff eyebrow, plain gray chest, stripes of black and buff on brown back. ♪ **Voice**: variety of chirping and chattering notes.

EURASIAN TREE SPARROW   *Passer montanus*

Introduced into St. Louis in 1870, this sparrow has survived but has not spread far. Small colonies live around farms, parks, suburbs in the St. Louis region of Missouri and Illinois, locally into southeastern Iowa. ▶ Both sexes resemble male House Sparrow, but crown *brown* (not gray), *black ear spot* on white cheek, usually smaller black bib. ♪ **Voice**: varied chirps and twitters, sometimes higher-pitched than those of House Sparrow.

AMERICAN SPARROWS

(part of **family Emberizidae**) include a variety of species. Many of these have attractive (if subtle) color patterns, and some have beautiful songs. Sparrows can be hard to identify at first; here are some clues to consider.

• **Pattern of the underparts**: is the bird streaked across the chest or down the sides, does it have a dark chest spot, or is it plain below?

• **Head pattern:** look for things like stripes on the crown, dark whisker marks (angling down from the bill), an eye-ring, or contrasting color on the throat.

• **Shape:** does the tail look relatively short (as on Savannah Sparrow) or long (as on Song Sparrow)? Does the bird seem flat-headed or large-billed? It takes some experience to see these subtleties, but after you know a few sparrows, you'll notice shape differences when you see new ones.

Savannah Sparrow   Song Sparrow

SPARROWS

females

House
Sparrow
6"

fall
male

spring
male

Eurasian
Tree Sparrow
5¾"

MORE CLUES FOR IDENTIFYING NATIVE SPARROWS:

• **Habitat:** Sparrows may pause anywhere during migration, but at most times they have clear habitat choices. You're not likely to find a Swamp Sparrow in the desert, nor a Sage Sparrow in the swamp. Sparrows are grouped by habitat type on some of the following pages.

• **Social life:** Sparrows (like most birds) are in pairs or family groups during nesting season, but at other seasons, some species are usually in flocks while others are usually solitary. This is often a very helpful clue, and it is mentioned in the species accounts that follow.

• Finally, is the bird really a sparrow? Sparrows have short thick bills for cracking seeds, but some other birds have similar bills. Before you give up on a mystery sparrow, ask whether it might belong to another group.

sparrow

blackbird
p. 332

Dickcissel
p. 334

finch p. 366

grosbeak p. 396

SPARROWS

These four usually stay low in brushy places and marshes; sometimes hard to see. They may be in pairs or family groups, but not flocks.

SONG SPARROW *Melospiza melodia*

Common and widespread. Likes dense low cover, but becomes rather tame around gardens, parks. Overall color varies by region, from widespread typical look to darker birds in northwest and paler, redder birds along desert streams. ▶ Fairly long tail, striped face, streaks on chest often run together into a central blotch. See Lincoln's Sparrow. Savannah Sparrow (p. 354) has shorter tail, usually lives in open fields. ♪ Song: short notes followed by trill, *twik twik twika to WEEE, trr, titititititititi*. Callnote: distinctively nasal, squeaky *chif*.

LINCOLN'S SPARROW *Melospiza lincolnii*

Common in west, usually scarce in east, in dense low thickets. Often shy, but (like other sparrows) will hop up to investigate squeaking noises, head feathers raised in a short perky crest. ▶ Contrasting face colors: buff "whisker," gray eyebrow, brown cheeks and crown. Rich *buff chest* has *narrow* black streaks. (Caution: juvenile Song Sparrows in summer can be buffy, with narrow streaks.) ♪ Song: short musical bubbling, shifts to higher pitch halfway through. Callnotes: *chep* and *szeet*.

SWAMP SPARROW *Melospiza georgiana*

A dark, richly colored sparrow that lurks in wet places: marshes, swamps, dense thickets near water. Sometimes common, but found singly, not in flocks. ▶ Looks rather dark overall, usually with *bright chestnut* on wings and back. Gray face contrasts with white throat and reddish cap in summer; cap is much duller in winter, brown with pale central stripe. ♪ Song: slow trill on one pitch. Callnote: sharp, ringing *peek*.

FOX SPARROW *Passerella iliaca*

On the ground under dense thickets, this big sparrow scratches in the leaf-litter with both feet at once. Generally seen only in small numbers. Color varies from foxy red (east) to gray-headed (mountain west) to sooty brown (Pacific Northwest); the different forms might be separate species. ▶ Large size, ground-scratching behavior. *Triangular* spots on underparts; rather *plain face*. Most forms have *reddish tail* (see Hermit Thrush, p. 258). Often has two-toned bill. Some in California very large-billed. ♪ Song: surprisingly musical, includes rich whistles, sliding notes, short trills. Callnote: varies by region, either *chep* or metallic *tink*.

SPARROWS

salt marsh
(California)

Pacific
Northwest

widespread
form

desert
rivers

Song Sparrow
5½"–7"

Lincoln's Sparrow
5½"

summer

fresh
fall plumage

Swamp Sparrow
5¾"

summer

immature

winter

sooty
form

large-billed
form

red
form

grayish
form

Fox Sparrow
7"

347

"AIMOPHILA" SPARROWS

large and long-tailed, usually hide in dense cover. Alone or in pairs or family groups, not in flocks. Voice is important for identification.

RUFOUS-CROWNED SPARROW *Aimophila ruficeps*

A long-tailed skulker of rocky, brushy hillsides and canyons. Usually in pairs. More often heard than seen. ▶ Rusty crown, white eye-ring, heavy dark *whisker mark;* looks big-billed, flat-headed. Swamp Sparrow (previous page) in very different habitat; Chipping and other rusty-capped sparrows (next page) more petite, less secretive. ♪**Song**: short jumble of notes, suggests House Wren. **Callnotes**: include nasal *dear-dear-dear.*

CASSIN'S SPARROW *Aimophila cassinii*

In brushy grassland, often unnoticed except during its flight-song. Rather nomadic, numbers and range vary from year to year. ▶ Long-tailed, gray-brown, confusingly plain. Dull white tail corners; dark marks on back and flanks can be obscure in faded summer plumage. Best known by habit of fluttering up in air and gliding back down while singing. ♪**Song**: short notes before and after long musical trill, *titi-trrrrrrrrrrr, tyew tyew.*

BOTTERI'S SPARROW *Aimophila botterii*

Uncommon and local in desert grassland and coastal prairie near Mexican border. Secretive, hard to see when not singing. ▶ Large, long-tailed, lacks obvious marks. Cassin's Sparrow less uniformly colored, may show streaks on flanks or dark scallops on back, but song is best field mark. ♪**Song**: given while perched, long irregular series of sharp notes, accelerating into trill.

BACHMAN'S SPARROW *Aimophila aestivalis*

A shy, uncommon sparrow of southern pine woods, palmetto stands, and brushy fields, staying near the ground in dense grass. Seldom seen except when singing. ▶ Large and long-tailed, relatively plain brown. Botteri's Sparrow very similar, but *no overlap in range.* ♪**Song**: beautiful clear whistles, usually one long note followed by slow musical trill on a different pitch.

RUFOUS-WINGED SPARROW *Aimophila carpalis*

Southern Arizona only. Very localized in desert with tall grass and scattered mesquite shrubs. Usually in pairs, hiding in grass except when singing. ▶ Rusty crown stripes, dark eye-line. *Two short whisker marks* distinctive. Rufous on wing is hard to see. Chipping Sparrow (next page) smaller, less secretive, lacks double whisker. ♪**Song**: two or three short notes followed by a fast trill; pitch of song is variable.

SPARROWS

Rufous-crowned Sparrow 6"

Cassin's Sparrow 6"

Bachman's Sparrow 6"

Botteri's Sparrow 6"

Rufous-winged Sparrow 5¾"

are small, with medium to longish tails. Usually seen in small flocks in winter, often perching up in the open in brushy places.

CHIPPING SPARROW   *Spizella passerina*

A summer backyard bird in many areas, hopping on lawns, nesting in hedges. Winter flocks forage around woodland edge, thickets. ▶ In summer, has chestnut cap, *white* eyebrow, *black* eyeline. Less contrast in winter; chestnut partly obscured. Juvenile streaky at first, retains some streaks into fall. Dull fall birds can suggest next two species, but have *rump gray,* not brown. ♪ **Song:** rapid, hard, dry trill. **Callnotes:** hard *chip* and thin *ssip.*

CLAY-COLORED SPARROW   *Spizella pallida*

Common on Great Plains, rare visitor to east or west coast. Likes shrubby areas in open country. ▶ Brown ear patch with darker outline; whitish central stripe on crown. Gray neck may contrast with buff on chest. Fall Chipping Sparrows can be similar, but Clay-color *lacks* dark line from eye to bill, has *brown rump.* See Brewer's Sparrow. ♪ **Song:** four flat, scraping buzzes on one pitch.

BREWER'S SPARROW   *Spizella breweri*

A pale little western sparrow with a blank expression. Common on sagebrush flats in summer. In winter, flocks in open desert, brushy spots. Sometimes sings on winter mornings. ▶ Lacks obvious marks. Plainer face than Chipping or Clay-colored Sparrows. Those nesting high above treeline from Montana to Alaska might be separate species, "Timberline Sparrow." ♪ **Song:** fast, variable trills and buzzes, running on and on.

AMERICAN TREE SPARROW   *Spizella arborea*

A cold-weather sparrow. Seen south of Canada in winter only, when flocks roam brushy fields, forest edge, gardens, often with juncos or other sparrows. Nests at edge of Arctic tundra. ▶ Rusty cap, *two-toned bill,* dark chest spot, two white wing-bars. Compare to Chipping and Field Sparrows. Swamp Sparrow (p. 346) chunky, more secretive, lacks white wing-bars. ♪ **Song:** musical clear whistles, warbles. **Callnote:** musical *twiddle-eat.*

FIELD SPARROW   *Spizella pusilla*

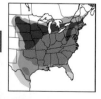

A baby-faced sparrow, common in brushy overgrown fields, often in small flocks. ▶ Rusty cap, *pink bill,* faint *whitish eye-ring,* pale rusty eyeline. Looks long-tailed for its size. Chipping Sparrow in winter may have pink bill, but has stronger dark eyeline. ♪ **Song:** short plaintive whistles in minor key, speeding up to trill; may descend or stay on same pitch. **Callnote:** soft lisping notes.

SPARROWS

Chipping Sparrow
5½"

juvenile

winter adult

summer adults

Clay-colored Sparrow
5½"

Brewer's Sparrow
5¾"

Field Sparrow
5¾"

summer

winter

American Tree Sparrow
6¼"

351

SPARROWS

These five all live in open, fairly dry places, mostly in the west, although the Lark Sparrow extends farther east.

LARK SPARROW *Chondestes grammacus*

A striking sparrow, common in the west, scarce in the east. Likes bare ground near brushy areas: farms, horse corrals, prairie edges. Often in small flocks, perching conspicuously in the open. Rare stray to east coast in fall. ▶ Strong *face pattern,* dark spot on chest. White *edges and corners* on long tail. Young bird duller, has recognizable face and tail patterns. ♪ **Song:** long series, starts with clear notes, then buzzy or gurgling notes tossed in. **Callnote:** metallic *tchip,* often in flight.

BLACK-CHINNED SPARROW *Spizella atrogularis*

In chaparral and oak scrub of western foothills, this small sparrow is quiet, easily overlooked. ▶ Gray head and chest, pale bill suggest a junco (p. 360), but back and wings patterned like Chipping Sparrow (previous page). Black on chin mainly on summer males. Long tail for its small size. ♪ **Song:** series of short notes speeding up into a very rapid dry trill. **Callnote:** thin *seeet.*

BLACK-THROATED SPARROW *Amphispiza bilineata*

A desert sparrow, very rarely straying away from dry country. Not shy; pairs or small groups forage on ground, making tinkling musical notes. ▶ *Black throat* and mask set off by *white* eyebrow and whisker stripes. Plain gray-brown above, with narrow white tail edge and corners. Juvenile has white throat, streaked chest; suggests Sage Sparrow (below) but has stronger white eyebrow. ♪ **Song:** two or three short metallic notes followed by trill; variable. **Callnote:** very high thin notes.

SAGE SPARROW *Amphispiza belli*

Favors barren country: sagebrush and saltbush flats, other desert types in winter. (Darker Pacific Coast form lives in denser chaparral.) Wags or dips tail often while perched. On open ground, runs with its tail held high. ▶ Inland form pale and drab with gray head, white whisker stripe, dark chest spot. Behavior is best clue. Coastal form darker gray, more contrasty. ♪ **Song:** high-pitched musical series. **Callnote:** thin high notes.

FIVE-STRIPED SPARROW *Aimophila quinquestriata*

Arizona only. A rare summer resident of a few rugged canyons near Mexican border; mostly absent in winter. ▶ Looks dark, with brown back, gray chest, five stripes on throat (three white, two black). ♪ **Song:** variable short metallic series, *chip-chip, tink . . . tick, wheesk . . . chep, tictictic . . . ,* etc.

SPARROWS

Lark Sparrow
6½"

immature

adults

Black-chinned Sparrow
5¾"

female and winter

summer male

juvenile

Black-throated Sparrow
5½"

adults

Five-striped Sparrow
(rare)
6"

Sage Sparrow
6¼"

inland form

coastal form

All marked with lots of streaks. Savannah and Vesper are often easy to see; Henslow's and Baird's are much more elusive, hiding in the grass.

SAVANNAH SPARROW *Passerculus sandwichensis*

Around fields, marshes, or beach grass, a streaky little sparrow that sits in the open is very likely to be this species. Common and widespread, often in small, loose flocks. Worth learning as a basis for comparison to other sparrows. ► Heavily streaked on chest, strong face pattern, narrow white central crown stripe. Often shows yellow in front of eye. Many local variations; extremes are blackish **"Belding's"** form (California salt marshes) and large, pale **"Ipswich"** form (Atlantic beaches in winter). ♪ **Song:** short notes before and after trill, *sip sip sip sreeeeeeee, sip.* **Callnotes:** *tsip* and *seet.*

VESPER SPARROW *Pooecetes gramineus*

This pale, streaky sparrow likes open prairies, farm fields, dry country, so it is more common in west than in east. Never in large flocks, but may gather with other sparrows in winter. Named for the impression that it sings most beautifully in late evening. ► *White* outer tail feathers (hard to see until bird flies). Heavy *dark outline* of cheek patch, *white* eye-ring, *narrow* streaks on crown. Chestnut spot on shoulder is often hidden. ♪ **Song:** musical and clear, two long notes followed by shorter notes and slurred trills. **Callnote:** sharp *ssip.*

HENSLOW'S SPARROW *Ammodramus henslowii*

Uncommon and very localized (and probably declining), in weedy overgrown fields, eastern prairies. Shy, hard to see; seldom perches in the open except when singing. When flushed, flies low and then drops into grass again. ► Small, short-tailed, with flat-headed look. *Olive-green* wash on head contrasts with rich *rusty brown* back and wings. Sharp streaks on whitish chest and sides. ♪ **Song:** odd, flat little noise, *hslick,* almost one-syllabled. May sing at night as well as by day.

BAIRD'S SPARROW *Ammodramus bairdii*

Dry prairies of midcontinent host this uncommon, elusive sparrow. Very hard to see during migration and winter, when not singing; flushes and flies low, dropping into grass again and then running. ► Short-tailed and flat-headed. *Mustard yellow tinge* on head, may show up as rich *ocher stripe* on center crown. Whitish below with necklace of dark streaks on chest. Streaky or scaly look on back. ♪ **Song:** surprisingly musical, three to five short notes followed by long trill.

SPARROWS OF OPEN FIELDS

typical
adults

"Belding's"
form

"Ipswich"
form

Savannah
Sparrow
5½"

Vesper
Sparrow
6¼"

Henslow's
Sparrow
5"

Baird's
Sparrow
5½"

These are all shy, solitary birds, never in flocks. Staying low in the grass, they are often hard to see well except when they are singing.

GRASSHOPPER SPARROW   *Ammodramus savannarum*

In dry, grassy fields, this sparrow is often common but easily overlooked. Even its song suggests the buzz of a grasshopper. ▶ Big-headed, short-tailed, with flat forehead. Crown has central white stripe bordered by thick *dark stripes,* otherwise mostly *plain buff* on face and chest. Gray nape with fine pink stripes, heavily striped back. ♪ **Song:** insectlike buzz, *pt-tup-bzzzzeeeeeee.*

LE CONTE'S SPARROW   *Ammodramus leconteii*

Very damp fields or very shallow marshes hide this shy, colorful little sparrow. If disturbed, it flies weakly and low before dropping into the grass again. ▶ *Orange-buff face stripes* around gray cheek; white central stripe on black crown. Gray nape has fine pink stripes. Suggests Grasshopper Sparrow, but has sharp *black streaks* on *sides.* ♪ **Song:** weak gasping hiss, *tk-ksssssssshh-tk.*

SALTMARSH SHARP-TAILED SPARROW   *Ammodramus caudacutus*

Along the central Atlantic Coast, this bird and Seaside Sparrow are common where undisturbed salt marsh still remains. ▶ Smaller and paler than Seaside Sparrow, with stronger face pattern. Very similar to Nelson's Sharp-tail (which occurs in same marshes in winter), but has whiter (less buffy) chest with heavier streaking. ♪ **Song:** wheezy hissing, often run into sputtering series.

NELSON'S SHARP-TAILED SPARROW   *Ammodramus nelsoni*

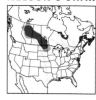

The two sharp-tailed sparrows were formerly considered one species. Nelson's is the only one likely to be seen away from the Atlantic Coast. It nests in coastal marsh from Maine north and in prairie marshes of the interior. ▶ Gray cheek patch surrounded by triangle of orange or buff stripes. Suggests Le Conte's Sparrow but has central crown stripe *gray* (not white), nape smooth gray (no stripes). ♪ **Song:** wheezy hissing *psshhhhhh-tk.*

SEASIDE SPARROW   *Ammodramus maritimus*

This gawky sparrow hugs the salt marshes of the Atlantic and Gulf Coasts. ▶ Long-billed for a sparrow, with short spiky tail. Has striking *pale spot* before eye, pale whisker stripe. Usually looks dark and drab, but overall color varies with range. Habitat is one of best field marks. Endangered south Florida race, "Cape Sable Sparrow," is greenish above, heavily streaked blackish below. ♪ **Song:** buzzy hissing, *tuk tuk zzzhheeee.*

FIELD AND MARSH SPARROWS

Grasshopper
Sparrow
5"

juvenile

Saltmarsh
Sharp-tailed
Sparrow
5"

Le Conte's
Sparrow
4¾"

Nelson's
Sharp-tailed
Sparrow
5"

widespread
form

northeast
coast
form

Seaside
Sparrow
6"

spend summer in cool climates, move south in flocks for winter. Open cup-shaped nest is placed on ground or in shrub.

WHITE-THROATED SPARROW   *Zonotrichia albicollis*

Flocks of White-throats haunt the undergrowth of woods, parks, and gardens in winter, foraging on the ground, often with other sparrows or juncos. Very common in east, scarce in west. Summers in northern forest. ▶ Conspicuous white throat, dark bill, yellow spot before eye. Adults have two color morphs; white-striped birds usually mate with tan-striped ones. Some first-winter birds are duller, with blurry streaks below. ♪ **Song:** clear whistled *oh, sweet, kimberly-kimberly-kimberly*. **Callnotes:** *sseeet* and metallic *chink*.

WHITE-CROWNED SPARROW   *Zonotrichia leucophrys*

Very common in west, uncommon in east is the elegant White-crown. Flocks in winter live in thickets, woodland edges, deserts, and may sing in rambling chorus from bush tops on warm winter days. Most spend summer in far north or mountains; some live all year along Pacific Coast. ▶ Usually grayer than White-throat, with *pink or yellow bill*. Crown stripes black and white on adults, chestnut and gray in first winter. Pattern in front of eye varies with range. ♪ **Song:** varies, with local dialects. Usually includes clear whistles and buzzy or trilled notes. **Callnotes:** metallic *pink* and thin *seeet*.

GOLDEN-CROWNED SPARROW   *Zonotrichia atricapilla*

In winter in the Pacific states, these big sparrows flock in undergrowth of woods and parks, often with White-crowned Sparrows. Farther east, they are very rare visitors. For summer, they go north to thickets and tundra. ▶ Striking black head stripes of summer plumage give way to duller winter pattern; some drab young birds suggest female House Sparrow (p. 344). Unlike White-crown, bill is mostly dark. ♪ **Song:** clear whistles, a sad, descending *oh, dear, me*. **Callnotes:** *tchip* and *szeeet*.

HARRIS'S SPARROW   *Zonotrichia querula*

On the southern plains in winter, Harris's Sparrows flock around thickets and woodland edges. Strays turn up elsewhere, with other sparrows or juncos. In summer they retire to open spruce forest of central Canada. ▶ Adults distinctive (see Black-throated Sparrow p. 352, House Sparrow p. 344). Immature lacks black throat; note large size, *pink bill*, bright white belly. ♪ **Song:** slow clear whistles in minor key. **Callnotes:** sharp *pink*. Flocks make musical *chug-up, chug-up*.

"CROWNED" SPARROWS

immature

tan-striped

**White-throated
Sparrow**
6¾"

white-
striped

**White-crowned
Sparrow**
7"

adults

west coast
adult

immature

dull
winter bird

adults

**Golden-crowned
Sparrow**
7¼"

**Harris's
Sparrow**
7½"

immature

adults

359

are gray sparrows with white outer tail feathers. Cool-weather birds, they nest mostly in the north or the mountains and spread southward in winter, often visiting backyard bird feeders.

DARK-EYED JUNCO   *Junco hyemalis*

"Slate-colored"

For many regions this is a "snowbird," visiting only in winter. Except when they pair up for nesting, juncos are usually in small flocks, feeding on the ground near thickets or forest edge. Several types (once regarded as full species) can be identified. All have separate ranges in summer; but in winter, west of the plains, several kinds may mix in the same flock. ▶ All of these have white outer tail feathers, and all but the last have pale pink bills. Juveniles of all are streaky brown at first.

"**Slate-colored Junco**" is the only form usually seen in the east. Solid gray on head, back, sides. Females and first-winter birds slightly browner than adult males.

"Oregon"

"**Oregon Junco**" is widespread in west, rarely appears in east. Male has solid black or slaty hood, chestnut back, rusty sides. Female paler, with gray hood.

"**Pink-sided Junco**" nests in north-central Rockies region, winters farther south (no map). A bit larger than most juncos, with pale blue-gray hood, pink sides, brown back. Female "Oregon" can be very similar.

"White-winged"

"**White-winged Junco**" nests in Black Hills region of South Dakota. Like "Slate-colored" but larger and paler, with *white wing-bars,* more white in tail. (Other juncos rarely can have wing-bars also.)

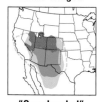

"Gray-headed"

"**Gray-headed Junco**" nests mostly in central Rockies and mountains of Great Basin. Reddish patch on back contrasts with gray hood. Unlike "Oregon Junco," sides and flanks are *gray,* not brown or tan.

"**Red-backed Junco**" (no map) is resident in mountains of northern Arizona and New Mexico, seldom moves far from nesting areas. Gray sides and reddish back like "Gray-headed," but has pale throat, mostly *dark bill.*
♪ **Song:** simple musical trill on one pitch. **Callnotes:** include dry clicking *tic* and harder *smack.* (Note: "Red-backed" has more varied song and callnotes.)

YELLOW-EYED JUNCO   *Junco phaeonotus*

In mountain forest near the Mexican border, this junco shuffles along on the ground or sings from the pines. ▶ Bright *orange-yellow eye* gives "fierce" look. Gray head, pale throat, reddish on back and wings, two-toned bill. Juvenile streaked, and has dark eyes at first. ♪ **Song:** more varied than in other juncos, usually includes trills and musical notes. **Callnotes:** *chip* and *tsst.*

JUNCOS

Dark-eyed Junco 6"

"Slate-colored Junco"

"Oregon Junco"

juvenile juncos are streaked

"Pink-sided Junco"

"White-winged Junco"

"Red-backed Junco"

"Gray-headed Junco"

Yellow-eyed Junco 6¹/₄"

juvenile Yellow-eyed

adult

live on the ground, and they live in flocks at most seasons. Winter flocks frequent plowed fields, short-grass plains, lake shores. If approached too closely, the flock rises and swirls about in undulating flight. Their winter plumages can be drab and confusing; focus on tail patterns (seen best on takeoff and landing) and callnotes, often given in flight.

LAPLAND LONGSPUR   *Calcarius lapponicus*

Typical of Arctic tundra in summer, the males singing from atop boulders or while flying. In winter, abundant on Great Plains, fairly common elsewhere, often in plowed fields with Horned Larks (p. 270). ▶ Summer male has black face, chestnut nape. Female and winter birds variable, usually show black mottling or streaking on chest sides, rich *reddish chestnut* in wings. Tail has *narrow* white outer edges. ♪ **Song:** short melodious warble, often given in flight. **Callnotes:** rough rattle, *tridit*, and whistle, *teeuw*, often alternated.

SMITH'S LONGSPUR   *Calcarius pictus*

Uncommon, localized, mostly in midcontinent. Nests at edge of tundra, areas with scattered low spruces; winters in short-grass fields of the southern Great Plains. ▶ Summer male orange-buff below, with contrasty face triangle. Females and winter birds much plainer; *more buffy* than other longspurs, with hint of face pattern. Tail has *narrow* white edges. ♪ **Song:** thin whistles, *sweetew weeteeteetew, weechew.* **Callnote:** dry ticking rattle, thinner than that of Lapland Longspur.

CHESTNUT-COLLARED LONGSPUR   *Calcarius ornatus*

Favoring taller grass than other longspurs, this species nests on northern plains, winters on southern plains and in southwest. ▶ Strong *tail pattern* (mostly white, with black triangle). Summer male black below, with chestnut nape, pale face. Female and many winter birds more sparrowlike; tail pattern and calls are best clues. ♪ **Song:** short warbling phrases, often given in flight. **Callnote:** very distinctive squeaky *cheedle-lup.*

MCCOWN'S LONGSPUR   *Calcarius mccownii*

Overlaps with Chestnut-collared Longspur, but likes areas with shorter grass or no grass; in winter, often on plowed fields, barren flats. ▶ Strong *tail pattern* (like Chestnut-collared, but black is shaped like inverted T). Summer male has black chest and cap, rusty shoulder; female duller. Winter birds *paler and chunkier* than most longspurs, with bigger bill. ♪ **Song:** short melodious warble, often given in flight. **Callnotes:** odd ringing *pwoik* and short dry rattle.

LONGSPURS

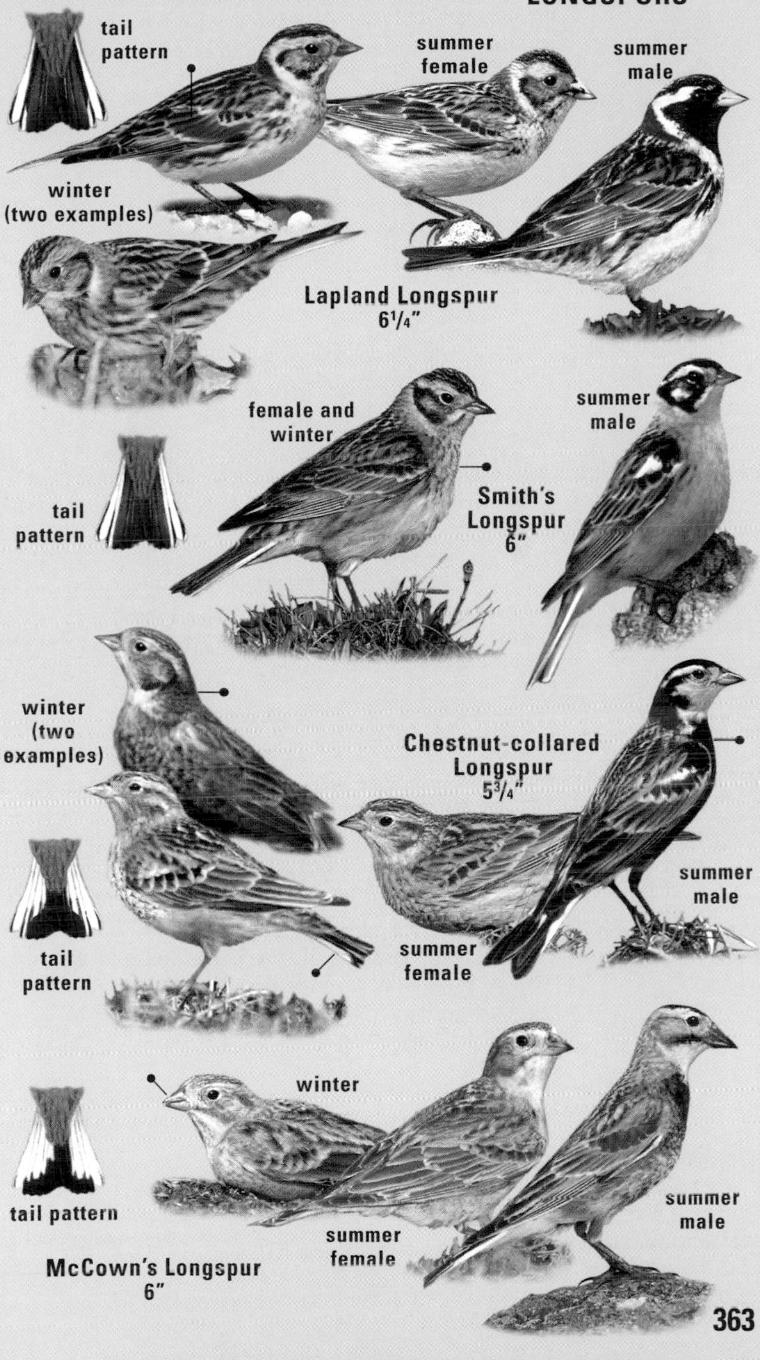

tail pattern
summer female
summer male
winter (two examples)
Lapland Longspur
6¼″
female and winter
summer male
tail pattern
Smith's Longspur
6″
winter (two examples)
Chestnut-collared Longspur
5¾″
tail pattern
summer male
summer female
winter
tail pattern
summer female
summer male
McCown's Longspur
6″

SNOW BUNTINGS AND ROSY-FINCHES

These two buntings are related to longspurs and sparrows. The rest on this page are the first of the true finches (**family Fringillidae**).

SNOW BUNTING   *Plectrophenax nivalis*

In winter in cold country, flocks of these pale buntings walk on the ground on barren fields, shores. For summer, they go to Arctic tundra. ▶ In winter, pale brown and white, with big *white wing patches,* black in tail and wingtips. Summer male clean black and white, female duller and grayer. Beware confusion with partial albinos of other species. ♪ **Song**: in summer only, rich warbling. **Callnotes**: musical rattle, soft *teew.*

MCKAY'S BUNTING   *Plectrophenax hyperboreus*

Rare Alaska specialty, nesting on Hall and St. Matthew Islands, rarely other islands. Winter visitor to Alaskan mainland. ▶ Much whiter than Snow Bunting. Similar birds away from Alaska are probably albino sparrows.

BROWN-CAPPED ROSY-FINCH   *Leucosticte australis*

Rosy-finches nest in barren rocky places in the highest mountains, may move downslope in winter. Usually in flocks. Forage at edges of snowfields, eating frozen insects. ▶ Pink wash on belly, rump, and wings, much less obvious on females. Male Brown-cap lacks gray nape of next two species. Note *range* (Colorado and nearby areas). ♪ **Voice**: rough *dzzeew* (all three rosy-finches).

BLACK ROSY-FINCH   *Leucosticte atrata*

The three species of rosy-finches have separate ranges in summer, may mix in winter. They forage on ground, but may visit feeders in mountain towns. ▶ Male shows striking contrast between black body plumage and gray nape band, rosy belly and wing patches. Female much plainer, may be darker than other species. All rosy-finches have black bill in summer, yellow in winter.

GRAY-CROWNED ROSY-FINCH   *Leucosticte tephrocotis*

The most widespread rosy-finch, high mountains from California to Alaska, also Alaskan islands (Pribilofs, Aleutians). Rarely wanders onto plains in winter. Nests are usually hidden in crevices in rock cliffs. ▶ Not as contrasty as Black Rosy-Finch. Male has *gray band* across nape, wider in some races than others. Females may be very similar to other female rosy-finches.

BRAMBLING   *Fringilla montifringilla*

Rare spring and fall migrant in western Alaska; very rare winter visitor to much of U.S. and Canada, sometimes at feeders. ▶ Spring males have sharp pattern, but females and winter males are plainer. Note *white rump,* tawny chest, stripes on nape.

BUNTINGS, ROSY-FINCHES

Snow Bunting
7"

winter flock

winter (two examples)

summer male

summer female

summer male

summer female

McKay's Bunting
(Alaska only)
7"

summer male

male

Brown-capped Rosy-Finch
6"

female

male

Black Rosy-Finch
6"

winter male

Brambling
(rare)
6"

female

Gray-crowned Rosy-Finch
6"

three variations

RED FINCHES

HOUSE FINCH
Carpodacus mexicanus

An abundant and familiar bird of back yards, cities, open woods, deserts, canyons. Native to the west, it was accidentally introduced to the New York area in 1940 and spread from there to occupy the east as well. Commonly visits bird feeders, often in flocks. Nest is hidden in sites such as dense trees, palms, vines on walls, and hanging pots. ▶ Female and young have rather *plain* brown face, blurry stripes *all over* pale underparts (sharper stripes on juveniles). House Sparrows (p. 344) lack stripes; native sparrows (pp. 346–363) all have different patterns, and most are more secretive. Male House Finch has red eyebrow and forehead contrasting with brown cap. Throat and chest red, lower underparts whitish, with dark *stripes on sides.* Compare to redpolls (next page). Some males have red replaced by orange or yellow. ♪ **Song:** fast cheery warbling, usually with loud rough note at end. **Callnotes:** musical chirping.

PURPLE FINCH
Carpodacus purpureus

Fairly common in north and northeast and along Pacific Coast, but usually outnumbered by House Finch, especially around towns and cities. Feeds mostly up in trees on seeds and berries, also visits bird feeders. Winter numbers in the east vary from year to year. ▶ Similar to House Finch but looks chunkier, shorter-tailed. Adult male more *uniformly* washed with dull red on head and foreparts, *lacks* obvious dark stripes on sides. Female and young show much stronger face pattern than House Finch, including dark whisker and whitish eyebrow. In mountain west, see Cassin's Finch. ♪ **Song:** rich mellow warbling, without rough notes. **Callnotes:** hard, loud *pik*, often given in flight; musical *chuwee*.

CASSIN'S FINCH
Carpodacus cassinii

Fairly common in high mountain forests of the west. When not nesting, wanders in small flocks, often feeding on buds and seeds in treetops. In some winters, may appear in lowlands of southwest, even out onto plains. ▶ Very similar to Purple Finch (which is absent from many areas of the west). Cassin's is slightly larger, with slightly longer bill. Note *dark streaks* on white undertail coverts. Male has sharply defined *red cap*, paler pink chest. Female has plainer face, sharper streaks below than female Purple; often shows *pale eye-ring*. Compare also to House Finch, usually at lower elevations. ♪ **Song:** rich mellow warbling, sometimes includes imitations of other birds. **Callnote:** musical *giddy-up*.

RED FINCHES

females

House Finch
5³/₄"

males

male color
variant

Purple Finch
6"

females

males

Cassin's Finch
6¹/₄"

females

male

nest in the north (or high mountains), wander in flocks when not nesting. Erratic in winter; may invade large areas one year and be absent the next.

RED CROSSBILL *Loxia curvirostra*

Chunky nomads of evergreen forest, prying open cones with their odd bills to eat the seeds. Wander in flocks, may nest at almost any season. ▶ Females and some males dull yellow, most males dull brick red, darker wings and tail. Crossed bill hard to see at distance. Note flocking and feeding behavior. Might represent up to eight species, differing only very slightly in callnotes and bill shape. ♪ **Voice**: hard *kip-kip*, often in flight.

WHITE-WINGED CROSSBILL *Loxia leucoptera*

Often farther north than Red Crossbill, though they overlap widely. Prefers spruces, feeding on cones. Wanders erratically, may be common or absent at a given place. ▶ Broad *white bars* on black wings (Red Crossbill sometimes has very thin wing-bars). Adult male mostly rose-red, female dull yellow with blurry streaks. ♪ **Voice**: dry slow rattle, often given in flight.

PINE GROSBEAK *Pinicola enucleator*

A big, sluggish finch of conifer forest (mostly spruce and fir, not pines). Typically uncommon and quiet. Sometimes wanders south in winter; small flocks may feed on berries, maple buds. Can be very tame. ▶ Long tail, stubby black bill, two wing-bars. Adult male mostly pink and gray, female and young gray, with yellow or orange on head. ♪ **Song**: rich warbling. **Callnotes**: musical *chyew-wee*, whistled *tew-tew-teew*.

COMMON REDPOLL *Carduelis flammea*

A tiny Arctic finch, nesting in birch or willow scrub around forest edge, tundra. Winter flocks may wander far south, visiting weedy fields, bird feeders. ▶ Small size, *red* forehead, *black chin*. Darker overall in summer. Male has variable pink wash on chest. Compare to red finches on previous page. ♪ **Song**: rapid, varied twittering. **Callnotes**: varied, including thin *queee-ee?* In flight, rattling *ch-ch-ching*.

HOARY REDPOLL *Carduelis hornemanni*

Tiny but tough, mostly in high Arctic year-round. Rare south of Canada, usually with Common Redpoll flocks. ▶ Very similar to Common Redpoll, hard to identify. Hoary has paler, "frosty" look; male has paler pink on chest; usually unmarked white on rump, flanks, undertail coverts. Bill may look stubbier. ♪ **Voice**: similar to Common Redpoll's.

WINTER FINCHES

Red Crossbill
6½"

female

juvenile

male

young
male

White-winged Crossbill
6½"

juvenile

male

female

male

female

**Pine
Grosbeak**
9"

**Hoary
Redpoll**
5¼"

**Common
Redpoll**
5"

369

GOLDFINCHES AND SISKIN

Tiny, sociable finches, feeding on seeds and other plant matter all year.

AMERICAN GOLDFINCH   *Carduelis tristis*

Lively, colorful, common around weedy fields, woodland edges, suburbs. Gathers in flocks in winter, often visiting bird feeders. ▶ Summer male bright yellow with *black wings, tail, and forehead.* Summer female duller yellow-green. Winter birds vary from yellowish brown to gray; note bold wing-bars (white or buff) on black wings, white tail spots. ♪**Song:** jumbled twittering, with variable pattern. **Callnotes:** clear thin notes. In bounding, dipping flight, a cheery *potato-chip.*

PINE SISKIN   *Carduelis pinus*

Like a goldfinch in camouflage. Despite its color pattern, the siskin acts like goldfinches and often flocks with them in winter. Sometimes oddly tame as it feeds at dried flower heads, bird feeders. ▶ Brown, usually with heavy streaking. Might suggest a sparrow, but note *narrower,* sharp-pointed bill, *plain face,* and edging of *yellow in wings and tail,* most obvious in flight. ♪**Voice:** varied calls include harsh, rising *zzsshreeee?,* clear *twee?,* and dry *cutcutcut.*

LESSER GOLDFINCH   *Carduelis psaltria*

Fairly common in the southwest, around streamsides, weedy fields, open woods. Usually seen in pairs or small flocks. ▶ Very small, with *white patches* in wings and tail. From Colorado to Texas, most males have black backs; farther west, most have green backs. Female is plainer; smaller than American Goldfinch, with undertail coverts *yellow,* not white. ♪**Song:** fast, musical twittering, includes brief imitations of other birds. **Callnotes:** plaintive *tweeyee;* in flight, dry chiming *eh-eh-eng.*

LAWRENCE'S GOLDFINCH   *Carduelis lawrencei*

Mainly California. Uncommon, elusive, unpredictable. In small groups in streamside trees in dry country, weedy fields. During some winters, many invade east to Arizona. ▶ Unlike other goldfinches, bold *yellow in wings.* Mostly pale gray or brown, with yellow on chest, white tail spots. Male has black face. ♪**Song:** fast, musical twittering, includes brief imitations of other birds. **Callnotes:** distinctive high *tink-ooo.*

EUROPEAN GOLDFINCH   *Carduelis carduelis*

Introduced in Bermuda and now very common there. Those seen occasionally in eastern U.S. are probably escaped cagebirds. ▶ Unmistakable. White border around *red face,* broad yellow band across black wings.

GOLDFINCHES, SISKIN

American Goldfinch 5"

summer male

winter (three examples)

summer female

Pine Siskin 5"

adults

pale variant

at bird feeder

Lesser Goldfinch 4½"

female

black-backed male

green-backed male

young male

European Goldfinch 5½"

Lawrence's Goldfinch 4½"

winter female

male

adult

summer female

371

These birds are named for their thick bill shape. Evening Grosbeak is related to finches on preceding pages; others below are in the **family Cardinalidae** (with the buntings on p. 374 and the grosbeaks on p. 376).

NORTHERN CARDINAL *Cardinalis cardinalis*

One of America's favorite backyard birds, very common in the east and in parts of the southwest. Lives in forest, swamps, deserts, suburbs, even city parks as long as there is some dense low cover. Comes to bird feeders to eat sunflower and other seeds. ▶ Male unmistakable, our only red bird with a crest. (See tanagers, p. 328.) Female duller, but shares *crest*, massive *pink bill*, rather long tail. In southwest, compare to Pyrrhuloxia. Juvenile has black bill at first. ♪ **Song:** bright clear whistles like *what-cheer, what-cheer,* or *teew teew teew;* many variations. **Callnote:** sharp, loud *tchip.*

PYRRHULOXIA *Cardinalis sinuatus*

This "desert cardinal" lives alongside Northern Cardinal in dry country of the southwest, in thickets, brush. May gather in flocks in winter. Odd name, from Latin and Greek, refers to shape of bill. ▶ Male gray and red, female buff with slight red tinges, with thin spiky crest. Separated from female cardinal by bill shape and color: thick, *curved, stubby bill* is dull *yellow* to yellow-orange. ♪ **Song:** rich whistles, can sound like cardinal; also rapid series of dry, thinner notes. **Callnote:** metallic *tchip.*

EVENING GROSBEAK *Coccothraustes vespertinus*

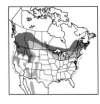

A nomad of the north and the mountains. Wanders unpredictably, often in large noisy flocks, like the "winter finches" on p. 368 (and related to them). May be common in a region one year, absent the next. Usually feeds up in trees, on seeds, buds, berries. Flocks visit feeders, consuming vast amounts of sunflower seeds. ▶ Gray and gold, with big white patch in black wings. Big pale bill turns greenish in spring. Male has yellow eyebrow on dark head. Goldfinches (previous page) have much smaller bills. ♪ **Voice:** loud *peeyr,* with ringing quality.

BLUE GROSBEAK *Passerina caerulea*

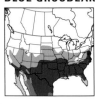

A dark, chunky grosbeak of summer, found mainly in the south. Favors bushy places such as riversides, woodland edge, desert washes. ▶ Very *thick bill,* wide *buff or cinnamon wing-bars.* Male very dark blue, female warm brown. Indigo Bunting (next page) slimmer, has smaller bill, lacks obvious wing-bars; female Indigo has streaks or mottling on chest. ♪ **Song:** fast, low, husky warble. **Callnotes:** loud metallic *tink!,* also a dry buzz.

GROSBEAKS

females

males

juvenile

Northern Cardinal 9"

Pyrrhuloxia 9"

male

female

Evening Grosbeak 8"

male

females

young male

Blue Grosbeak 7"

female

male

373

BUNTINGS

INDIGO BUNTING *Passerina cyanea*

A classic summer bird of the rural east, in farmland, brushy pastures, woodland edges. Indigo-blue males (looking black at a distance) sing from wires, bush tops. Scarce in the west. Flocks of migrants feed on the ground near woods in spring and fall. ▶ Adult male is dark blue in spring/summer (see Blue Grosbeak, previous page). Female and fall male are brown, usually with fine streaks on chest, blue tinge on tail. One-year-old male in summer may be blue with white belly. ♪ **Song:** bright, sweet phrases, the notes often in pairs: *weet weet tsew tsew jif jif,* etc. **Callnotes:** hard *spuk* and thin *bzzzt.*

LAZULI BUNTING *Passerina amoena*

Fairly common in the west in summer, in brushy places, often near water. ▶ Sky-blue male has rusty chest, white belly, *white wing-bars.* Bluebirds (p. 256) have thin bills, lack wing-bars. Female brown; usually shows *cinnamon* wash on *unstreaked* chest, more obvious wing-bars than female Indigo. Lazuli and Indigo Buntings may hybridize on Great Plains, producing intermediates. ♪ **Song:** bright, sweet phrases, often ending in jumble of notes. **Callnotes:** hard *spuk* and thin *bzzzt.*

PAINTED BUNTING *Passerina ciris*

Beautiful but shy, Painted Buntings can be hard to see in southeastern thickets. Males often sing from perches well hidden among foliage in low trees. ▶ Adult male unmistakable. Female plain green, with no markings. Other small greenish birds have thinner bills, or show marks such as wing-bars. Juveniles are much grayer than adult females at first. ♪ **Song:** bright fast warble, *graffiti graffiti spaghetti-for-two.* **Callnotes:** sharp *chip.*

VARIED BUNTING *Passerina versicolor*

In canyons and streamsides near the Mexican border, this bunting is uncommon in summer. ▶ Male looks black at a distance. In good light, dull purple with red nape, blue forehead. Colors partly covered by brown edging in fall. Female very plain brown, lacking wing-bars or chest streaks. ♪ **Song:** short, lively series of sweet phrases and notes. **Callnotes:** hard *pik.*

BLUE BUNTING *Cyanocompsa parellina*

Rare visitor to southern Texas, mostly in winter, in riverside woods and brush. ▶ Suggests Indigo Bunting but has thicker, stubbier bill. Male shows contrasting patches of darker and brighter blue; female plain warm brown all over. No wing-bars (see Blue Grosbeak, previous page).

BUNTINGS

female

Indigo
Bunting
5"

males

juvenile
Indigo or
Lazuli

female

Lazuli
Bunting
5¼"

fall male

male

Painted
Bunting
5"

juvenile

female

male

male

female

Varied
Bunting
5"

male

Blue Bunting
(rare, Texas)
5¼"

Birds on this page have similar colors but different behavior. These grosbeaks usually stay among the foliage of trees; towhees feed mostly on the ground, scratching in leaf-litter with both feet. Towhees (and all birds on next page) belong to the sparrow family (Emberizidae).

ROSE-BREASTED GROSBEAK *Pheucticus ludovicianus*

Fairly common in summer in leafy woods of the east; a rare migrant in the west. Moves rather deliberately among foliage of trees; sometimes comes to ground or to bird feeders. ▶ Adult male has *rosy triangle* on chest, black head, big white spots in wings. Female and young dark brown above, striped below; may suggest sparrows, but note heavy bill, strong face pattern, bold white in wings. ♪ Song: rich whistled phrases, with robinlike quality but often faster, more varied. Callnote: sharp metallic *feek*.

BLACK-HEADED GROSBEAK *Pheucticus melanocephalus*

Often very common in summer in oak woods, canyons, riverside trees of the west. Very rare stray in the east. Sometimes interbreeds with Rose-breasted Grosbeak along rivers on Great Plains. ▶ Male dull orange-brown with black head, black and white wings. Female and young like those of Rose-breasted Grosbeak, but tinged *more orange* below, with *less streaking;* bill is often darker. ♪ Song: rich whistled phrases, with robinlike quality but faster, more varied. Callnotes: sharp *fik*.

EASTERN TOWHEE *Pipilo erythrophthalmus*

Common in the undergrowth of eastern woods, scratching among dead leaves on the ground under dense thickets. ▶ Dark hood and rusty sides set off by *white stripe* down center of belly. Upperparts mostly black (male) or chocolate-brown (female). Tail has big white corners. Compare to American Robin (p. 252). Eyes usually red; white-eyed form occurs in Florida. ♪ Song: usually two short notes followed by trill, *Drink-your-teeeeeeee*. Callnote: sharp nasal *chwink*.

SPOTTED TOWHEE *Pipilo maculatus*

Very common in parts of the west, in chaparral, open woods, brushy hillsides. Forages on the ground, but males sing from bush tops. Moves well out onto Great Plains in winter, sometimes straying as far as east coast. ▶ Rusty and white below, dark on hood and back, with bold white spots on back, wings, tail corners. Upperparts and hood are black on males and may be black or gray on females. ♪ Song: variable. Harsh buzzy trill, may be preceded by shorter notes. Callnotes: harsh whines.

GROSBEAKS, TOWHEES

young male

Rose-breasted Grosbeak 8"

female

male

Black-headed Grosbeak 8"

females

male

female

white-eyed male

male

Eastern Towhee 8"

juvenile

Spotted Towhee 8¼"

female

male

CALIFORNIA TOWHEE *Pipilo crissalis*

In gardens, parks, and chaparral of California and southwest Oregon, this drab towhee lurks in the bushes or shuffles about on the ground, often in pairs, scratching in the leaf-litter with its feet. ▶ Rather long-tailed. Plain dusty brown, more buffy under tail and on throat, with fine streaks around throat. ♪ **Song:** sharp, ringing notes, in a series that speeds up. **Callnotes:** single sharp *chik* or *tink;* also a squealing chatter.

CANYON TOWHEE *Pipilo fuscus*

Brushy places and dry hillsides in the interior southwest are home to this towhee. ▶ Very much like California Towhee, but easily identified by range, since the two do not overlap. Usually paler, grayer, with dark central spot on chest, more reddish brown on cap, very different voice. ♪ **Song:** variable series of clear musical notes. **Callnotes:** squeaky *cheeyilp;* also a squealing chatter.

ABERT'S TOWHEE *Pipilo aberti*

Locally common in limited range along southwestern rivers. Hides in dense underbrush, usually in pairs. Also fairly common in suburbs of a few cities at low elevations (such as Phoenix, Yuma). ▶ Slim and long-tailed. Warm buffy brown with *black face,* pale gray bill. ♪ **Voice:** sharp ringing *poik!,* run together into stuttering song; also harsh squealing chatter.

GREEN-TAILED TOWHEE *Pipilo chlorurus*

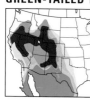

Common in summer in brushy thickets and chaparral of mountains. In migration and winter, favors dense low cover, especially near streams. Rarely wanders east in winter. ▶ Gray face and chest set off sharp *white throat, reddish cap.* Upperparts and tail olive green. Head feathers often raised in perky crest. ♪ **Song:** short sweet notes followed by dry trill. **Callnote:** catlike *meyew.*

OLIVE SPARROW *Arremonops rufivirgatus*

South Texas only, north to about Corpus Christi and Del Rio. Secretive, foraging on the ground under dense thickets. ▶ Dull olive above, grayish below. Head gray with dull *brown stripes* on crown. ♪ **Song:** hard *chip* notes accelerating into a dry rattling trill. **Callnotes:** light *tsit.*

WHITE-COLLARED SEEDEATER *Sporophila torqueola*

Rare and local in extreme south Texas (mostly Starr and Zapata Counties). Damp weedy fields, thickets near water. ▶ *Tiny,* with very *short stubby bill.* Male has blackish cap, partial buffy collar, white wing spot and wing-bars. Female and young plainer buff, with fainter wing-bars. Note bill shape. ♪ **Song:** thin clear whistles. **Callnotes:** thin *syoo.*

TOWHEES AND TEXANS

California
Towhee
9"

Canyon Towhee
8½"

Abert's
Towhee
9½"

Green-tailed
Towhee
7½"

Olive
Sparrow
6"

White-collared
Seedeater
4¼"

female   male

379

Sources of further information: If birding is a spare-time hobby for you, this may be the only bird guide you'll ever need. But if you become more deeply involved, you'll find many detailed references available.

The Peterson Field Guides (*Eastern Birds* and *Western Birds*), published by Houghton Mifflin, have wonderful paintings by the late Roger Tory Peterson plus very detailed maps and clear text. The Peterson series also includes specialized books on groups of birds such as hawks and warblers. These will always be valuable books for birders. For a more technical approach, see the *National Geographic Field Guide to the Birds of North America,* as well as the *National Audubon Society Sibley Guide to Birds.*

A compact field guide can't give much space to the fascinating things that birds actually *do.* For lots more about their feeding, nesting, and migration habits, see my *Lives of North American Birds* (Houghton Mifflin, 1996).

Many states and provinces have their own detailed bird books, and new ones are appearing constantly. Check with your library for information about such local books. For serious birders who want to track down new species, there are also bird-finding guides that give precise directions. Many of these guides are published by the American Birding Association (ABA), and all of them are available through its ABA Sales; contact them at P.O. Box 6599, Colorado Springs, CO 80934.

If you have access to the Internet, you'll find thousands of bird-related sites — some reliable and some not! Your best bet on the net is **BirdSource** (www.birdsource.org), sponsored by the renowned Cornell Laboratory of Ornithology and the National Audubon Society. BirdSource will connect you with the very latest and most accurate information as well as the chance to take part in ongoing field studies. Highly recommended.

Acknowledgments: It would take a bigger book than this one to list all the people from whom I've learned things about birds. Many who have helped me most were acknowledged in my *Field Guide to Advanced Birding* (1990), and my debt to those individuals continues.

There's a big difference between knowing a subject and knowing how to teach it. In recent years I've been obsessed with questions of how to teach people about nature. Thanks to the American Birding Association and Victor Emanuel Nature Tours, I was able to teach birding workshops in many regions, and these were more educational for me than for the students. I'm particularly grateful to Victor Emanuel and David Wolf of VENT, with whom I taught many sessions and from whom I learned a lot. Others who helped me understand teaching concepts were Capt. Ted Appell, Susan Roney Drennan, Kim Eckert, Scott Edwards, Jeff Gordon, P. J. Grant, Steve Hilty, Jeri Langham, Will Russell, Rich Stallcup, and Judy Toups.

Every field guide in the world is based ultimately on scientific collections of specimens in museums. In researching details, I made use of many such collections, especially those at the University of Arizona, Tucson; Lousiana State University, Baton Rouge; the American Museum of Natural History, New York; and the National Museum of Natural History, Washington.

People who helped in specific ways with this book were many. Thanks to Dick and Joan Bowers, Edward LaCambra, Greg Lasley, Linda Lucz, J.V. Remsen Jr., Andy Richford, Don Roberson, Brian E. Small, and Dale and Marian Zimmerman for going out of their way to help.

It was a pleasure to work again with the professionals at Houghton Mifflin. Editor and naturalist Harry Foster has been the backbone of that company's nature program for years; he was instrumental in getting this book rolling, and he improved every aspect of it. Super-designer Anne Chalmers, besides walking me through many graphics issues, developed the book's overall design; the usefulness of a field guide depends heavily on effective design, and Anne handles this better than anyone. Lisa White once again kept me (mostly!) from going astray on text matters, and brought clarity and order to the whole. Michaela Sullivan designed a strikingly beautiful cover. Barry Estabrook gave sage advice, and Liz Duvall caught many inconsistencies. Thanks also to Nancy Grant, Becky Saikia-Wilson, Lori Glazer, Terry McAweeney, Deborah DeLosa, Bridget Marmion, Rux Martin, Debbie Applefield-Milley, Bill McCormick, Julie Burns, Katie Dillin, and Beth Ineson, as well as Jim Allen and Meredith Oberfrank of Thomas Allen and Son. Special thanks to Wendy Strothman, who had the imagination to see the potential of this book's new approach.

More than eighty fine photographers gave permission to use their work in our illustrations. Bird photography is challenging, and it's a rare person who can take a great bird portrait and then allow it to be changed. All of these photos were excellent to begin with; my changes to them were for the sake of consistent illustration, not for quality. Complete photo credits begin on the next page, but the massive contribution of these photographers is evident throughout the book.

In the actual production of book materials in Tucson, I was lucky to be part of a terrific team, and I can't say enough good things about my coworkers. Lynn Hassler worked up the designs of all the color plates, rearranging birds for a more attractive composition. (If any plates don't look good, it means I messed up the design for labeling.) Lynn worked on virtually every other aspect of the book, from color and text decisions to the index. Rick and Nora Bowers, of Bowers Photo, handled the exhaustive correspondence to locate the tens of thousands of slides from which I chose the 2,000-plus used in the book. They also scanned slides to produce digital images with enough detail for editing, kept the scanner and several high-powered computers running in good order, and gave critical input based on their wide experience with birds. Most impressive, though, is the fact that nearly half the images used in this guide came out of the Bowers Photo collection itself, reflecting their prolific skill as photographers.

This updated printing for 2005 is not a revised edition, but it involved enough small changes to require a lot of work. Stacy M. Fobar did most of the work of putting the material into the new page layout program, a major feat of software skill. Others who helped in important ways included Megan Butler, Amanda Chatterton, Jennie Duberstein, Patricia Manzano Fischer, Kim Fredritz, Jean Iron, Dan O'Connell, Martin Reid, and Lynne Taylor. My sincere thanks to all.

PHOTOGRAPHER CREDITS

This book would not have been possible without the cooperation of many outstanding photographers, who not only allowed us to use their photos but gave permission to have those photos altered for the sake of illustration. An abbreviation (below) has been assigned to each photographer and/or stock agency consisting of first initials of the first, last, and sometimes middle names. In the case of duplicated initials, first and second letters of the last name are used. Plates are listed by page number (in bold). Read credits from left to right and top to bottom. Where needed for clarification the species name and the following abbreviations are used: Male = m, female = f, adult = ad, young = y, immature = im, juvenile = jv, hybrid = h, flying = fy, fall = a, summer/spring = s, winter = w, nest = n, and breeding = b. Photographer name and abbreviations: **AB/WR** Arnaud van den Berg/Windrush; **AC** Al Cornell; **AM** Anthony Mercieca; **AM/PP** Anthony Mercieca/Photophile; **AM/RR** Anthony Mercieca/Root Resources; **AMO/VU** ArthurMorris/Visuals Unlimited; **AMU** Alan Murphy; **AN/RR** Alan G. Nelson/Root Resources; **AS** Arnold Small; **BG/VU** Barbara Gerlach/Visuals Unlimited; **BH/WR** Barry Hughes/Windrush; **BHA** Bruce Hallett; **BM** Bruce Mactavish; **BP** Rick & Nora Bowers/Bowers Photo; **BPA** Brian Patteson; **BS** Brian E. Small; **BW** Bing Wong; **BZ** Barry Zimmer; **CAM** C. Allan Morgan; **CGI** Cathy & Gordon Illg; **CM** Charles W.Melton; **DE/RW** Dudley Edmondson/Raptor Works; **DR** Don Roberson; **DMZ** Dale and Marian Zimmerman; **DT/WR** David Tipling/Windrush; **DW** Donald E. Waite; **ES** Ervio Sian; **GE/WR** Göran Ekström/Windrush; **GJ** George M. Jett; **GK** Gary Kramer; **GL** Greg W. Lasley; **GLA/WR** Gordon Langsbury/Windrush; **GV** Gordon Vickrey; **GVE/VU** Gustav Verderber/Visuals Unlimited; **HB/VU** Hal Beral/Visuals Unlimited; **HC** Herbert Clarke; **HS** Hugh P. Smith, Jr.; **IJ** Ian L. Jones; **JB/NI** Jim Burns/Natural Impacts; **JBL** James D. Bland; **JH/WR** J. Hollis/Windrush; **JHO** John H. Hoffman; **JI** Jean Iron; **JM/VU** Joe McDonald/Visuals Unlimited; **JN** Jan Kåre Ness; **JP** John Pogacnik; **JS** John Sorensen; **JW/VU** Jan L. Wassink/Visuals Unlimited; **KTK** Kevin T. Karlson; **KK** Kenn Kaufman; **KZ** Kevin Zimmer; **LB** Lance Beeny; **LD** Larry Ditto; **LM** Larry Manfredi; **MB** Mark Bittner; **MD** Mike Danzenbaker; **MG/WR** Michael Gore/Windrush; **MT** Monte M. Taylor; **M/VU** Maslowski/Visuals Unlimited; **MW/WW** Mark Wallner/ Wing It Wildlife; **NH** Ned Harris; **NS** Nancy L. Strand; **PB/WR** Peter Basterfield/Windrush; **PD/WR** Paul Doherty/Windrush; **PL** Peter LaTourrette; **PP** www.petpix.com; **RA** Ron Austing; **RAS** Rob & Ann Simpson; **RAS/VU** Rob & Ann Simpson/Visuals Unlimited; **RB/WR** Richard Brooks/Windrush; **RC/EB** Rob Curtis/The Early Birder; **RD** R.H. Day; **RDI** Richard Ditch; **RH** Russell C. Hansen; **RK** Russ Kerr; **RL/VU** Robert Lindholm/Visuals Unlimited; **RS/VU** Rob Simpson/Visuals Unlimited; **RT/WR** Roger Tidman/Windrush; **SB** Steve Bentsen; **SS/NI** Scot Stewart/Nature's Images; **SVU/VU** Science VU/Visuals Unlimited; **SY/WR** Steve Young/Windrush; **TE/VU** Tom Edwards/Visuals Unlimited; **TL/WR** Tim Loreby/Windrush; **TV** Tom Vezo; **TW/VU** Tom Walker/Visuals Unlimited; **WB** William Bolte; **WC** W.S. Clark; **WG/VU** William Grenfell/Visuals Unlimited; **WM** William H. Mullins; **WT/VU** Will Troyer/Visuals Unlimited

7 BP **10** KK **14** *top:* JHO, PL, BP, BP *left middle:* BP *right middle:* BS *bottom:* KTK, BP, BP, DMZ **17** KK **19** KK **23** KK **27** *Mallard: all fy* TV, m KK, f & y BP, f BP, "Mexican" BP, h GK, eclipse RAS/VU *American Black Duck:* BP all *Mottled Duck:* KK, BS **29** *N. Pintail:* BP all *Gadwall:* BP, BP, fy MD, BP *Am. Wigeon:* KK, BP, BP, fy RK *Eurasian Wigeon:* BP **31** *Green-winged Teal:* fy RK, GL, MD, ad f BS *Blue-winged Teal:* fy RK, BP, BP, BP *Cinnamon Teal:* fy RK, BP, BP *Garganey:* PD/WR *N. Shoveler:* fy KK, BP *Lesser Scaup:* BP, BP, BP fy HB/VU *Gr. Scaup:* BP, BP, BS, fy TV *remainder:* BP **35** *Com. Pochard:* MD *Long-tailed Duck:* fy BP, s f BP, w f BS, s m BP, w m KTK *remainder:* BP **37** *Surf Scoter:* y m KTK, BS, BS *White-winged Scoter:* DMZ, BS, BS *Black Scoter:* KTK, MD, *Harlequin Duck:* BP all **39** KTK, TV, KTK, KTK, TV, AS, KTK, KTK, KTK, KTK, MD, MD **41** BS, BS, BS, BP, BS, BS, BP, BP, fy BS, BP, JHO, BS, BS, GL **43** CM, MD, fy BP, BS, BS, BP, BP, MD **45** *Wood Duck:* BP, BP, BP, fy MW/WW *remainder:* BP **47** fy RK, BP, KK, BP, *Cackling Goose:* JI, NS *Gr. White-fronted Goose:* BP, BP *Brant:* TV, CAM, BP **49** *Snow Goose:* KK, KK, fy BP, BS, BP *remainder:* BP **51** *Mute Swan:* ad KK, jv KK, fy BP, KK *Tundra Swan:* KTK, AM *Trumpeter Swan:* BP all *Swan Heads:* BP, *Tundra* KTK, *Mute* TV, *Whooper* GL **52** *Domestic:* KK, BP, KK, KK, BP *Swan Goose:* KK *remainder:* BP **53** *Ringed Teal:* AM/PP, GK *remainder:* BP **55** KK, BP, fy jv JS, KK, GL, BP, JHO, BP, jv BP, jv BP, BS, BP, GL, GL **57** KTK, BP, BS, BP, BS, BS, BP, TV, BP, KK, BS **59** BPA, TV, BZ, TV, BP, BP, JS, w ad MD, fy BP, BP, BP, SVU/VU, MD **61** BS, fy RD, BP, BP, BP, KTK, KTK, MD *Black Guillemot:* RT/WR, TV *Pigeon Guillemot:* RA, JHO **63** *Cassin's Auklet:* fy DR, MD, CAM *Ancient Murrelet:* MD, fy DW, JB/NI *Marbled Murrelet:* MD, ES, GL, GL *Kittlitz's Murrelet:* RD all *Xantus's Murrelet:* AM/PP, MD, MD *Craveri's Murrelet:* fy MD, DR, MD **65** *Dovekie:* AS, BPA, MD *Whiskered Auklet:* IJ *remainder:* BP **67** BS, KTK, BS, GL, TW/VU, KTK, BS, TV, JS, KTK, TL/WR **69** *Pacific Loon:* fy MD all *Great Cormorant:* DT/WR, JH/WR *remainder:* BP **71** *Pelagic Cormorant:* BS, BP *Anhinga:* m GL *remainder:* BP **73** *Am. White Pelican:* BP all *Brown Pelican:* fy KK, *remainder:* BP *Gannet:* DMZ, fy BM, fy TV, fy BPA, fy BP *Magnificent Frigatebird:* ad f KK, ad m BP, im BP, f BS *remainder:* BP **75** *Brown Booby:* BP, BP, JHO *Red-footed Booby:* BP, BP, KK *Red-billed Tropicbird:* TV all *White-tailed Tropicbird:* fy KTK, MG/WR *remainder:* KK **76** *Heads:* KK, KK, TV, TV *Herring Gull:* KK, TV, KTK, KK, MD, TV **77** BP **79** *Herring Gull:* im BS, w ad BP, s ad TV, fy im RC/EB *Ring-billed Gull:* fy BM, BP, fy KK, w ad KK, BP *California Gull:* im KK, w ad BS, *bottom* im DR, s ad BP *Mew Gull:* BP, fy JP, fy MD, BP **81** *Western Gull:* top im KK, fy MD, middle im MD, ad BS, bottom im KK, *Great Black-backed Gull:* im KK, fy AMO/VU, ad MD, bottom im KK *Lesser Black-backed Gull:* BM, GL *Slaty-backed Gull:* MD, fy BP *Yellow-footed Gull:* BP all **83** *Glaucous-winged Gull:* top im BP, fy ad MD, *middle* im KK, *bottom* fy im MD, h BP, ad BP *Glaucous Gull:* im KTK, fy MD, ad MD, im GL *Iceland Gull:* AS, fy PL, KTK *Thayer's Gull:* MD all **85** *Laughing Gull:* fy RDI, KK, KK, BP, im KTK, fy KTK *Franklin's Gull:* BS, BP, fy AM/PP, BS *Bonaparte's Gull:* fy KTK, fy BP, im BS, BP, BP *Black-headed Gull:* MD, BS, fy MD, MD *Little Gull:* SY/WR, AB/WR, fy AS, PL **87** *Black-legged Kittiwake:* n BP, fy MD, fy MD, w DMZ *Red-legged Kittiwake:* MD all *Sabine's Gull:* fy jv CAM, fy KTK, BS *Ross's Gull:* GL *Ivory Gull:* fy AS, DT/WR *Heermann's Gull:* BP, BP, BP, fy RK **89** *Forster's Tern:* BP, BP, w KK, s BS, fy jv KK, s BS *Com. Tern:* fy TV, fy KTK, jv TV, BP, BP *Arctic Tern:* jv PB/WR, BP, BP, BP, BP *Roseate Tern:* fy TV, jv AMP/VU, s TV, TV **91** *Caspian Tern:* BP, BP, BP, BP, w KK *Royal Tern:* BP all *Elegant Tern:* KTK, BS, BS *Sandwich Tern:* BP, KK, BP, BP **93** *Sooty Tern:* BS, fy BS, fy GL, fy jv BPA *Aleutian Tern:* fy BP, AM/PP *Bridled Tern:* BPA *Black*

Noddy: GL *Brown Noddy*: GL, fy KTK, fy KTK **95** *Black Tern*: fy jv BPA, w BH/WR, fy s BS, fy ad GL, BS *White-winged Tern*: PD/WR *Least Tern*: fy TV, jv GL, BP, BP *Gull-billed Tern*: fy BP, fy BP, GL, GL *Black Skimmer*: fy BP, fy BP, jv BS, BP **97** *Parasitic Jaeger*: jv JS, fy im JS, fy ad KTK, TV, KTK *Long-tailed Jaeger*: jv BPA, BP, BP *Pomarine Jaeger*: fy im MD, KTK, fy ad MD (small), fy ad BPA (large) *Great Skua*: BPA *South Polar Skua*: BP all **99** *Head*: BP *shearwater*: MD *storm-petrel*: CAM *Laysan Albatross*: BP all *Black-footed Albatross*: MD all **101** *Sooty Shearwater*: all fy MD, JS *Flesh-footed Shearwater*: MD *Short-tailed Shearwater*: MD all *Northern Fulmar*: fy BP, fy JS, fy BP, BP **103** *Greater Shearwater*: BZ, all fy BP *Cory's Shearwater*: BPA, MD *Manx Shearwater*: MD *Audubon's Shearwater*: MD all *Black-capped Petrel*: BPA all **105** *Pink-footed Shearwater*: JS, all fy GL *Buller's Shearwater*: MD all *Cook's Petrel*: MT *Black-vented Shearwater*: MD all **107** *Wilson's Storm-Petrel*: MD, BP, CAM *Leach's Storm-Petrel*: top DB, left DR, right BPA *Ashy Storm-Petrel*: MD, CAM *Band-rumped Storm-Petrel*: BPA *Black Storm-Petrel*: CAM, AS, n CAM *Least Storm-Petrel*: JB/NI *White-faced Storm-Petrel*: BPA *Fork-tailed Storm-Petrel*: fy RD, JS, fy MD **111** *Red-tailed Hawk*: BP, BP, fy typical ad RK, BP, fy light ad WC, fy dark WC, fy jv RK, ad TV *Rough-legged Hawk*: fy WC, fy WC, fy WC, BP, WC *bottom* fy BP *Ferruginous Hawk*: fy BS, fy WC, GL, BP **113** *Broad-winged Hawk*: fy KTK, fy KTK, fy WC, WC, WC *Red-shouldered Hawk*: fy jv RK, fy ad BP, fy ad BP, jv WC, ad WC, *bottom* fy ad WC *Hook-billed Kite*: WC, fy y m KTK, fy m BZ, fy f MD *Gray Hawk*: BP, fy jv WC, fy ad BS *Swainson's Hawk*: BP, BP, fy ad RK, fy BS, fy jv RK, BP *White-tailed Hawk*: GL, fy BS, WC *Short-tailed Hawk*: KTK, NH **117** *Zone-tailed Hawk*: fy BP, fy BP, JB/NI *Com. Black-Hawk*: fy KK, KK, fy jv WC *remainder*: BP **119** *Osprey*: BS, BS, BS n BP *Bald Eagle*: BP all *Golden Eagle*: fy im WC, BP, BP **121** *N. Harrier*: fy f DMZ, fy m RK, fy m WC, fy jv BS, fy f BS, fy m RK, jv DMZ *Turkey Vulture*: jv BP, fy BP, fy BS, fy JHO, ad BP *California Condor*: DS, fy AS *Black Vulture*: fy BS, BP, fy BS **123** *Mississippi Kite*: BS, fy WC, fy WC, fy WC *White-tailed Kite*: fy DS, fy BP, BS, BS *Swallow-tailed Kite*: fy BP, KTK, fy BP *Snail Kite*: WC, fy KTK, fy KTK, WC, BP **125** *Sharp-shinned Hawk*: fy TV, fy WC, fy WC, DMZ, DMZ, DMZ *Cooper's Hawk*: fy jv KTK, fy ad RK, WC, DMZ, fy KTK *Northern Goshawk*: fy jv DE/RW, fy ad MD, DE/RW, TV **127** *Am. Kestrel*: WC, RK, BS, BP *Merlin*: fy f KTK, fy m WC, f TV, m JS, prairie WC, black JS *Aplomado Falcon*: fy jv KTK, fy ad RK, WC, DMZ, fy KTK *Northern Goshawk* **129** *Peregrine Falcon*: WC, DMZ, fy BP, fy jv WC, fy ad BP *Prairie Falcon*: BP, fy upper wing surface BP, fy WC, fy CM, fy RK *Gyrfalcon*: AN/RR, JM/VU, fy BS, BS **131** *Long-eared Owl*: BS, BP, WM *remainder*: BP **133** *E. Screech-Owl*: brown TE/VU, red TV *remainder*: BP **135** *Snowy Owl*: JHO, BP *remainder*: BP **137** *Boreal Owl*: jv WG/VU, BP *N. Saw-whet Owl*: AN/RR, BP *N. Pygmy-Owl*: BP, BP, GL *Burrowing Owl*: jv JHO, BP, BP *Ferruginous Pygmy-Owl*: BS, BP **139** AC, AC, AC, BP, BP, BP, BP, BS, GL, GL **141** BP, BP, BP, BP, BP, KTK, KTK, BP, JBL, CM, BP **143** BS, BS, BS, LB, LB, GL, CM, GL, BP, MD, BS **145** DMZ, BS, BP, GK, JHO, BP, GK, BP **147** BP, BP, JHO, BP, BP, BP, MD **149** TV, TV, *remainder*: BP **151** *Glossy Ibis*: BS, KTK *White-faced Ibis*: w KTK *White Ibis*: fy BS *Roseate Spoonbill*: im TV *remainder*: BP **153** *Great Blue Heron*: "Würdemann's" GL, fy BS *Whooping Crane*: jv GL *remainder*: BP **155** BP, BP, KK, BP, BP, BP, BP, KK, BP, KK, BP, GL, BS, BP **157** *Reddish Egret*: white morph TV, head KTK *remainder*: BP **159** KTK, JHO, BP, fy KTK, BP, BP, fy KTK, BP, fy KTK, BP, BP, BP **161** *Clapper Rail*: BP, BS, BS *remainder*: BP **163** *Sora*: BP, BP, ad BS *Virginia Rail*: jv AS, BP, BP *Yellow Rail*: GVE/VU *Black Rail*: BP **167** *Killdeer*: TV, BP, TV, KK *Black-bellied Plover*: ad BP, jv BS, s ad BP, top fy KTK, w ad BS, *bottom* fy BS (3) *Pacific Golden-Plover*: BS all *Am. Golden-Plover*: BS, fy BM, DMZ, BP **169** *Semipalmated Plover*: GL, BS, BP *Wilson's Plover*: BP all *Piping Plover*: BS, BS, BP *Snowy Plover*: BP, BS *Mountain Plover*: s DMZ, w BP **171** *European Golden-Plover*: fy BM, MD, MD *N. Lapwing*: fy MD, GLA/WR *Mongolian Plover*: MD *Com. Ringed Plover*: MD *Eurasian Dotterel*: PL, MD **173** *Black-necked Stilt*: all fy TV, BP, BP *Am. Avocet*: BS, BP, BP *Am. Oystercatcher*: GL, BP, fy TV *Black Oystercatcher*: BP **175** *Sanderling*: s ad TV, w ad DP, fy DP (2), s ad BP, a jv BS, w ad GL *Dunlin*: BS, KTK, BP, BS, BP, BS *Red Knot*: DS, s ad BP, BS **177** *Least Sandpiper*: w JHO, a jv DP, s ad BP, a jv KTK, s ad BS *Semipalmated Sandpiper*: BS, BS, BS, BP *W. Sandpiper*: BP, BP, BS, BP *Red-necked Stint*: BS **179** *Pectoral Sandpiper*: BS, BP, BP *Sharp-tailed Sandpiper*: MD *White-rumped Sandpiper*: a ad KTK, fy MD, a jv AS, s MD *Baird's Sandpiper*: BP, KTK *Buff-breasted Sandpiper*: DS, KTK **181** BS, BP, JHO, RP, BP, BP, BS *Rock Sandpiper*: BS, BP *Purple Sandpiper*: BS, MD **183** *Spotted Sandpiper*: TV, w BP, TV, TV *Solitary Sandpiper*: BP, BZ *Lesser Yellowlegs*: BS, BP *Gr. Yellowlegs*: s ad BP, a jv TV, w ad BS, fy BP *Wandering Tattler*: BP all **185** *Am. Woodcock*: KTK all *Com. Snipe*: BP all *Long-billed Dowitcher*: w KTK, BP, fy MD *Short-billed Dowitcher*: w KTK, BP, a jv KTK, BP *Stilt Sandpiper*: BP, KTK, BP, TV **187** *Willet*: BP all *Marbled Godwit*: BP, BP, fy BS *Hudsonian Godwit*: a ad KTK, s ad KTK, a jv TV, fy KTK *Bar-tailed Godwit*: MD, BS **189** fy MD, BP, BP, fy KZ, BW, BW, BP, BP, fy BP, BP, BP, BG/VU **191** DS, AS, BS, AS, BS, BS, RK, BP, BS, KTK, BP, BP, BP, BP **193** *Ruff*: a jv MD, f AM/PP, m DT/WR, m DT/WR *Curlew Sandpiper*: MD, DT/WR, RB/WR *Wood Sandpiper*: MD *Gray-tailed Tattler*: KZ *Spotted Redshank*: MD *Com. Sandpiper*: DT/WR *Terek Sandpiper*: PD/WR **195** fy MD *remainder*: BP **197** *Mourning Dove*: JS, KTK, BP, BP, fy RH *White-winged Dove*: DMZ, BP, GL, fy RH *Eurasian Collared-Dove*: KTK all *remainder*: BP **199** fy RH, BP, BP, BS, BS, BP, BP, BP, BP **201** *Yellow-billed Cuckoo*: KTK all *Mangrove Cuckoo*: BS *Black-billed Cuckoo*: KTK, M/VU *Com. Cuckoo*: IJ, MT *Groove-billed Ani*: DMZ *Gr. Roadrunner*: BP **202** *Black-hooded Parakeet*: PP *Monk Parakeet*: BS *Yellow-chevroned Parakeet*: MT *White-winged Parakeet*: BHA *Peach-faced Lovebird*: JHO *remainder*: BP **203** *Red-crowned Parrot*: AM/RR *Rose-ringed Parakeet*: DMZ *Green Parakeet*: GL *Blue-crowned Parakeet*: MB *Mitered Parakeet*: BS *Red-masked Parakeet*: MB *remainder*: BP **205** *Com. Nighthawk*: BP, BP, BP, fy TV, fy TV, fy TV *Lesser Nighthawk*: m CAM, f AM/PP, fy GV, fy MD *Antillean Nighthawk*: KTK, fy BHA *Com. Pauraque*: BP, MD, fy JHO **207** *Whip-poor-will*: f KTK *Chuck-will's-widow*: KTK, KTK, tail BP *remainder*: BP **209** *Belted Kingfisher*: TV, BS, SB *Green Kingfisher*: BP all *Ringed Kingfisher*: BS all *Eared Trogon*: f BS, m BP *Elegant Trogon*: f BS, m BP **211** *Acorn Woodpecker*: BP all *Red-headed Woodpecker*: KTK, fy GJ, KTK *Lewis's Woodpecker*: BS, fy HS, BS *White-headed Woodpecker*: BS all **213** *Golden-fronted Woodpecker*: f GL, BP *Ladder-backed Woodpecker*: BS all *Nuttall's Woodpecker*: BS all *remainder*: BP *Downy Woodpecker*: BP, f BS, f TV *Hairy Woodpecker*: BS all *Black-backed Woodpecker*: BS all *Three-toed Woodpecker*: BS, BP *Red-cockaded Woodpecker*: RAS/VU, GL **217** *Red-naped Sapsucker*: BS, DMZ *Yellow-bellied Sapsucker*: jv TV, BP, m BS *Red-breasted Sapsucker*: GL, BS *Arizona Woodpecker*: BP, BS *Williamson's Sapsucker*: BS all **219** *N. Flicker*: red-shafted BS all, yellow-shafted DMZ, TV *Gilded Flicker*: DMZ, BP *Pileated Woodpecker*: BP, f BS, fy BP **221** BP all **223** *Broad-tailed Hummingbird*: BP, DMZ, DMZ *Allen's Hummingbird*: MD *remainder*: BP **225** *Buff-bellied Hummingbird*: BS *Magnificent Hummingbird*: BS, BP *remainder*: BP **227** *Green-breasted Mango*: GL *remainder*: BP **229** *Chimney Swift*: BP, all fy MD *Vaux's Swift*: MD all *White-throated Swift*: AN/RR, all fy MD *Black Swift*: MD all **231** *Purple Martin*: n KTK, fy KTK, fy KTK, BP, BP *Tree Swallow*: BP, TV, KTK, BP *Violet-green Swallow*: AM/PP, RP, BP *Bahama Swallow*: MD, KTK,

KTK **233** *Barn Swallow:* BP, RH *Cliff Swallow:* n BP, fy MD, BP, AM/PP *Cave Swallow:* BP all *N. Rough-winged Swallow:* MD, BP *Bank Swallow:* AS, n TV(2) **235** *E. Kingbird:* BP all *Gray Kingbird:* GL all **237** DMZ, GL, BP, BP, BS, BP, BP, RC/EB, BS **239** *W. Wood-Pewee:* BS all E. *Wood-Pewee:* GL, KTK *Olive-sided Flycatcher:* DMZ, RAS remainder: BP **241** BP all **243** *Ash-throated Flycatcher:* DMZ, KTK, BP *Great Crested Flycatcher:* KTK, TV *Dusky-capped Flycatcher:* BP, BS *Brown-crested Flycatcher:* SB, BS **245** *Yellow-bellied Flycatcher:* BP, RAS *Acadian Flycatcher:* BS, GL remainder: BP **247** *Hammond's Flycatcher:* BS, MD remainder: BP **249** *Scissor-tailed Flycatcher:* TV, BS *Fork-tailed Flycatcher:* KTK *Sulphur-bellied Flycatcher:* BS all *Great Kiskadee:* BP all *Rose-throated Becard:* RC/EB, KZ, RC/EB **253** BS, BP, KTK, BP, BS, BS, BS, BS, BP **255** KTK, BS, BS, KTK, TV, BS, DT/WR, MD, DT/WR, SB, DMZ **257** *E. Bluebird:* JHO, TV, TV *W. Bluebird:* jv BP, BP, BS, GL *Townsend's Solitaire:* BS, BP *Mountain Bluebird:* TV **259** TV, BS, BS, KTK, BP, BP, RAS/VU, BS, KTK **261** *Sage Thrasher:* BS, DMZ *Gray Catbird:* GL, BP remainder: BP **263** *Le Conte's Thrasher:* MD, BS remainder: BP **265** RH, BS, BP, BS, KTK, BS, BS, KTK, RA, MD **267** *Cedar Waxwing:* KTK, BP, BP *Phainopepla:* BP, fy MD, BP *Bohemian Waxwing:* PD/WR *Red-whiskered Bulbul:* WB **269** BP, BP, BP, BS, BS, MD, BP, BP **271** *Horned Lark:* LB, BS, BS, BS *Sky Lark:* MD *Am. Pipit:* BS, BS, RC/EB *Red-throated Pipit:* HC, BS *Sprague's Pipit:* BP all **273** *Brown Jay:* BS, BS, remainder: BP **275** *W. Scrub-Jay:* BP, BP, BS *Florida Scrub-Jay:* BP *Island Scrub-Jay:* PL *Mexican Jay:* BP all *Pinyon Jay:* BS all **277** CM, CGI, BS, BP, BP, BP, GL, BP, BP **279** KK, BP, BP, BP, KTK, GL, CGI, DMZ, BP, BP, BP **281** *Black-capped Chickadee:* BP, GL, TV *Mountain Chickadee:* BP all *Carolina Chickadee:* BS, BP **283** BS, BP, WT/VU, BP, BM, JN, DT/WR, BP **285** BP, BP, BP, BP, BP, DMZ, BP, BS **287** *White-breasted Nuthatch:* BP all *Brown-headed Nuthatch:* RAS *Red-breasted Nuthatch:* BP, BS *Brown Creeper:* KTK, BS *Pygmy Nuthatch:* BP all **289** CM, BP, KTK, BS, TV, JHO, BP, BP, BP **291** *Sedge Wren:* KTK, BS *Marsh Wren:* BS, TV *Canyon Wren:* BS, BP remainder: BP **293** BS, TV, BP, AS, JHO, BS, BP, BP **295** BS, JHO, KTK, TV, BP, JHO, BS, BP, BS, BP, BP **297** *Ruby-crowned Kinglet:* BS remainder: BP **299** BS, KTK, DMZ, MD, BP, BP, BP **301** *Philadelphia Vireo:* BS all *Warbling Vireo:* BP all *Red-eyed Vireo:* KTK, BS, BP *Yellow-green Vireo:* AS *Black-whiskered Vireo:* BS **305** *Yellow Warbler:* bottom f BS *Prothonotary Warbler:* BS all remainder: BP **307** BS, BS, BS, y f TV, BS, BS, BP, BS, BS, BS, BP **309** TV, TV, GL, RL/VU, BS, BS, DMZ, KTK, BS, BS, BS, BP, BS, BS **311** *Tennessee Warbler:* MD, RAS/VU, s m BS, BP *Orange-crowned Warbler:* BS, KTK, BP, BP *Blue-winged Warbler:* BP, BS *Golden-winged Warbler:* BS all *Brewster's Warbler:* BP *Lawrence's Warbler:* AMU **313** *Virginia's Warbler:* DMZ, DMZ remainder: BP **315** *Blackpoll Warbler:* dull TV, KTK, KTK, KTK *Bay-breasted Warbler:* KTK, KTK, KTK, s f BS *Pine Warbler:* RAS/VU, KTK, TV *Black-and-White Warbler:* f BP, BS, s m KTK **317** BP, BP, KTK, BS, BP, BP, BS, DMZ, HC, BS, BS, BS **319** *Chestnut-sided Warbler:* BS, BS, m BP *Blackburnian Warbler:* RAS/VU, s m BS, MW/WW *Yellow-throated Warbler:* BS, BP *Grace's Warbler:* BP all **321** *Palm Warbler:* KTK, KTK, s BS *"Yellow" Palm Warbler":* s SS/NI, a RAS/VU *Prairie Warbler:* KTK, TV *Kirtland's Warbler:* RA all *Yellow-breasted Chat:* BP all **323** BP, BP, KK, BP, KTK, BS, BS, KTK **325** *Com. Yellowthroat:* BP, f KTK, BP, BP *MacGillivray's Warbler:* BP, BS *Kentucky Warbler:* BS, KTK *Mourning Warbler:* RC/EB, BP, BP *Connecticut Warbler:* M/VU, RS/VU **327** *Am. Redstart:* im m BS *Olive Warbler:* f BS *Bananaquit:* KTK remainder: BP **329** *W. Tanager:* BS, BP *Scarlet Tanager:* BP, BS *Hepatic Tanager:* BP all *Summer Tanager:* BS, BP *Flame-colored Tanager:* HC, JB/NI *Stripe-headed Tanager:* BHA **331** *European Starling:* TL/WR, BP, BP, fy RT/WR, KTK, TV, JHO *Crested Myna:* ES *Com. Myna:* BP *Hill Myna:* AM/PP **333** *Red-winged Blackbird:* f TV, "Bicolored" JHO, m TV, f DMZ, fy BP, w m BP remainder: BP **335** DMZ, BS, DMZ, BP, BS, TV, BS, BS, BS, RS/VU, BS, BP, fy RH, BP, JW/VU 337 jv KTK, "purple" KTK, TV, AC, BP, BP, BP, BP, BS, BP, BP, BP, DMZ **339** *Brown-headed Cowbird:* BP, BP, BP, BP, jv BS *Shiny Cowbird:* BS *Bronzed Cowbird:* DMZ, BP, BS *Rusty Blackbird:* AM/PP, MD, a BS *Brewer's Blackbird:* TV, BP **341** *Baltimore Oriole:* BS, KTK, TV, TV *Bullock's Oriole:* BP, BP, DMZ *Hooded Oriole:* BS, BS, w m BP, BS *Orchard Oriole:* BS all **343** *Spot-breasted Oriole:* LM *Streak-backed Oriole:* CAM *Audubon's Oriole:* MD, GL remainder: BP **345** *House Sparrow:* BP all *Eurasian Tree Sparrow:* MD **347** *Song Sparrow:* BS, TV, KTK, TV, desert BP *Lincoln's Sparrow:* BP all *Swamp Sparrow:* BP, KTK, BS *Fox Sparrow:* MD, MD, red TV, grayish BS, KTK **349** *Bachman's Sparrow:* RC/EB, GL remainder: BP **351** *Am. Tree Sparrow:* w MD, BS remainder: BP **353** *Lark Sparrow:* BP, GL, BP *Black-chinned Sparrow:* m DMZ, JHO *Black-throated Sparrow:* im DMZ, BP, BP *Five-striped Sparrow:* BP all *Sage Sparrow:* BS, BP **355** *Savannah Sparrow:* "Ipswich" KTK remainder: BP **357** MD, BP, BP, MD, KTK, MD, MD, BS, BS, BS, KTK **359** *White-throated Sparrow:* BP all *White-crowned Sparrow:* MD, BP, BS, im JHO *Golden-crowned Sparrow:* MD, TV, BP *Harris's Sparrow:* RC/EB, BP, BP **361** *Dark-eyed Junco:* TV, KTK, BS, BS, BP, DMZ, JHO, MT, BP, BP *Yellow-eyed Junco:* BP all **363** *All tail patterns:* KK *Lapland Longspur:* TV, TV, BP, MD *Smith's Longspur:* TV, KTK *Chestnut-collared Longspur:* w HC, w MD, s f AM/PP, s m BS *McCown's Longspur:* MD, BS, BS **365** *Snow Bunting:* fy GE/WR, TV, BS, BS, MD *McKay's Bunting:* PL all *Brown-capped Rosy-Finch:* CM, BP *Black Rosy-Finch:* BS *Brambling:* MD all *Gray-crowned Rosy-Finch:* BS all **367** *House Finch:* BP, BP, BP, BS, BP *Purple Finch:* f BS, f KTK m BS, m BS *Cassin's Finch:* DMZ, BS, DMZ **369** BS, BS, GL, DMZ, RC/EB, CGI, TW/VU, BS, BS *Hoary Redpoll:* DT/WR all *Com. Redpoll:* AN/RR, AN/RR, RS/VU **371** *American Goldfinch:* BS, TV, KTK, s m BP, s f CGI *Pine Siskin:* KK all *Lesser Goldfinch:* BP all *European Goldfinch:* DT/WR *Lawrence's Goldfinch:* CM, BS, BS **373** *Evening Grosbeak:* BP, DMZ, DMZ *Blue Grosbeak:* BP, BS, BP remainder: BP **375** KTK remainder: BP **377** BS, BS, BS, DMZ, BP, BS, KTK, BS, KTK, PL, JHO, BP 379 BP, BP, BP, BP, DMZ, KTK, KTK, BS

INDEX OF ENGLISH NAMES OF BIRDS

You can keep track of your "life list" here, by checking off the boxes in front of the names of birds you've seen. A box is provided for every full species included in the book that is either native to or naturalized in North America.

Short index: KAUFMAN FIELD GUIDE TO BIRDS OF NORTH AMERICA

(Some rare birds, unlikely to be seen by most readers, are excluded here but included in regular index.)